The CAREER FITNESS PROGRAM

EXERCISING YOUR OPTIONS

FIFTH EDITION

DIANE SUKIENNIK

WILLIAM BENDAT

LISA RAUFMAN

Prentice Hall
Upper Saddle River, New Jersey 07458

Library of Congress Cataloging–in–Publication Data

Sukiennik, Diane.
    The Career fitness program : exercising your options / Diane
Sukiennik, William Bendat, Lisa Raufman. — 5th ed.
       p.   cm.
    Includes bibliographical references and index.
    ISBN 0-13-780826-7
    1. Vocational guidance. 2. Job hunting. 3. Personality
assessment.   I. Bendat, William. II. Raufman, Lisa. III. Title.
HF5381.S914 1998
331.7'02—dc21   97-31188
                                              CIP

Acquisitions Editor: *Todd Rossell*
Managing Editor: *Mary Carnis*
Production: *Holcomb Hathaway, Inc.*
Production Liaison: *Adele Kupchik*
Director of Manufacturing and Production: *Bruce Johnson*
Manufacturing Buyer: *Marc Bove*
Marketing Manager: *Frank Mortimer, Jr.*
Editorial Assistant: *Amy Diehl*
Marketing Assistant: *Christopher Eastman*
Cover Design: *Marianne Frasco*

© 1998 by Prentice-Hall, Inc.
Simon & Schuster / A Viacom Company
Upper Saddle River, New Jersey 07458

Printed in the United States of America

10 9 8 7 6 5 4 3 2 1

ISBN 0-13-780826-7

Prentice-Hall International (UK) Limited, *London*
Prentice-Hall of Australia Pty. Limited, *Sydney*
Prentice-Hall Canada Inc., *Toronto*
Prentice-Hall Hispanoamericana, S.A., *Mexico*
Prentice-Hall of India Private Limited, *New Delhi*
Prentice-Hall of Japan, Inc., *Tokyo*
Simon & Schuster Asia Pte. Ltd., *Singapore*
Editora Prentice-Hall do Brasil, Ltda., *Rio de Janeiro*

Brief Contents

For the complete Contents, see page VII.

Contents

Introduction
On Your Mark . . .
Get Set . . .

The world of work is spinning at a dizzying pace. As we approach the new millennium the job market is more unpredictable than ever. Companies are downsizing, rightsizing, restructuring, outsourcing, and undergoing radical technological change. Bigger mega-mergers are occurring and more small businesses are being created. The globalization of industries and organizations presents us with competitive challenges and unprecedented opportunities. You can benefit from becoming aware of the changing job market, by keeping up with trends and identifying how they fit your personal preferences. Six major trends are shaping the workplace:

1. The majority of jobs are created by small businesses employing fewer than 50 employees. *Trends*

2. The traditional hierarchical organization is changing into a variety of forms with a "flat" (reduced middle management) organizational chart becoming more common. Flexible networking of specialists who come together for a short-term project, then reform into a new group for the next project will be commonplace. (See the discussion of the virtual workplace in Chapter 6.)

3. Smaller companies are able to expand and contract with the changing economy by increasingly employing temporary and contract employees.

4. Just as manufacturing used to be our mainstay, we are now considered a "service economy" that depends on "knowledge workers." (See Chapter 6: "the learning organization" and "knowledge workers.")

5. Lifelong learning is the rule; getting a degree to get a job may get you an entree into a company, but if you don't continually upgrade your knowledge you will lose your competitive edge. The winners are rethinking, reinventing, and re-engineering products, ideas, and services to meet continually changing needs.

6. Global competition and multinational corporations will influence more and more companies. The most valuable employee will be the one most familiar with several languages and cultural customs. The number of women and immigrants will continue to increase in the workforce.

A broad rainbow of possibilities makes this an exciting time in history. Yet many of us are overwhelmed by lack of knowledge about our choices and our place and purpose in the world. One thing that is certain is change. It is essential to prepare ourselves to expect change, accept it, and plan for it. We can best prepare for it by learning "who we are" in terms of lifetime goals and by

taking responsibility for shaping our lives. As we gain information about our-selves and begin to make our own decisions, we acquire self-confidence. In a deep, personal way we begin to realize that no matter how drastically the world changes, we can deal with it.

The expectations and demands of today's job market require us to be phys-ically agile, mentally alert, and psychologically able. *The Career Fitness Pro-gram* will prepare you to exercise your options whether you are planning for your first job, reentering the workforce, or recareering. This program will help you build the mental stamina and psychological strength you need to be successful and satisfied today. You will also develop the mind-set and acquire the tools for continuing success despite the inevitable surprises and challenges that will face you. *The Career Fitness Program* is designed to assist you in the process of self-discovery and realization. The main goal of this book is to lead you through the process of career planning, which includes self-assessment, decision making, and job search strategy; our primary objective is to assist you in making satisfying career choices. By following our chapter-by-chapter pro-gram, you will learn more about yourself and how self-knowledge relates to your emerging career plan.

Let's review the contents of this book to see how it will help you achieve your career goals. The career-planning process is divided into two main parts: personal assessment and career exploration, Chapters One–Eight, and job search strategy, Chapters Nine–Eleven.

- In Chapter One, you will come to understand how the process of self-assessment *begins* the process of career planning. You will explore the con-cept of *life stages* and give thought to your current life stage. Chapter One also discusses the difference between a job and a career.

- In Chapter Two, you will learn how building self-esteem greatly affects your actions. This chapter's goal is to help you develop a positive approach to life and career planning.

- In Chapter Three, you will identify your needs, wants, and values and explore how they influence your career choice.

- In Chapter Four, you will develop an understanding of and appreciation for your unique personality and interests—factors that will influence your career choice.

- In Chapter Five, you will learn about different types of skills; you will learn to identify and describe your own skills with job requirements in mind.

- In Chapter Six, you will explore societal and cultural norms and biases that may affect your career choices. In this chapter you will also read about workplace trends, promising occupations, and salary predictions.

- In Chapter Seven, you will investigate published and computerized sources of information about careers and specific jobs, including govern-ment publications and Internet resources.

- In Chapter Eight, you will identify how people make decisions and learn how to improve your own decision-making skills. This process includes learning to set and pursue short- and long-term goals.

- In Chapter Nine, you will learn about job search strategies, including infor-mational interviewing, networking, and electronic job search techniques.

- In Chapter Ten, you will write an effective resume and cover letter.
- In Chapter Eleven, you will prepare for job interviews. This chapter discusses all aspects of the interview process, includes sample questions that you may encounter, and advises you about handling illegal employer queries.

Even if you are not yet in the full-time job market, the job search strategy chapters (Nine–Eleven) will be a valuable resource for you now. If you are in school, planning to work part-time, already employed, or seeking an internship, you can begin to prepare your resume and practice interviewing skills.

THE PROCESS

In many ways, the process of preparing to meet job and career challenges is much like the process by which athletes prepare to meet the challenges of competition in their particular sport. It involves establishing a fitness program in which the competitor sharpens existing skills, adds needed skills, and, most important, develops a mental attitude of success.

Meeting the challenges

Any good fitness program is a combination of theory and exercise, and our career fitness program maintains this balance. For each step of the planning process, we will explain the theory behind that step, how it relates to the previous and next steps, and how it moves us closer to our final goal of identifying career options.

The chapters conclude with a series of exercises designed to bring each step of the process to life. These exercises will help make you more aware of your strengths, weaknesses, and attitudes, and they will also help you summarize what you think is important to remember after each chapter. Remember that reading a chapter or a book is a passive activity. However, responding to questions makes you an active participant in the career exploration process. You may find that it helps to share your answers with at least one other person; a classroom setting in which group discussion is encouraged is even better because it adds to your own awareness and perspective.

Becoming an active participant: commitment

It is easy for someone to sit back and read about career planning and simply agree with the text, theories, and exercises. *But until you make the commitment to actually get involved in the process, to actively participate, and to experience both progress and occasional discomfort along the way, you will not be able to reap the benefits of the process.*

THE CHALLENGE

Yes, we did mention the word *discomfort* just now. What do we mean by that? Anytime you begin a new physical exercise program, even if you start cautiously and sensibly in relation to your current level of activity, new muscles are stretched, and they let you know about it. They feel awkward. They ache. You become aware of parts of your body that you may never have noticed before. You can also expect this to happen in the process of career planning. Along the way, confusion and some discomfort may occur. We will ask questions to help you dig deep into yourself for answers. In this process of enhancing self-awareness, you will discover much about yourself that you like, as well as some things that you would like to change.

The process of change and personal growth

Because of this self-discovery process, at certain points along the way in our fitness plan you may feel a bit confused, a bit anxious, a bit impatient. All of these feelings are normal. When you start out on a physical fitness program you idealistically hope that in a week or two you will have the body that you visualize in your mind, even though you know realistically that developing a good physique is going to take a lot longer. Similarly, with your career plan you may begin to feel impatient and want things to move along more quickly or more clearly. It is important to remember that any change or growth typically includes some discomfort, uneasiness, or anxiety. Frankly, if you begin to experience some of those feelings, it is a good sign! It indicates that you are stretching, that you are growing, and that you are moving toward a newly developed awareness of who you are and how you relate to the world of work.

COMMITTING TO THE PROCESS

Benefits of perseverance and belief

Whether you are taking the time at the beginning of your adult career to carefully and thoroughly examine your options, or are finding at midlife it is time to explore new directions, you will reap tremendous benefits in the future. The satisfaction you experience at "the finish line" will be directly proportional to your willingness and ability to deal with the anxiety and uncertainty you will experience at some points in the career-planning process. In essence, the more you put into any activity, the more you are likely to get out of it. Stories that we have heard and read about our cultural heroes and heroines, whether athletes, performers, scientists, or political figures, tell us that the results they achieve, which look so easy and so glamorous, are always and only the consequence of tremendous sustained effort, commitment, and perseverance. A statement attributed to famed artist Michelangelo seems to say it all: "If people knew how hard I had to work to gain my mastery, it wouldn't seem so wonderful after all."

Your career search requires a similar commitment. It requires your willingness to go with the process; to seek out specialized assistance; and to move through points of frustration, uncertainty, and confusion in the belief that you will come out with more awareness and a good sense of the next steps to take along your career path. We invite you to participate in an adventure and endeavor that are every bit as exciting and rewarding as preparing for the Olympics. You are identifying your own mountain peaks and are setting out to climb them. Among your resources is this career-planning textbook, which incorporates the insights and experience of the authors and other successful career planners over several decades. Most of all, the important attributes of your own spirit, vitality, and intuition, together with the desire to improve yourself, will serve you well throughout your search. This career fitness program will help you master the inevitable changes that occur within yourself and are associated with your evolving career choices and the work world around you. It will help you identify options that are consistent with who you are. It will enable you to be the champion of your own career.

PART ONE

PERSONAL ASSESSMENT

O N E

Taking Stock

LEARNING OBJECTIVES

At the end of the chapter you will be able to . . .

Differentiate between a job and a career

Identify life stages as they relate to career planning

Understand why personal assessment is the key factor leading to career satisfaction

Self-awareness = first step

Do you want to have a career that meets your needs, complements your personality, and inspires you to develop your potential? Are you someone who deliberately chooses the type of life you live rather than settling for what's convenient and available? If so, you need to set goals that will lead you from where you are now to where you want to be. However, to be realistic, goals must reflect your experiences, desires, needs, interests, values, and vision of the future.

PERSONAL ASSESSMENT

As the first step in self-assessment, this chapter helps you examine your personal experiences, who you are right now, your current stage of career and life development, and your ability to deal with new information. Once you begin to identify what energizes you about life, you can begin to incorporate those insights into a career. Self-awareness is the first stage of both the career choice and career change process. As we look for insights that will help us chart our careers well into the 21st century, it is useful to take a look at career development models. Renowned psychologist Donald Super (1957) is credited with developing the theory that a career makes it possible for you to actualize or express your

self-concept. Your **self-concept** is essentially *how you see yourself*. Consider the following principles of Super's theory on career development and how they relate to you.

Super's Self-Concept Theory

1. We differ in abilities, interests, and personalities.
2. Every occupation requires a characteristic pattern of abilities, interests, and personality traits. Within each occupation are workers with varying degrees of these characteristics.
3. Each of us is qualified for a number of occupations.
4. Vocational preferences and skills, the situations in which we live and work, and our self-concepts change with time and experience. These factors make choice and adjustment a continual process based on our maturity and lifestyle.
5. Selecting a career involves the following stages. As we will discuss later in this chapter, many people experience these stages more than once in life. Thus, although Super discusses the stages in a more traditional sense, remember that you may return to the stages discussed below at various times in your life.

   a. GROWTH: This includes both physical and emotional growth as you form attitudes and behaviors that relate to your self-concept. What did you learn about yourself from childhood games or family roles? For example, "I am a team player," "I am an individualist," "I am a mediator," or "I would rather read than play games." A child begins having fantasies during this period, e.g., a dream of becoming a doctor.

   b. EXPLORATION: This is divided into *fantasy* (e.g., a child's dream of becoming a doctor), *tentative* (e.g., high school and post-high school periods of exploration in which ideas are narrowed down), and *reality testing* (e.g., in high school or early college, working part-time or volunteering in a hospital, taking math and science classes, or raising a family). You start learning about the kind of work you enjoy and the kind of worker you are, for example, "I am good with detail," "I enjoy working with people," "I enjoy working alone," "I take criticism well."

   c. ESTABLISHMENT: This includes initial work experience that may have started only as a job to earn a living, but offers experiences for growth so that it becomes part of the self-concept. For example, "I am an assistant manager, I am responsible for the bookkeeping, and I look forward to becoming the manager," rather than, "This is just a job, and I will be doing bookkeeping until I can finish my bachelor's

My life is my message.
Mahatma Gandhi

degree and get into law school." Very often several changes in jobs will occur over a few years.

    d. MAINTENANCE: This is a time when we maintain or improve in our career area. Advancement can be to higher levels or laterally across fields. For example, you may start thinking: "I am extremely competent," "I can compete with others," "I can cooperate and share my knowledge," or "I can train others."

    e. DISENGAGEMENT: Super defines this as the stage just before retirement or one when we see no new challenges or chances for mobility. Traditionally, it is a period during which there is a shift in the amount of emphasis you place on your career; you may even seek a reduction of the hours you work. Disengagement may also occur some time prior to retirement. You may think: "I have many things other than this job I want to do." "I want to spend more time at home," "I want to work on my hobbies," "I want to travel more," or "I want to make a living from my leisure pursuits." Job or career changes are a form of disengagement, whether prompted by personal choice or circumstances beyond your control (a layoff, for instance).

6. The nature of any career pattern is influenced by parental socioeconomic level, mental ability, personality characteristics, and the opportunities to which the individual is exposed. Both limitations and opportunities may be apparent as a result of these factors. People are affected by the realities of everyday life. A teenager living in an affluent suburb may have unlimited opportunity to focus on high school classwork because of ample financial support. On the other hand, a teenager living in the inner city with several siblings may work 20 hours or more each week to help out with the family finances. Such limitations can be overcome with effort and perseverance.

7. The process of career development is essentially that of self-concept development and implementation. All of us try to maintain a favorable picture of ourselves.

8. Work satisfactions and life satisfactions depend on the extent to which our work and our life provide adequate outlets for our abilities, interests, personality traits, and values.

What has influenced your self-concept? Do you have an accurate view of your likes and dislikes, desires, attributes, limitations, needs, wants, and values? An accurate self-assessment will enable you to make better career decisions by increasing your personal awareness and understanding. Self-awareness improves the probability of seeking and selecting jobs that fit your unique self-concept. Super's theory applies each time you make a career change: you will reexperience the stages of growth, exploration, establishment, maintenance, and disengagement.

UNDERSTANDING THE DIFFERENCES BETWEEN A JOB AND A CAREER

We will be using the words *job* and *career* throughout this book, so let's define them. There is an important difference between them. Basically, a job is a

series of tasks or activities that are performed within the scope of what we call work. These tasks relate to a career in that a career is a series of jobs. But more than jobs, a career is a sequence of attitudes and behaviors that are associated with work and that relate to our total life experience. *A career is really an integration of our personality with our job activities.* Therefore, our career becomes a primary part of our identity or our self-concept.

A career is the integration of personality with work activities

In the past, people chose a career early in life, and they tended to stay in it most of their lives. Farmers worked on their farms, secretaries stayed in the office, and teachers taught until retirement. More recently the trend in America has shifted toward multiple careers. We can now expect to have four or more careers in our lives. Furthermore, with the rapid changes in society as well as in economic conditions, jobs, and technologies, many traditional jobs are becoming obsolete. In fact, William Bridges in his book, *Jobshift* (1995), suggests jobs as we know them will not exist in the next millennium. Although that may sound like a radical concept, he means that a person hired to take a particular job can be certain the job tasks will change rapidly. Even if the job title remains the same, new and different skill sets will continually be required—the original position may become dramatically different or even disappear altogether.

This is markedly different from the world in which your family worked. Thus, the expectation that once you find a job you are "home free," "secure," or "set for life" is no longer realistic. The traditional "employee contract," although unwritten, implied an honest day's work for an honest day's wage, employee loyalty in exchange for job security, and raises and promotions in return for seniority. Today's new employee contract simply implies continued employment for individuals who possess skills that continuously meet a business need.

More than ever it is important to give considerable thought to what you want to do and structure your training and education to be relevant both to your interests and to trends in the job market. You will find it beneficial to assess your skills and identify those that are transferable from a previous career to a newly emerging field with a minimum amount of retraining. Knowing yourself and developing a plan of action based on both your needs and the needs of the job market will help you embark on the career most satisfying for you rather than just following the latest trends in one field or another.

Follow intuitions and not trends

Demands in the job market rapidly come and go. Some time ago, teachers were in great demand. Then, for about a decade, there was a glut of teachers on the market. Now there seems to be a renewed need for teachers in the workforce. The same is true of engineers. If you base your career decision primarily on current trends, by the time you obtain the training necessary to get into the "hot" field, it may well have cooled down. This strategy leaves you with slim prospects for a job that can lead to a career, and quite possibly with skills and training in a field that you weren't terribly excited about in the first place (except as a quick opportunity).

Each of us has the potential to be satisfied in any number of occupations. Getting to know yourself better through self-assessment will help you identify careers that are best suited to your personality. People who are not prepared for change allow that change to make decisions for them. They are often frustrated and unhappy because they are forced to work at jobs they don't enjoy. They may never have realized that they have choices, or perhaps they never took the time or energy to become aware of their preferences. They settle for less than

Be prepared to manage your career

what might be best for them. Dad says "get a job in business" even though his child has a special talent in art. The high school adviser recommends engineering because scholarships are available. The employment department directs a job applicant into an electronics training program because there's an opening. By knowing your own preferences you will be ready to manage your career path instead of merely following others' suggestions.

Striving for Career Satisfaction

Survey after survey on job satisfaction among American workers indicates that well over 50 percent are dissatisfied with their jobs. In a 1995 study for *U.S. News & World Report*, people were asked to name the three things that contribute most to their quality of life. The top categories for men and women were "job/career satisfaction," "relationship with family," and "money." Because people may be changing jobs and careers several times in their lives, it is more important than ever before to have accurate knowledge about yourself and the world of work. Two-thirds of a group of adults surveyed (Gallup Organization, 1994) said if they were starting all over they would try to get more information about their career options. You will face the need to continually reevaluate yourself and your career path. It is useful to know about the changing world of work and which occupations allow you to best express yourself and best use your strengths and talents. When analyzing your personal assets, it is to your advantage to ultimately think about the total job market. Search for jobs that will lead you into a career. You will benefit greatly from identifying a variety of alternatives that allow you to express your personality. Once you have looked within yourself and identified what you want and need in a job, changes will be easier to make because you'll know when you have outgrown one job and need a new one.

Greatest Contributors to Quality of Life

Men
- "Job/Career Satisfaction" – 32%
- "Relationship with Family" – 28%
- "Money" – 18%

Women
- "Job/Career Satisfaction" – 28%
- "Relationship with Family" – 33%
- "Money" – 17%

Be prepared to continually revise your career plan

For most of us, career planning is not a simple, straightforward, linear process in which we follow certain prescribed steps, end up at a specific destination, and live happily after. It is instead a feedback loop that continues to self-correct as we add information about our changing self and the world around us. We are constantly revising our career plan as we grow and change. This means that there isn't any one "right" career. Instead, there are many careers in which we could be equally happy, equally successful, equally satisfied.

There is no single "right" career

We are looking, then, not for the *one* right career but for the series of alternatives and career options that seem to make sense for each of us given our background, our personality, our career and life stages, and the changing world. Our discussion of Super's theory briefly mentioned the general career stages that many people have experienced: Growth, Exploration, Establishment, Maintenance, and Disengagement. Since you are probably somewhere between the stages of Exploration and Maintenance right now, it is useful to understand that you are also experiencing the transitional stages that relate to your age and affect your career planning.

An Overview of Life Stages

The following life stage descriptions, derived from a variety of research on adult life stages suggest that we emphasize different needs at different times of our lives. Planning a career involves thinking about the past, present, and future. Reviewing life stage information allows a career searcher or changer to gain and accept insight regarding certain personal and emotional issues that tend to influence values, planning, and goal setting.

Needs will change throughout life

Ages 16–22—late adolescence.

Leaving parents' world, independence being established but not stable, unsure of ability to make it in the adult world, open to new ideas.

Ages 22–28—provisional adulthood.

Gaining independence in work, marriage, or intimate relationships, testing all of the parental shoulds and oughts, and choosing which to retain in adulthood. Still proving competence to parents; more self-reliant, building for the future; marriage and family considerations.

Ages 28–32—the thirties transition.

Questioning the early commitments to marriage and relationships, family and career; reassessments and changes may take place. A particularly vulnerable stage for continuity, although many choose to continue their earlier choices.

Ages 32–39—the time of rooting.

Involved in career; helping children grow, giving priority consideration to childbearing; recognizing parental messages; modifying personality; accepting choices; giving more attention to business matters; establishing reputation—until about age 35 when the question "Will I have time to do it all?" begins to arise; more awareness of time and renewing the important matter of "What do I really want to be?" This may be the first time a woman experiences freedom from child rearing and begins to consider career options.

Ages 39–43—the turning point years.

Experience a period of great upheaval and midlife crisis; may appear that earlier dreams may not be attainable; wondering "Why am I here, where am I going?"; potential lifestyle changes, often not planned; feeling there is something missing in life, possible further thoughts about raising a family; starting or changing a career.

Ages 43–50—restabilization/bearing fruit.

More at peace with questions of mortality, career and lifestyle transitions; children testing their independence; personal review of child-raising patterns; career blossoming; attention to personal growth; activity in community; reevaluating relationships as one's children become adults.

Ages 50–65—renewal.

Either enjoying a time of relative calm, boredom, or acceptance and enjoyment of life; or facing new challenges due to an abrupt career

change; planning for retirement; physical energy and strength may decline; spouses and/or friends die; new life structure emerges, risk taking seems less likely to occur; acceptance of parents' role in one's life; spiritual questioning; potential for creative growth; disengaging from concept of "work," though some people will start a new career at this time; dealing with caretaking responsibilities for aging parents; possible tension between a wife in the prime of her career after completing child rearing and a husband eager to retire and start a new phase of life.

Ages 65 and up—transition toward retirement.

As life is extended and retirement is not mandatory, this period may become the true "golden years" of continued usefulness to society and growth for oneself.

Retirement.

Ending traditional work patterns for extended time with hobbies and interests; opportunities to increase social and civic activities, enjoying travel, family, and leisure.

Remember that these life stages are based on social norms of the past and present. The world is changing at such a rapid pace that social norms will surely be different in future studies. For example, two-career families, single-parent households, later marriages, alternative lifestyles, longer life spans, fewer entry-level jobs, and the need for lifelong learning will all influence the directions of people's lives and thus impact future life stages.

Author Gail Sheehy has explored how people change as they age and found that as longevity has increased, so have concepts and definitions of career and retirement. There is no longer a clear-cut point when we end our training or move into retirement. Finding challenging or rewarding employment may ultimately mean retraining and an early exit from a stale or boring job in order to find one's passion and pursue it. The idea is to think long-range and anticipate an active lifestyle into later years—perhaps into one's 80s or 90s. Being personally productive may now mean anticipating retiring in stages. This may mean going to an alternate plan should a primary career end either by choice or economic factors.

Since it will take longer to grow up and grow old, we need to seek meaning to our existence and be open to new experiences. These can include nonprofit ventures, volunteering, turning hobbies into businesses, or using part-time hours to help others and increase earnings. Taking risks to supplement and expand our personal horizons is encouraged at any age to avoid becoming vulnerable, "stuck," or even being directed by unforeseen events. In essence, our later adulthood can be a time of renewal, leisure, service to society, activity, and productivity.

CHOOSING AND CHANGING CAREERS

Each one of us, regardless of our stage in life, is in some phase of career development. You may be starting your first job or looking for a job. You may be planning for your first career, reentering the job market after some time at home, considering your next career, planning for part-time employment, or looking for meaningful volunteer experience.

As there is no crystal ball that will predict the one right career for you, you will want to consider several options as you explore career development. The previous examples described people who reassessed their needs and made satisfying changes. It is also possible to survey your needs, values, interests, skills, aptitudes, and sources of information about the world of work in order to create a broader career *objective*. Some careers do have established or common career paths. In teaching, one often starts out as a tutor, works up to student teacher, and then becomes an assistant teacher before becoming a full-time teacher. In the marketing profession, people often start in sales. Therefore we need to think about career goals in the sense of their being both short-term and long-term. A short-term career goal is one that can be rather quickly attained. For instance, in the process of career planning, you may discover you want to be a lawyer. We would normally consider law a long-term career option because it generally takes many years of study and preparation. However, a short-term career goal related to law might be obtaining a job as a legal secretary or a paralegal. Either of these would give you the opportunity to work in an environment that excites and energizes you long before you actually achieve your final and ultimate career goal. In addition, relevant experience enhances your appeal to future employers.

Preparation = short- and long-term goals

If you examine enough options during the career-planning process, you may be able to use career experiences to move into related areas just as Sandra did. Subsequent chapters in this book will help you identify your related options.

There is a final, very important reason that this effort at personal assessment is crucial as the first step in your career-planning process. Once you know who you are and what your preferences and talents are, you can better make sense of the information that continually bombards you regarding the world of work. It's almost impossible to read a newspaper, listen to a news broadcast, visit a Web site, or watch a television show that does not have some implication for you and your career. In fact, you may feel you suffer from information overload. Looking at the want ads and reading about employment projections and trends can cause confusion, frustration, and often discouragement about what place you might have in this elusive job market.

Sandra was 17 when she started her first secretarial job. By luck, it was in a legal office. For ten years she was happy being a secretary involved with the legal profession. This left her time to raise her family. But her employers encouraged her to continue her education. Not only did she attend evening courses, but she also became involved with the Professional Secretaries' Association. By the time her children were grown, she had completed a two-year college degree program, served as president of her association, started a training course to become a paralegal, been promoted to legal assistant, and is now teaching legal terminology at a local community college.

One of the best ways to achieve a sense of control and perspective on this constant stream of information is to know who you are, so that when you are listening, reading, watching, and experiencing, you will have a means of processing information through your consciousness, through your personality and preferences, and through your values and skills. Eventually, you will be able to recognize and reject information that does not apply to you, and to internalize and add to your career plan information that does. If a group setting such as a career class is available to you, all the better! The opportunity to discover yourself and expand your horizons is multiplied by the added benefit of group interaction.

Self-knowledge helps decision making

Sample career changers

Here are some examples of the kinds of career selection we've been discussing.

- Professor Nguyen had reached his life goal, or so he thought. He was one of the few chosen to be a professor of religion at a small college in the San Francisco area. One day he woke up with stomach pains and body aches and had little energy. He dragged himself out of bed. When the pains lasted longer than three days, he visited his family physician only to find there was no medical reason for his discomfort. He then began some soul searching. His pains and nightmares continued over a period of months and seemed to occur only during the work week. On weekends, when he was with his family or volunteering at a hospital, he felt energetic and healthy. Soon he took a leave of absence from his job and devoted more time to his hospital avocation. The physical ailments mysteriously disappeared. He spent one year examining his needs, consulting with a career counselor, and talking things over with friends. He found that his real satisfaction came from helping people in the hospital rather than from teaching religion. Shortly thereafter, a friend told him about a job opening as an ombudsman in a hospital. He got the job and now lectures to local classes in career development on the hazards of keeping a job that is making you ill! Professor Nguyen needed to reexamine his original goals to discover why his career as a professor wasn't meeting his needs.

- David Chan spent two years at a state college with a major in pre-law, but a love for art. He wished to choose a career with strong financial potential that would be acceptable to his parents. During his junior year David realized he constantly daydreamed about a career in art. So he enrolled in an evening community college class and then transferred full-time to a technical art school where he specialized in drawing and sketching. David completed his degree, sought career counseling, and decided to try for his dream job. Within two years, he had a part-time job with an animation studio. He is now a full-time animator, creating characters for feature films. David was able to find a career which used his artistic talents and surpassed his financial goals.

- Taylor Jordan is a sophomore at a community college. For the past two years, largely on the advice of her parents, she has been preparing to transfer to the local university to complete a degree in business. Taylor now realizes that she wants to follow her true talents and interests, and pursue a career in interior design. Although she has spent much time and effort accumulating credits toward a bachelor's degree in business, she knows that many of her core courses will apply toward her associate's degree in interior design. She is determined to do what is necessary to achieve her new goal. To prepare for her discussion with her parents, Taylor has researched local job opportunities with furniture and home improvement stores, home builders, and interior design firms. She has talked to a college adviser about possible internships and volunteer work. Most important, she believes that her decision is the right one and is determined to follow through with it.

- Jose Marcade emigrated to the United States in the 1980s. In 1990, after improving his language skills by attending adult school, he enrolled in a restaurant and hotel management program at a community college and began working as a parking attendant. Jose was very sociable and positive, often making friendly conversation with his customers. By the time he finished his schooling, he was the supervisor of parking facilities. One of his customers told him about a job possibility with a large hotel chain and recommended he apply. Jose not only got the job, but within three years was managing the hotel's restaurant at an annual salary of $60,000. His ability to network, be friendly, learn on the job, and combine studies and work experience led him to a great job.

- Rhonda Speer spent five years in college completing a bachelor's degree program in teaching with an emphasis in special education. After 2½ years working in the field she decided that she needed a change. Working with children all day was making it difficult for Rhonda to concentrate at the end of the day on her own young daughter at home. She found a job as a stockbroker trainee. Within six months she was a full-fledged stockbroker. Now she's a corporate financial adviser.

Summary

The best approach to the process of career planning is first to examine who you are, what you know about yourself, and what you need and want, and then to mesh that information with the world of work. You then have the distinct advantage of being able to choose training for a career about which you are truly excited and enthusiastic. These two qualities are among the most important to potential employers. Even if the job market for the field you have chosen is extremely competitive, you will have an edge because of your sense of commitment, your passion, and joy for what you are doing. We will elaborate further on these "attitudes for success" in Chapter Two and will identify and discuss the attitudinal components that will make you a success in whatever career you choose.

Attitude influences action: knowing yourself is critical in an unpredictable job market

The first set of exercises will help you explore your current feelings and attitudes and thus better understand yourself. Begin with Exercise 1.1, First Impressions. This will help you take stock of where you are currently. Exercise 1.2 is a review of where your life focus has been. You will learn more about how personality and interests relate to career planning in Chapter Four. For now, Exercise 1.3 asks you to begin thinking about your interests, and Exercise 1.4 asks you to identify your personal strengths. (Later when you are reading about the personality requirements of different careers, you can use this list as another piece to complete the "personality puzzle.") The final exercise, 1.5, encourages you to identify job preferences by ranking occupations according to how you perceive their status.

1.1 First impressions

Here is your first chance to think about yourself and record your responses. Fill in each blank carefully and honestly. Be true to yourself; don't try to please anyone else with your answers. Try to be spontaneous; the longer you think before answering, the more likely you are to censor your answers.

a. I am ....

b. I need ....

c. I want ....

d. My current life stage in selecting a career is: ....

e. I would like to change ....about myself.

f. If all goes well in the next five years, I will be doing the following things: ....
....
....
....

g. If things go poorly in the next five years, I will be doing ....
....
....
....

h. Reviewing past jobs or volunteer experiences I have had, what did I like best/least about each one? Is there a pattern? ....
....
....
....

1.2 Your lifeline

Review the information on life stages. As we noted, these life stage descriptions suggest that we emphasize different needs at different times of our lives. Can you remember the highs and lows in your personal and career life and then place them on a line? It is helpful to place symbols on a line graph of your life indicating times of major decisions such as moves or new jobs; periods when mentors or other influential people entered or affected your life; and times when you had particular problems or acquired important new skills. To assist your memory, divide your life into four time periods and write four important memories (activities, people, events) in each group.

Childhood/Preteen, Ages 0–12

(Try remembering friends, birthday parties, holidays, or school events to recall your earliest memories. What did you excel at?)

1. ....
2. ....
3. ....
4. ....

Teenage Years, Ages 13–19

1. ....
2. ....
3. ....
4. ....

Early Adult Years, Ages 20–38

1. ....
2. ....
3. ....
4. ....

Adult Years, Ages 35 Plus

1. ....
2. ....
3. ....
4. ....

Now you can transfer these memories onto the lifeline. It may help to use symbols to save space, e.g., A = people, B = events, C = jobs, etc.

EXHIBIT 1.A

A sample lifeline and space to draw your own lifeline.

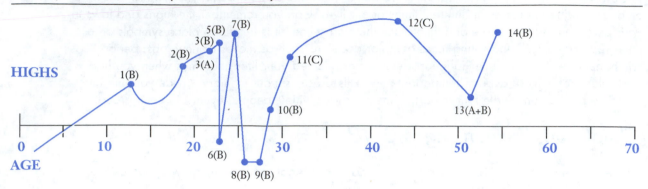

1. Leadership award in sixth grade (age 12).
2. Chosen student ambassador to France—sophomore in college (age 19).
3. Spent senior year in France (age 21).
4. Met significant person in my life (age 21).
5. Graduate school in New York (age 22).
6. Move from New York to Missouri (lost friends and career contacts) (age 23).
7. First professional job (but not my ideal job) (age 24).
8. Fired! (A bona fide case of sexual harassment!) (age 25).
9. After being unemployed for nine months, I volunteered at a career planning center and learned new skills (age 26).
10. Began my own serious job search, identified my ideal job (career counselor) in the ideal setting for me (a community college) (age 27).
11. Success! Landed the perfect job for me! (age 30)
12. Still learning on my job and beginning to explore further options and/or career enrichment opportunities (age 44).
13. Dealing with my parents' mortality and my own aging (ages 50–54).
14. Seeking balance, giving back to the community, planning for increased leisure and continuous life-long learning (age 55).

NOW DRAW YOUR OWN LIFELINE BELOW:

HIGHS

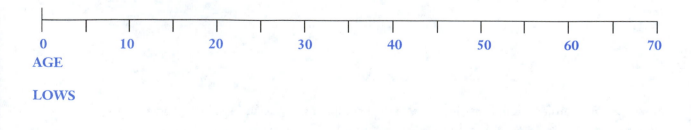

AGE

LOWS

1.3 Identify your interests

a. What subjects in school do I like? ....

....

....

b. What books or magazines do I read? What kinds of music, art, theater, and cinema do I like?

....

....

....

c. What do I like to do for fun? How do I spend my spare time? ....

....

....

....

d. Jobs I've had and what I liked about them, including volunteer work: ....

....

....

....

1.4 Describe yourself

Circle those adjectives that best describe you. Place an "X" in front of those adjectives that are least like you.

R Realistic	I Investigative	A Artistic
practical	careful	emotional
conforming	introverted	expressive
persistent	curious	imaginative
stable	precise	unordered
down-to-earth	independent	creative
rugged	achieving	impulsive
athletic	confident	flexible
frank	analytical	idealistic
self-reliant	intellectual	original

S Social	**E** Enterprising	**C** Conventional
helpful	energetic	conscientious
insightful	adventurous	efficient
kind	ambitious	organized
friendly	competitive	obedient
responsible	enthusiastic	dependable
understanding	driving	moderate
popular	powerful	orderly
cooperative	persuasive	persistent
tactful	assertive	detailed
flirtatious		thorough

Next, review the adjectives you circled. Note it is divided into six clusters known as Realistic, Investigative, Artistic, Social, Enterprising, and Conventional (RIASEC). Which groups of adjectives best describe you? Also note that most of the words are positive personality traits. This exercise gives you a chance to acknowledge your positive attributes.

From which three of the six groups do most of your adjectives come? Rank the group from which most of them come as 1, the least as 3.

#1 _____   #2 _____   #3 _____

Each group of adjectives describes a certain kind of person. What kinds of people do you like to be around? Rank those you most like to be around as 1, the least as 3.

#1 _____   #2 _____   #3 _____

1.5 Considering occupational "status"

Rank the following occupations in numerical order according to the *status* you attribute to them. Number 1 should be the occupation that in your mind is most significant—how you define "significant" is, of course, up to you. For example, a police officer could appear as number 1 on your list if you place most value on societal order and safety. Number 20 should reflect the occupation you regard as least significant.

_____ administrative assistant	_____ engineer	_____ police officer
_____ agriculture supervisor	_____ hairdresser	_____ psychiatric nurse
_____ auto technician	_____ landscape designer	_____ public school teacher
_____ computer operator	_____ lawyer	_____ restaurant manager
_____ construction worker	_____ movie director	_____ robotics technician
_____ dental hygienist	_____ musician	_____ salesperson
_____ doctor	_____ plumber	

Think about the aspects of these positions that impress you or seem of value to you. Next, think about how you define status. Is it based on probable income, amount of education required, societal standards? How individualistic do you think your rankings are? For example, was *musician* ranked in your top five because you appreciate music? There are, in actuality, no correct or incorrect answers in this exercise. However, your rankings may reflect some of your basic preferences. If most of your top-ranked occupations were higher-salaried or if your ranking was based on potential for high pay, you may be motivated by a need for security; if your highest rankings were for service-related occupations (e.g., doctor, public school teacher), your motivation might be different.

1.6 Exercise summary

Write a brief paragraph answering these questions

What have I learned about myself? My current life stage? How does this knowledge relate to my career/life planning? How do I feel?

*Go to page 157,
of the Part One Chapter Summaries,
and fill out the Chapter One exercise summary now.*

TWO

Programming Yourself for Success

Through the process of career planning, you learn how to take what you've got (values, skills, interests, aptitudes, qualities, limitations) and do what it takes (job search strategy) to reach your career goal. A satisfying career *is* attainable *if* you decide you want it. We begin the process of career planning with an assessment of your self-esteem and your attitudes, because your mental outlook is the crucial variable that will move you toward or keep you from identifying and achieving your career goals. No book, set of exercises, system, or counselor will affect your future as much as your own belief system and your own commitment to achieving success. Your beliefs are reflected by your actions. How many times have you told yourself, "I'm going to start on a new exercise program today" and then found a "legitimate" excuse to postpone your efforts? Are you really ready to work on your career fitness? If so, let's examine some of the beliefs and attitudes that can assist you with your plan.

Because we believe in positive attitude and imagery (both of which we'll discuss shortly), we have used positive statements to begin each section in this chapter. This is done to provide you with models of statements that reflect attitudes that lead to successful behavior.

I am building self-esteem

Our sources of self-esteem are deeply rooted; at a very young age we begin to formulate a concept of ourselves based on our upbringing, our schooling, our culture, and a multitude of other factors. It is an unfortunate truth that many of us reach adulthood with low self-esteem, which manifests itself in many ways. For example, we may be afraid to try new things for fear of being embarrassed. We may let others make decisions for us, or we may stay in a job that we dislike rather than risking loss in order to find one we do like.

Obviously, one book or course cannot miraculously repair low self-esteem, and we do not mean to imply that such a quick fix is possible. *However*, this book can help you identify possible problem areas, give you the incentive to make changes, and start you in the right direction. Today, many colleges offer courses on building self-esteem, learning to be assertive, and related issues. Thus, you have resources available if you discover you need help; making that discovery is an important step in the right direction.

The ultimate goal is to like yourself. The higher your appreciation of yourself, the greater your chances of feeling and being successful in your personal and career goals. This chapter identifies several building blocks of self-esteem. As you read each section, take a quick pulse. How would you rate yourself on each of these essential components? Which ones do you need to work on first? As you identify the areas in your life that need work, pay attention to the suggestions for improvement. Later, Exercises 2.1 and 2.3 will help you further your goal of building self-esteem. This should be a lifelong goal. Establish small goals that you can meet along the way and give yourself credit for small successes.

Although the word "success" means many things to many people, success in general usually means the progressive external demonstration of internalized life goals. In other words, success refers to the step-by-step movement toward the attainment of an object, quality, or state of mind that we value and wish to possess.

Sooner or later, the person who wins is the person who thinks, "I can!"
Anonymous

I maintain a positive outlook

Do you have your own personal definition of success? Regardless of the particular goals you have in mind, you need to think positively to attain them.

Have you ever heard the saying, "It's all in your head"? People who say this believe that our mental attitudes have control over our body and our life and can, therefore, program our success or failure. Although many of our attitudes and beliefs come from early messages we received from our parents and teachers, as

If you think you are beaten, you are;
If you think you dare not, you don't;
If you like to win, but you think you can't,
It is almost certain you won't.

If you think you'll lose, you've lost,
For out of the world we find
Success begins with a person's will;
It's all in the state of mind.

If you think you are outclassed, you are;
You've got to think high to rise.
You've got to be sure of yourself before
You can even win a prize.

Life's battles don't always go
To the stronger or faster man,
But sooner or later, the person who wins
Is the person who thinks, "I can!"

Anonymous

adults we can choose to keep or change these messages depending on how helpful they are to us in achieving success and satisfaction in life.

Examine your philosophy of life. How you see life in general is how you lead your life. A quick way to identify your philosophy is to examine how you visualize the future.

Read the following scenarios and select the one that best relates to your point of view (Kauffman, 1976).

The future is a great roller coaster on a moonless night. It exists, twisting ahead of us in the dark, although we can see each part only as we come to it. We can make estimates about where we are headed and sometimes see around a bend to another section of track, but it doesn't do us any real good because the future is fixed and determined. We are locked in our seats, and nothing we may know or do will change the course that is laid out for us.

The future is a mighty river. The great force of history flows inexorably along, carrying us with it. Most of our attempts to change its course are mere pebbles thrown into the river: they cause a momentary splash and a few ripples, but they make no difference. The river's course can be changed, but only by natural disasters like earthquakes and landslides or by massive, concerted human efforts on a similar scale. On the other hand, we are free as individuals to adapt to the course of history either well or poorly. By looking ahead, we can avoid sandbars and whirlpools and pick the best path through any rapids.

The future is a great ocean. There are many possible destinations, and many different paths to each destination. A good navigator takes advantage of the main currents of change, adapts the course to the capricious winds of chance, keeps a sharp lookout posted, and moves carefully in fog or uncharted waters. Doing these things will get the navigator safely to a destination (barring a typhoon or other disaster that one can neither predict nor avoid).

The future is entirely random, a colossal dice game. Every second, millions of things happen that could have happened another way and produced a different future. A bullet is deflected by a twig and kills one person instead of another. A scientist checks a spoiled culture and throws it away or looks more closely at it and discovers penicillin. A newly renovated home is destroyed by an earthquake. Since everything is chance, all we can do is play the game, pray to the gods of fortune, and enjoy what good luck comes our way.

One of these scenarios may reflect your perception of life. Is your life a roller coaster, beyond your control; a mighty river to which you must adapt; a great ocean with many directions and options; or just a game of chance? Are you a positive thinker or a negative thinker? The second and third scenarios are the more positive reflections. Your belief system will affect how you see life. Have you ever noticed how your most dominant thoughts reinforce what happens to you? This phenomenon is called the "self-fulfilling prophecy."

Your mind tends to believe what you tell it. And, yes, you can if you *think* you can. Cultivating a positive, assertive outlook on life is the most crucial factor in the difference between those people who have successful, satisfying lives/careers and those who don't. Let's examine some of the aspects of this positive, assertive outlook so that we can get into a mind-set for success.

I am assertive

One of the basic choices we make moment to moment is whether to be assertive, aggressive, or passive in response to life situations. Being assertive means being the ultimate judge of our own behavior, feelings, and actions and being responsible for the initiation and consequence of those actions. In essence, assertive people choose for themselves and build themselves up *without* putting others down. Aggressive people choose for themselves and others; they build themselves up *by* putting others down. Passive people allow *others* to choose *for* them; they put themselves down or allow others to do so.

An assertive attitude will help you maintain some control over today's competitive job market. An assertive outlook enables you to be persistent, seek more information when you run out of leads, weigh all alternatives evenly (incorporating both your logic and your intuition), revise your goals when necessary, and pursue your goals with commitment and purpose. Assertiveness specifically enables you to say what you feel, think, and want. It allows you to be expressive, open, and clear in communication. You are able to say no under pressure, recognize and deal with manipulation, and stand up for your rights in negative, confrontational situations. You gain the ability to be a better listener. Others appreciate your directness and ability to hear them. You enjoy more positive interactions with people and feel more positive about being able to handle life situations.

Assertive personal traits include body language as well as words. Studies indicate that 93 percent of the meaning of any message is communicated nonverbally. Look at your appearance, facial expressions, and typical physical movements and stance when you are feeling assertive compared with when you are feeling passive. What does your style of dress say about you? Can changing the color or style of your outfit change the mood you project to others? Have you ever noticed your gesturing? Assertiveness is often associated with expansive gestures rather than limited ones. Finally, how do you deal with touch or physical closeness? Being assertive means feeling comfortable within your own body space.

Positive, assertive behavior suggests that you truly have confidence in yourself. This behavior conveys verbally and nonverbally that you believe in your abilities and in your own worth. That positive, confident, and enthusiastic self

Remember the times you've thought the following:

"That's just the way I am."

"I can't control what I do."

"I just can't seem to finish anything I start."

"I would like to do that differently, but it's just too hard to change."

"Yes, it happened again."

"I've never been good at that."

An assertive attitude helps to maintain control

Positive, assertive behavior shows self-confidence

will set you apart, make people take notice of you, and ultimately enable you to exercise control over your career and your life.

I have a sense of humor

According to journalist Norman Cousins, laughing is internal jogging, and when you laugh you are exercising all your internal organs. Not only does laughter feel good, it is essential to good health and a sense of well-being. Cousins has good reason to believe this: some years ago he was diagnosed with a terminal illness and given just two months to live. Instead of spending his precious time remaining in the hospital, he checked into a hotel and watched, read, or listened to every humorous movie, book, and audiotape he could get his hands on. He virtually laughed himself well. Many years later, still in excellent health, Cousins was convinced, as were his doctors, that laughter accounted for his recovery! In fact, the medical school at U.C.L.A. invited him to join its faculty to teach interns how to "lighten up."

Cousin's amazing story holds a lesson for all of us. We can all stand to lighten up a little, to find the genuine humor in an embarrassing moment, in a mistake, in a situation that is so serious that we need to laugh to keep from crying. Humor at its best means being able to laugh at yourself. Look for opportunities to see the lighter side of life and to share the experience of being human with others who can laugh with you, not at you. Cultivate the habit of walking on the "light" side of life.

I am self-confident

Discover your own self-worth

Self-confidence, perhaps more than any other factor, is the secret to success and happiness. It is the ability to recognize that even though you are imperfect, you are a unique, worthwhile, and lovable person who deserves and can attain the best in life. You project a sense of self-confidence in your body language, your dress, your pace, your ability to take pride in your accomplishments, your ability to learn from your mistakes, and your ability to accept suggestions and praise from others. Because you believe you deserve the career of your choice, you can attain it.

You can begin to develop more self-confidence by recognizing and rewarding yourself for something you do *well* each day. It may feel more natural for you to review, in great detail, each and every negative event that has occurred. This is a common and understandable human reaction that can be neutralized by deliberate positive thinking. At times you may have to force yourself to think of something positive and give yourself a pat on the back. Better yet, make it a point to share the good news with a friend, a support person, someone who you know will delight in your small personal achievement. Consider starting a support group consisting of individuals who want to share their personal victories with each other. The reinforcement and support of others are powerful tools in our personal quest for success. Start small, remembering that an Olympic gold medal, just like self-confidence, is built on hours, days, weeks, months, and years of small personal victories.

I am enthusiastic

You can identify achievers by their consistently optimistic and enthusiastic demeanor. They know that life is a self-fulfilling prophecy, that people usually get what they actively imagine and expect. They choose to start the day on a positive note by listening to music, singing in the shower, or telling themselves this will be a good day. They view problems as opportunities to be creative. They learn to stay relaxed and calm under stress. They associate with people who share their optimism about life and who support each other through praise, encouragement, and networking. When asked about their career goals, instead of saying, "I don't know," they say, "I'm in the process of discovering my career goals."

Employers rate enthusiasm highly

When employers are asked what traits they look for in prospective employees, enthusiasm is always among those at the top of the list. What kind of people do you want as friends, associates, and colleagues? Chances are you want people who are optimistic and have a zest for life. You can become more enthusiastic about life by getting involved in something that has meaning for you. A hobby, volunteer work, mastery of a skill, a new relationship all provide opportunities to generate and express enthusiasm. On the job, displaying a professional attitude includes acting as if things are fine even when you feel upset or depressed. While it may seem phony, you will find that acting positively pays off. Not only do you come across as mature and professional, but as you begin to "act" enthusiastically you receive positive feedback from others. The smiles, nods, and positive words of others begin to make you feel enthusiastic, and you soon discover you are no longer acting: you genuinely feel better!

I use positive self-talk (affirmations)

One of the most effective ways to improve your self-image is the deliberate use of positive self-talk. You already talk to yourself; we all do, constantly! But we usually do not consciously listen to our internal dialogue; consequently, we often hear only negative, self-defeating messages that create and reinforce a poor self-image. Once you decide to take charge of your self-talk, you can begin to repeat positive messages that will reinforce a positive self-image. This process is commonly called affirmations.

Positive self-talk improves self-image

An *affirmation* is a statement or assertion that something is *already* so (Gawain, 1995). It is an existing seed or thought in the here and now that will grow as life unfolds. It is not intended to change what already exists but to create new, desired outcomes. Remember, all events begin with a thought. If you think you can, you can! Anything a person can conceive can be achieved. Good gardeners cultivate not only flowers but also the soil in which they grow. The thoughts you are thinking and sending out are the "soil" of your life. If you constantly project thoughts of lack of ability, you will have barren soil. If you project thoughts of ability and strength, your soil will be rich. Therefore, any career in which you can imagine yourself being happy and successful can be achieved.

However, when developing your affirmations, remember that you are planting a seed and that the seed must carry information on the exact thing

Here are some hints to follow when stating or writing down your own affirmations.

1. Always phrase the affirmation in the present, never in the future; otherwise it may remain in the future. For example, if your goal is to be less tense or nervous in challenging and stressful situations, use an affirmation like "I *am* calm; I *am* in control of my feelings and this situation," rather than "I *will be* calm."

2. Phrase your affirmation in the positive rather than the negative. In other words, avoid affirming what you don't want. Instead of writing "My present job doesn't bother me anymore," it would be much more effective to write, "My work is wonderful" or "I enjoy my job."

3. Maintain the attitude that you are creating something new and fresh. You are not trying to manipulate, redo, or change an existing condition.

you want to grow into, or produce—the result you desire. When you become specific about what you want, you are focusing the power of your mind's energy (your thoughts) on your desires. The more specific you are about your goals, the more focused you become about what must be done to reach them. You know you are being specific enough when you can visualize details about what you want. For example, if you want to become a college professor, you must be able to see yourself on a college campus, in a specific classroom, standing before a room of students, lecturing, interacting with other professors, and correcting papers!

Let's put this technique into action. Think of a quality that you want to develop in yourself; we'll use enthusiasm as an example. Your first instinct might be to say or think, "I'm not very enthusiastic." As soon as this thought comes to mind, replace it with the opposite thought, "I am enthusiastic." Repeat the phrase over and over, day and night, until you feel you own it; soon it will feel comfortable. At the same time, picture yourself doing something enthusiastically, such as explaining to your boss why you deserve a day off, starting a conversation with a stranger, or confidently disagreeing with an instructor during class. Picture yourself making your statement and being positively reinforced: your boss says yes, you deserve it; the stranger becomes a friend; the instructor praises you for your insight.

Thus, even before you implement your affirmation by enthusiastically taking some action, you have prepared yourself mentally for a positive outcome of your action. Your chances of experiencing the positive outcome improve because you are projecting a positive self-image. Try it!

I visualize success

Visualization, much like affirmations, is mental practice. It is the conscious implanting of specific images in your mind. Through repetition, these images will become part of your unconscious and then conscious mind, evoking and enhancing abilities, habits, and attitudes. Visualization differs slightly from affirmations because it involves specific mental imagery as opposed to verbal expression of positive thoughts. Visualization is also referred to as *mental imagery* and *mental rehearsal*.

Use mental rehearsal for success

Although we marvel at the mastery of an expert, we often assume that the person was born with superhuman talents or skills. We forget that every champion athlete, every great performer, every skilled surgeon, and every professional developed expertise through endless hours of physical and mental practice. They visualize their performance, they engage in positive self-talk ("I can," "I'll do better next time"), and through repetition they become more and more of what they desire to be.

Until you begin to understand yourself, it is difficult to fully contemplate success, both in personal matters and a career. Choose your own vision where specific results, qualities, and abilities are evident and consistent with "winning."

Visualization is one of the most powerful tools promoting personal change. It is the process of maintaining a thought long enough for the mental picture we create to evoke an emotional response. This emotion causes conviction, and conviction influences reality. Thus, a change in reality begins with visualization, which turns to emotion, and results in conviction.

Visualization can have a profound impact on your mind. Your subconscious does not distinguish between imagining something or actually experiencing it. (Try imagining you are biting into a lemon; can you taste it?) You can change your opinions, beliefs, aspirations, and levels of expectation by vividly imagining the circumstances and experiences you select. Of all the species on earth, only human beings can visualize the future and believe it can happen (Dyer, 1992).

A pessimist says, "I will believe it when I see it," whereas an optimist says, "I always see it when I believe it." What you see is what you get. The critical first step is a mental one. You must believe in and be able to see the possibilities and outcomes in your mind before you can hope to realize them in your life.

A high-jumper visualizes a successful route to clear the bar; a golfer sees in his mind the putt dropping into the cup and follows that vision. Strong visual messages are often reinforced with appropriate positive affirmations. This process will assist you in achieving what you want to accomplish. Conscious visualization of you as a "winner" is a key step toward a self-fulfilling prophecy.

Those who use visualization successfully do so regularly over a period of time. This is the key to the success of mental rehearsal. Research indicates that a goal must be visualized a minimum of 30 minutes a day for at least a month to obtain results. This discipline distinguishes visualization from random daydreaming, an effortless activity in which we all engage from time to time!

I have a positive self-image

Successful people *like* themselves, visualize themselves at their best, and monitor their self-talk to reinforce their images of success in word and action. They know that self-image acts as a regulator, an unconscious thermostat. If you cannot picture yourself doing, being, or achieving something, you probably will not be able to do, be, or achieve it. Your self-image absorbs information, memorizes it, and guides your actions accordingly. Every time you say, "I can't," you are adding to a negative self-image. Every time you say, "I can and will," you are giving yourself permission to be your best. Successful people recognize how potent their beliefs about self are, and they take responsibility for shaping their own self-images, rather than allowing others' opinions to shape or limit them.

I learn from role models

So far we have explored the components for developing a positive self-image, that is, personal behaviors and attitudes that help us identify and best use our

values, skills, and interests. Now it's time to look outside ourselves at people who display the qualities of success we want to cultivate. Think about who you admire and begin to make a list. First, think globally about prominent individuals on the national and international scene. Then, think locally about people with whom you work; individuals who are part of your community, your neighborhood, or your religious affiliation; those who attend your school; or those who share your hobbies. Finally, think of the people who are most dear to you—your family and friends. Which of their qualities do you admire? In what ways do you want to be more like them?

First steps in networking and information interviewing

Spend time observing them in action. You may want to consider telling them what you admire about them and asking them to tell you how they developed those qualities. Ask them for insights and suggestions that you might use in developing your own success profile. Make these people part of your network of contacts. You will probably find that even the most successful people have struggled with moments of self-doubt or crises of self-confidence. Ask them what they do when the going gets rough.

No doubt you choose your friends and associates deliberately and carefully, knowing that you are influenced by the attitudes of the company you keep. Similarly, when you seek out individuals and acknowledge the qualities you admire in them, you are giving them the gift of recognition and appreciation, a valuable commodity in today's fast-paced, all too impersonal world. Also, in speaking with your role models you are practicing "information interviewing" (to be discussed in Chapter Nine) and taking the first steps in developing networking skills.

In fact, this is a good time for doing some volunteer work, exploring internships, and getting involved in the community. It is not too soon to use the newspaper or local magazines to find leads and meet people who can give you ideas. Look for articles describing successful people or interesting jobs. Then call these people and interview them about how they chose and trained for their careers. Their strategies may also work for you. (See Exercise 2.6.) You are making connections that can later assist you in the job search process. Of course, you are also projecting the positive self-image you are cultivating.

Allan had been laid off after working for a company for twelve years. After the shock and disbelief of his involuntary career change had passed, he began to ask himself what he would really enjoy doing. He realized that the hours he spent in the library provided some of his most rewarding experiences. Because he was not a librarian, he could not imagine himself working in a library in any capacity and could not even bring himself to volunteer his services. His fears about lacking the qualifications (fear of inadequacy) prevented him from moving in the direction of his desire (to work in a library). After many months of fruitless job hunting, he finally mustered up the courage to become a volunteer at the library. In less than two months, the staff recognized his valuable contributions, and he was offered the next paid position that became available.

I initiate action

Successful people realize that goals activate people and fears stop people. If you dwell on your fears, whether real or imagined, you will be immobilized in the pursuit of your goals. If you concentrate on your goals, you will move toward them. People who are afraid to tell the world what they want don't get it. The difference between those who are successful and those who are not is attitude. What side of the coin do you choose to look at—fears or goals? In what direction are you going—away from or toward your goals?

Imagine yourself in your dream job, your fantasy career, the kind of job you would pay to do. Take the job of cruise ship director, for example. Now identify someone who has that occupation. If you don't know of anyone, ask your friends, relatives, neighbors, and classmates, all of whom are part of your extended network (see Exercise 9.1 for a list of people who make up your network). Ask if they know someone who actually has your dream job. Next, contact that individual in person, if possible, and arrange a brief information interview. Read the section in Chapter Nine on information interviewing, and plan to ask the sample questions.

After you have gathered some facts about your fantasy career, ask yourself if it still holds its appeal for you. If so, you may wish to talk to others in the field to further develop an accurate and detailed assessment. If not, you may want to choose another fantasy career to investigate.

I am persistent

Persistent people take responsibility for initiating desired action. They know that life is full of choices, not chances. They realize they have the personal power, both physical and psychological, to take control of their own lives. They know that blaming Mother Nature for a less-than-perfect body or calling it fate when they don't get a job is simply "copping out." Successful people make things happen for themselves. What appears to be luck is usually opportunity met by preparation.

Luck = opportunity, preparation, and persistence

Perhaps nowhere is this more evident than in the Olympics. Only the most persistent and committed athletes will be chosen to participate, and all know full well the slim chance of coming home with a medal. Nevertheless, many return time after time, and some eventually triumph. Those fortunate enough to compete gain public acclaim knowing their participation places them in elite company. The successful person is the one who keeps trying after *not* reaching a goal or after rejection, the one who keeps trying until the dream is attained.

In today's unpredictable economy, many of us feel like we, too, are preparing for the Olympics; this especially holds true for students and job seekers, who must face such hurdles as degree and training decisions, finances, interviews, and rejections. Never has persistence in the face of limited opportunity been more necessary.

Through tenacity, determination, and consistent effort, you can achieve much. Talent and education are not automatic keys to success: nothing can take the place of persistence and enthusiasm.

I am disciplined

Self-discipline can also be called *self-control*. It is the ability to control or manage some aspect of your life, to have power over it. A simple example is that most of us have the self-discipline to get out of bed every morning at a particular time even though we'd probably prefer to sleep later.

Use mental rehearsal for success

Self-discipline is a vital component of success. If you lack the discipline to complete a task or spend the hours needed to accomplish your immediate goal (e.g., to contact four potential employers, study for an important test), your long-term goals will not be accomplished. Each time we allow a task to go

undone or a goal to go unaccomplished, we train ourselves to believe that it is okay, that there's always tomorrow. In the meantime, someone else is out there doing it. As is true of persistence and attitude, self-discipline is part of the foundation for success; it must be the basis of other strategies for success we have discussed.

I demonstrate emotional intelligence

Our competitive and achievement-oriented society places great value on intellectual ability. Early in your life your parents and teachers probably tried to determine your IQ (intelligence quotient). The results of such tests are highly regarded, even though these tests are often judged to be inaccurate and incomplete. The results are often unreliable predictors of future success in life. Were you labeled an overachiever or underachiever? Average, or below average? Were you inspired by these labels—or did they cause you to lose motivation? We have all heard stories of high IQ individuals who were not successful at chosen paths or who were unhappy in life. Conversely, many people with low to average "intelligence" have defied all predictions and become successful by any definition of the term. In fact, research on college grade point average as a predictor of success indicates the B to C student often enjoys more success in later life than the solid A performer! What explains this apparent paradox?

Recent research completed by Daniel Goleman and discussed in his book *Emotional Intelligence* (1995) offers some answers. The common sense, wisdom, maturity, humor, and street smarts that distinguish successful individuals is the manifestation of emotional intelligence (EQ). It is the awareness of and ability to monitor and control our emotions, thoughts, and feelings and the ability to be aware of and sensitive to others that define emotional intelligence. Complete Exercise 2.3 to test your own EQ. The better developed your EQ, the more successful you are likely to be. Although you are born with IQ, you can learn and cultivate EQ. It may be IQ that gets you the job, but it's EQ that keeps you employed and gets you promoted!

I identify my goals

People who succeed have clearly defined plans and objectives that they refer to regularly to keep in mind their lifetime goals, as well as to order their daily priorities. Clearly defined, written goals help move us to completion. The reason most people don't reach their goals is that they don't identify them. They don't know what they want. (See Chapter 8 for information on setting goals.)

If you don't know where you are going, you probably won't get there. Even though you're just embarking on your career fitness plan and you probably don't have a specific career in

---

What makes workers succeed . . .

Executives say these personality traits are most important:

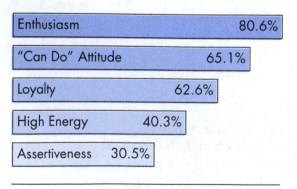

Enthusiasm	80.6%
"Can Do" Attitude	65.1%
Loyalty	62.6%
High Energy	40.3%
Assertiveness	30.5%

Source: Management Dimensions Inc.; Survey of 241 executives from all types of companies. Elys McLean-Ibrahim, *USA Today*.

mind as yet, you can still begin the process of goal setting. Your *first goal* might be to read this book one chapter a week, and complete all the exercises after each chapter with the intent of learning more about yourself so you can make appropriate career choices when the time comes. Ideally, you should set aside a specific time and place each week so that you will get into the habit of working on your career fitness plan in the same way that you would work on a physical fitness plan—with consistency and commitment.

Knowing what you want is step number one

I am self-reliant and career resilient

In the face of events such as downsizing and rightsizing, successful employees must demonstrate self-reliance and resilience. These involve the ability to continually learn and develop new skills, initiate activities, demonstrate flexibility, and continuously align work with the business need. It is essential to ask constantly—and be able to answer—the question, "How does my work add value to the organization?" As the job tasks and business needs change, those who want to remain employed must be in a *continuous learning* mode. Simply doing a good job is no longer enough!

SUMMARY

Career success is based on a knowledge of self. The more you understand and accept your uniqueness, the better able you will be to make appropriate life and career choices.

Programming yourself for success is the first step of your personal assessment program. As you cultivate and engage in each of the practices addressed in this chapter, you will raise and reinforce your self-esteem, the root of all success. *Your opinion of yourself will grow in proportion to the time and energy you give to developing your most valuable asset—yourself.*

These exercises are designed to review your attitude and assertion skills. Try to answer the first set of questions as quickly and spontaneously as possible. Do not censor your answers. These are called open-ended questions. Open-ended questions sometimes make people think about different responses each time they see them, so it's all right to have more than one answer, as well as to change an answer whenever you review the questions.

These questions will also cause you to review past actions so that you can better identify how they affected who you are today. Answer the questions in the rest of the exercises to reflect your ideal environment and how you see yourself.

2.1 Past actions and influences

Fill in each blank carefully and honestly. Be true to yourself; don't try to please anyone else with your answers.

a. I am proud that ....

....

....

b. One thing I can do now that I couldn't do a few years ago is ....

....

....

c. Name the person you most admire. This person can be living, historical, or fictional. Write down the specific characteristics that you admire in this person (e.g., smart, famous, rich, loving, generous). ....

....

....

d. Name a person who is like you, and describe this person. ....

....

....

e. In the last two weeks, what activities or people gave you a feeling of being energized? ....

....

....

....

f. What have you always wanted to do in your life? What's keeping you from doing it? What action could you take in the next year to get closer to this goal? ....

....

....

....

g. What negative habit have you successfully changed? ....

....

....

....

h. What three words would you like others to use in describing you? ....

....

....

2.2 Two perfect days

a. **Written description**

In order to be clear about what you want in life, write a **one-page description of two ideal days in your future.** One day should be related to leisure, and one day should be related to work. Think about where you would be; what you'd be doing; who, if anyone, would be with you, etc. Try to be as detailed as possible. **Use Chapter 7, Exercise 7.4 as your outline for the workday.**

Use this space for notes: ....

....

....

....

....

....

b. **Summary in two or three words**

Write down three or more words or phrases that capture the *essence and quality of each of these two days*, e.g., peaceful, challenging, fun, harmonious, exciting, restful, productive.

Leisure day: ....

....

....

Workday: ....

....

....

2.3 Emotional intelligence checklist

Answer the following questions for a better idea of how your attitude is reflected in your actions. Consider asking several important people in your life to also respond to these questions about you. Compare their answers with yours. Choose two or three areas to work on to improve your attitude and emotional intelligence.

	Satisfied	Need to Improve
a. Do I always do my best?		
b. Do I tend to look on the bright side of things?		
c. Am I friendly and cooperative?		
d. Am I prompt and dependable?		
e. Do I do my share (or more than my share)?		
f. Do I appear confident, poised?		
g. Am I believable?		
h. Do people ask my opinions?		
i. Do I appear to be trustworthy?		
j. Am I well-mannered, tactful, considerate of others?		
k. Do I dress appropriately?		
l. Do I put others before myself? To what extent?		
m. Can I accept compliments?		
n. Do I give compliments?		
o. Do I make suggestions?		
p. Can I say no?		
q. Do I wait for others to decide for me?		

2.4 Positive self-talk (affirmations)

a. Write six affirmations related to being successful in your career and life planning. Put them on 3 x 5 cards (one per card). Some examples:

1. *I am a confident and competent person.*
2. *I have many transferable skills.*
3. *I am a valuable employee.*
4. *I am a risk taker.*
5. *I am a skilled networker.*
6. *I enjoy talking to people about their careers.*

1. ....

2. ....

3. ....

4. ....

5. ....

6. ....

b. Read your affirmations to yourself two times during the day, once in the morning as you awake and once just before going to sleep. Consider sharing your affirmations with a close friend or a classmate.

c. To accelerate their effectiveness, try the following suggestions.

   1. *Write your affirmations in longhand while speaking them aloud to yourself ten, twenty, or more times.*

   2. *Try writing in different persons, such as "I, Marilyn, am highly employable." "You, Marilyn, are highly employable." "She, Marilyn, is highly employable."*

   3. *Record your affirmations on a cassette tape recorder and listen to them as you drive or while doing chores around the house.*

   4. *Before going to sleep at night or on rising in the morning, visualize yourself as you are becoming. For example, see yourself as more assertive, loving, social, enthusiastic.*

   5. *Chant or sing your affirmations aloud while driving or during any appropriate activity.*

   6. *Meditate on your affirmations.*

   7. *Tape them up around the house, on the telephone, on the mirrors, on the refrigerator, on the ceiling above your bed, on the dashboard of your car, in your dresser drawers.*

   8. *Use affirmations as bookmarks.*

d. Finally, ask yourself: is it what you really want? George Bernard Shaw once commented, "The only thing worse than not getting what you want is getting what you want!" In other words, many go fishing all their lives, only to realize it wasn't the fish they wanted.

2.5 Your fantasy careers

"Wouldn't it be great to be . . ."

List your current fantasy careers below. Then think back chronologically to earlier age levels and try to recall some of your past fantasy careers; list them as well. We develop fantasy careers at a very young age. Most children see cartoons, television dramas, and movies about doctors, lawyers, police officers, firefighters, astronauts, teachers, and scientists, to name a few popular careers. Books about solving mysteries create an image of excitement about being a detective. Current movies influence many to dream of being a jet pilot or gifted performer. What have you read about, seen in the movies, or dreamed about doing?

a. For each career on your list, ask yourself this question: "What about this career is or was appealing to me?" Many of us might have the same fantasy career but for different reasons.

Current   What about this career appeals to me?

1. ....

2. ....

3. ....

4. ....

Chronological past,   What appealed most to me about
by age   this fantasy career?

1–10 ....

....

....

11–15 ....

....

....

16–20 ....

....

....

21–30 ....

....

....

31–40 ....

....

....

41–50 ....

....

....

51 plus ....

....

....

b. Now choose the one fantasy career that is most appealing. Try to locate someone who earns a living in this career. If you are part of a class, ask your instructor and classmates if they can refer you to someone. Otherwise, try to make a connection by asking people you know at school, work, and social gatherings. Read the section on information interviewing in Chapter Nine. Arrange an interview, preferably in person, and ask the questions in the sample list of typical questions under Information Interviewing Outline.

2.6 Making a fantasy real

a. Find a newspaper or magazine article describing a job that seems like a "fantasy job" to you. Or find a story about a person you consider to be truly "successful." (Remember, you have a right to your own definition of success.)

b. Summarize the features that make the job or the successful person interesting. What are the personality traits of the person holding the job? What adjectives best describe this person? (See Exercise 1.4.) How do these traits relate to your own personality traits?

2.7 Exercise summary

a. What have I learned about myself?

b. I want to improve the following:

c. I admire the following qualities in people:

d. My affirmations are

e. What can I do in the next two weeks to improve my self-confidence?

Go to page 158,
of the Part One Chapter Summaries,
and fill out the Chapter Two exercise summary now.

THREE

Values Clarification

What is it that causes someone to study for years to enter a career such as medicine or law while others are looking for the quickest, easiest way to make money? What causes someone to switch careers midstream after spending years developing mastery and a reputation in a field? The answer to these questions is *values*. Your values are the often unidentified forces that guide and influence your decisions throughout your life. Values are *the deeply held commitments that influence your thinking when you are faced with choices*. They provide you with a frame of reference for evaluating information and options. If you value fitness and good health, you make time for daily exercise, positive self-talk, and proper nutrition. If you value career satisfaction, you will take time to examine your values and make choices consistent with them.

DEFINING VALUES

Values are the self-motivators that indicate what you consider most important in your life. Values are reflected in what you actually do with your time and your life. This chapter will help you identify what is needed in your work environment to make

you feel satisfied with your job. You may discover that the reason you are dissatisfied with your present job is that it incorporates few of your values and interests.

From time to time it may be necessary to settle for a job just to pay the bills; in such circumstances you may feel empty, frustrated, and unfulfilled by the job. Once you learn how to identify your values, it will be natural for you to take them into account and make meaningful and satisfying decisions about jobs. In other words, your decisions can be based on what's really important to you. If you are determined to follow your chosen career path and stay committed to your values, you will find that even when times are tough you will make every effort to stick to your long-range goal.

CLARIFYING YOUR VALUES

Now that you have begun to take charge of your mental attitude, identifying your values becomes the next step in your personal assessment program. By the age of 10, most of us have unconsciously adopted the values of our parents, teachers, and friends. By adolescence, we have begun to sort out which of these adopted values we want to freely choose as our own. This process of rejecting some of our family's values and developing our own is often called "teenage rebellion." Parents, in particular, often take offense when we question or reject a value they believe important. In fact, however, this process of values clarification is an essential part of growing up. Mature, independent, successful individuals act upon their own values rather than those of others. This frees them from unnecessary guilt ("What would my mother say if . . . ?") and indecision ("What would my boss do in this situation?"). It fosters satisfaction and self-confidence ("Regardless of the outcome, I'm in control of my life").

Adults often fail to reassess their values as life goes on. Research about life stages indicates that adults can and do make dramatic changes in their personal and career lives based on changes in values. This process of change can be less traumatic for all individuals involved if, as adults, we periodically review and reassess what is important to us.

How can you identify your values? The more intense your favorable feelings are about some activity or social condition, the more you value it. Is there an issue currently in the news that excites you or makes you angry? Are there certain activities that energize you? Are there circumstances in your life that lead you to certain activities? All of these are indicators of your values.

For the secret of man's being is not only to live but to have something to live for.
Dostoyevsky

Mary was one who benefited from reviewing her values. A secretary for an air freight carrier, she was delighted when the company contracted for the services of a career counselor. She couldn't wait to get help in choosing a new job. She felt bored and stagnant where she was. As the counselor helped her identify her values, Mary realized she liked security and didn't mind routine, structure, or taking orders. As she further explored her feelings of boredom, she remembered that the main reason she had chosen to work at an airline was for the travel privileges. Yet it had been years since she had actually taken advantage of the travel opportunities. Once she remembered and reevaluated her desire for travel, she began to use this benefit and was quite content to continue working for her current employer.

More specifically, the following criteria will help you determine your values. Values that are alive and an active part of you have the following qualities:

Prized and cherished. When you cherish something, you exude enthusiasm and enjoyment about it. You are proud to display it and use it.

Publicly affirmed. You are willing and perhaps even eager to state your values in public.

Chosen freely. No one else is pressuring you to act in a certain way. You own these values. They feel like a part of you.

Chosen from alternatives. If given a choice to play a leading role in a Hollywood film or be provided with a full scholarship to study at Harvard Business School, which would you choose? Choosing to act in Hollywood highlights such values as creativity, prestige, glamour, monetary returns, and risk taking, whereas choosing to acquire a Harvard MBA suggests prestige, monetary returns, education, intellectual stimulation, and security.

Chosen after consideration of consequences. We usually consider the consequences before we make an important decision. What impressions come to mind when you consider the following scenarios?

- You have been offered a job at a firm across the country far from the place you've lived all your life.
- You are offered a well-paying job as a defense contractor in your town.
- You are presented with a dinner check that doesn't charge you for all the food ordered.

What values come into play as you think about the decisions involved and their possible consequences?

Acted upon. Again, values are reflected in what you do with your time and your life; they are more than wishful thinking or romantic ideals about how you *should* lead your life.

Acted upon repeatedly and consistently, forming a definite pattern. The premise here is that you repeatedly engage in activities that relate to your highest values. To identify specific examples for yourself, complete the Values Grid in Exercise 3.1 at the end of this chapter. List five aspirations or goals you have achieved in your lifetime (e.g., finished high school, member of debate team, planned a surprise party, found a job), and then check the values that were involved in each goal. When you're done, the values with the most checks are those most important to you.

As you begin to think about it, you will come to realize how much you rely on your values to make decisions. People facing career planning often wonder how they will ever choose a career when they have so many possibilities in mind. This is precisely the time when knowing your values is most important. Let's say you've discovered that economic return, helping others, and security are your top three values. You are thinking about becoming an artist, an actor, or a speech teacher. You might well be able to do all three, even simultaneously! However, in order to choose one direction, try deciding which career would best satisfy your top three values. You are likely to experience the most success and happiness from this kind of choice. In this case, "speech teacher" most closely incorporates the values mentioned.

NEEDS AND MOTIVATORS

So far we have discussed motivation based on successful personal attitudes and values. In addition, inner drives or needs also influence how you choose a career. People experience psychological discomfort when their needs are unmet. We best satisfy our needs by identifying them and then engaging in behaviors that meet them. Once our needs are met, tension and discomfort are reduced. You may have read about five primary types of needs as identified by Abraham Maslow (1970), a famous psychologist.

As you can see, these needs progress from the most basic and biologically-oriented (survival needs) to more complex and socially-oriented levels of needs. When people are preoccupied with finding ways to put food on the table (physiological needs), they have little time or desire to work on developing relationships or to search for a job that can utilize their talents. Rather, they tend to work at any job that will immediately bring in money. A person becomes aware of a higher-order need only when a lower-order need has been met. These basic needs are such primary and intense self-motivators that our *values* may be eclipsed when we are struggling to meet primary *needs*.

One example of changing needs often occurs among divorcing couples with children. Most newly single parents have to readjust from the shared responsibilities of a two-parent family and the greater financial security of a two-person income. For some, the reduction in income and addition of responsibilities may be so great that the individual returns to a focus on meeting survival needs such as securing food and shelter. If parents in this situation are out of work, they will likely be far less concerned about the perfect job than with simply finding a job. As we discussed earlier, however, people should certainly take their values into account in career decisions whenever possible.

It is also important to assess needs from a cultural perspective and to realize that individuals may function and see things differently depending on the cultural context. For example, recent immigrants need time to adapt or adjust to a new environment. Even if their survival needs for

---

Maslow's types of needs

1. *Physiological needs.* Basic survival needs such as food and water.
2. *Safety needs.* Both physical (security, shelter, protection, law and order, health insurance, pension plans, secure job) and psychological (freedom from fear and anxiety).
3. *A sense of belonging and love.* Friends, affiliation, affection, relationships, love.
4. *Self-esteem/ego status.* Prestige, self-respect, competence, self-confidence, sense of self-worth.
5. *Self-actualization.* Achieving one's potential, being creative, serving a cause, contributing to society.

food, clothing, and shelter are met in the new culture, their lack of familiarity with local customs and their homesickness for familiar people and customs may diminish their sense of security, psychological well-being, and competence, as outlined by Maslow.

Job satisfaction: Internal vs. external motivators

When your ability to meet your physiological and safety needs is stable, you may find that you demand more feedback (satisfaction of social needs) in your work environment. Renowned industrial psychologist Frederick Herzberg (1966) examined the factors that produce or contribute to job satisfaction for most workers. We have already discussed how a job that reflects your top values contributes to job satisfaction. Herzberg also found that we have both external motivators and internal motivators. External motivators include salary, working conditions, company policies, and possibility for advancement, elements that fulfill physiological and safety needs. However, internal motivators involving amount of responsibility, type of work accomplished, recognition, and achievement all contribute to job satisfaction. These motivators appear to be most important for people with values and needs related to status and self-actualization. People do not necessarily respond to each need with identical intensities of desire. For your own benefit, it would be useful to examine what brings you satisfaction on the job. Exhibit 3.A illustrates how Herzberg's research on job satisfaction overlaps with Maslow's identification of needs.

FINDING BALANCE

Balance is the ability to include all your top priorities and values in your career and life plan. Some people who live to work *(workaholics)* and claim to be happy may not experience balance.

In today's challenging economic environment, it may seem more difficult than ever to consider your values, interests, and overall happiness when making career decisions. Nevertheless, as you learn more about what makes you happy and successful, you are indeed more likely to take all factors into account when choosing schooling or training and when making job and career decisions, even in tough economic times. Ideally, this process of identifying interests, talents, and values will begin much earlier in life for the generations to come. More and more high schools, for example, are offering career courses and encouraging students to find volunteer jobs and internships and take courses in those subjects and areas that interest them. When these students reach college or some other form of post-high school training, they are likely to have a much better idea of what they want to do and to have more experience to offer.

THE ROLE OF LEISURE

At one time, an employee who diligently honored family obligations and pursued leisure and other nonwork activities may have been considered uncommitted. The workplace now, however, acknowledges and even often encourages these pursuits. A satisfied, balanced individual is likely in the long run to be a more productive employee. Leisure activities allow individuals to "let go," be spontaneous, and tap into their creativity, self expression, and personal growth. All these qualities enhance performance on the job and counteract the negative effects of stress in many work situations. (In addition, many people have turned leisure pursuits into careers. Consider Mrs. Fields

Needs and motivators.

EXHIBIT 3.A

MASLOW'S NEED HIERARCHY

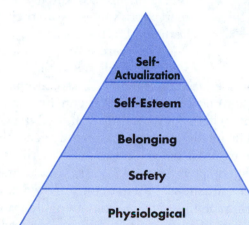

HERZBERG'S THEORY OF MOTIVATION

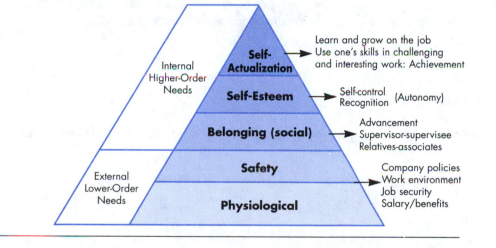

and her cookies and Tiger Woods and his golf.) The more an individual can balance the demands of family, work, and personal leisure, the better he or she can embrace the inevitable changes that challenge us daily.

Even in these challenging economic times, today's workers place a higher premium on leisure and family than in the past. Despite evidence that some employees are working longer hours to make up for corporate downsizing, employees today, when given the choice, typically place greater emphasis on finding quality time for family and outside interests than on increasing their wages by working extended hours.

SUMMARY

In Chapters Two and Three, we discussed several types of forces that propel you to act on your goals: attitudes, values, and needs. In Chapter Four you will learn more about your specific interests and personality type and how these can and should affect your career decisions.

The following exercises will help you identify your own specific values. As you complete the exercises, look for the values that occur repeatedly in your answers. By the end of the exercises you will have identified the five values that come up most often. These are your primary work values. Note them in Exercise 3.5 at the end of the chapter.

The exercises are divided into six parts. Exercise 3.1 is called the Values Grid. It will demonstrate how activities that you consider accomplishments or aspirations reflect your values. It also shows how your highest values recur and are implemented repeatedly in a variety of activities. Exercise 3.2 seeks to clarify what is important to you in all aspects of your life, from hobbies to work environments. The job descriptions are actually general descriptions of both jobs and values. Try guessing the name of the value and jobs described. The names of the values can be found at the end of this chapter. Exercise 3.3 asks you to rank your values in the order of importance in four different situations. Often, in our career decisions and in life in general, we do not get all that we want and must give up something desirable to get something *more* desirable. Exercise 3.4 asks you to examine what you say you want to do in your life. If you haven't taken any action to get what you want, your goals need to be reevaluated. The premise is that what is really valued serves as a driving force that motivates you to take action. Exercise 3.5 asks you to identify the types of careers that would utilize the values you hold dear. Exercise 3.6 explores the relationship between values and ethics.

3.1 Values grid

a. Fill out the Values Grid on the following page. Once you have completed the grid, respond to the questions in parts (b) and (c) below.

b. List your top five values (#1 is the value that received the greatest number of checks).

1. .... 2. .... 3. ....

4. .... 5. ....

c. Using the Values Grid and the list of values in the Job Description Answers (Exercise 3.7), first identify five jobs that best express your values, then those that least express your values.

Best Express Values

1. ....

2. ....

3. ....

4. ....

5. ....

Least Express Values

1. ....

2. ....

3. ....

4. ....

5. ....

VALUES GRID	ACCOMPLISHMENTS					

Above the numbers 1 through 5, *list* five accomplishments you have achieved anytime throughout your life. Use only a key word or two to represent the accomplishment. (If you wish, use the space below this chart to list your accomplishments in more detail.) *Check* the values that were involved in each accomplishment.

VALUE	DEFINITION	1	2	3	4	5	Total checks
accomplishment	knowing you've done well						
advancement	moving up						
aesthetics	caring about beauty and harmony						
cooperation	living in harmony with others						
creativity	developing new ideas or things						
economic return	working at a job that pays well						
education	appreciating learning						
family	caring about parents, children, & relatives						
freedom	having free choice of thoughts and actions						
health	feeling emotional/physical/spiritual well-being						
helping others	being of service to people						
independence	planning your own work schedule						
integrity	displaying behavior consistent with beliefs						
loyalty	showing devotion to someone or something						
management	planning and supervising work						
pleasure	seeking enjoyment or gratification						
power	having influence & the ability to act on it						
prestige	becoming well-known and respected						
recognition	gaining respect and admiration						
security	being certain of something						
teamwork	working together productively						

If desired, describe your accomplishments 1 through 5 in more detail here:

1. ....
2. ....
3. ....
4. ....
5. ....

3.2 Explore your values

a. List five things you love to do. What values are reflected in these activities? (See 3.1 Values Grid for ideas.) ....

....

....

b. What is one thing you would change in the world? In your town? About yourself?...................

....

c. What is something you really want to learn before you die? ....

....

d. List several values that are most important to you in your job (e.g., independence, creativity, working outdoors, environment). ....

....

e. Work environments are people environments. Some people add to your energy, productivity, and self-esteem; others drain you. Think of three people and describe their influence on you.

....

....

f. If you had unlimited funds so that you would not have to work:

1. How would you spend your time? (Try to think beyond "summer vacation," into a daily lifestyle.) ....

....

2. To what charities or causes would you contribute?...

....

Job descriptions

From the list of fifteen on the following pages, choose the three job descriptions you find most interesting as career possibilities. Then list the values each of those job descriptions implies. Some possible answers follow the exercise summary at the end of the chapter.

1. ....

....

2. ....

....

3. ....

....

.... 1. An opportunity to help people in a personal way. Meet and deal with the public in a meaningful relationship. Help to make the world a better place to live. Pay and benefits in accordance with experience.

.... 2. Do your own thing! Work with abstract ideas. Develop new ideas and things. Non-routine. A chance to work on your own or as a member of a creative team. Flexible working conditions.

.... 3. A professional position. Position of responsibility. Secretarial assistance provided. Pay dependent on experience and initiative. Position requires a high level of education and training. Job benefits are high pay and public recognition.

.... 4. A job with a guaranteed annual salary in a permanent position with a secure, stable company. Supervisory assistance is available. Minimum educational requirement is high school. Slightly better pay with one or two years of college or vocational training. Position guarantees cost-of-living pay increases annually. Retirement benefits.

.... 5. Looking for an interesting job? One that requires research, thinking, and problem solving? Do you like to deal with theoretical concepts? This job demands constant updating of information and ability to deal with new ideas. An opportunity to work with creative and intellectually stimulating people.

.... 6. This job requires an extraordinary person. The job demands risk and daring. Ability to deal with exciting tasks. Excellent physical health a necessity. You must be willing to travel.

.... 7. An ideal place to work. An opportunity to work with people you really like, and, just as important, who really like you. A friendly, congenial atmosphere. Get to know your coworkers as friends. Pay and benefits dependent on training and/or experience.

.... 8. Work in a young, fast-growing company. Great opportunities for advancement. Starting pay is low, but rapid promotion to mid-management. From this position, there are many opportunities and directions for further advancement. Your only limitations are your own energy and initiative. Pay and benefits related to level of responsibility.

.... 9. Set your own pace! Set your own working conditions. Flexible hours. Choose your own team or work alone. Salary based on your own initiative and time on the job.

.... 10. Start at the bottom and work your way up. You can become president of the firm. You should have the ability to learn while you work. Quality and productivity will be rewarded by rapid advancement and recognition for a job well done. Salary contingent on rate of advancement.

.... 11. Ability to direct work tasks of others in a variety of activities. Leadership qualities in controlling work force and maintaining production schedules. Ability to maintain a stable workforce. Coordinate work of large management team. Instruct workforce. Evaluate work completed. Hiring and firing responsibilities.

.... 12. Great opportunity for money! High salary, elaborate expense accounts, stock options, extra pay for extra work. Christmas bonus. All fringe benefits paid by company. High pay for the work you do.

.... 13. Are you tired of a dull, routine job? Try your hand at many tasks, meet new people, work in different situations and settings. Be a jack-of-all-trades.

.... 14. Does the thought of a desk job turn you off? This job is for the active person who enjoys using energy and physical abilities, since it requires brisk and lively movement.

.... 15. Opportunity to express your personal convictions in all phases of your job. Devote your lifestyle to your work.

3.3 Your values–some hard choices

In this exercise you are asked to choose the best and worst among sets of options, all of which are more or less undesirable. Rank the situations and individuals, however unpleasant, that you could best and most easily accept as number one, and the "worst bad case," the situations you would find hardest to accept, as number five, with the intervening cases ranked accordingly.

Job situations

.... To work for a boss who knows less than you do about your work and over whom you have no influence.

.... To be the key person in a job, while someone else gets better pay and all the credit for what you do.

.... To work with a group in which trust is very low.

.... To work in an organization whose job is to serve the poor but which wastes huge amounts of its resources on red tape.

.... To work day-to-day with someone who is always putting in second-rate work.

Environment

.... The desert (120 degrees F.) with a well-paying job.

.... A small subsistence-level farm in Appalachia.

.... An efficiency apartment in New York on a tight budget.

.... A congested, smoggy urban area that is a short walk to work from your comfortable low-rent apartment.

.... A middle-income suburban housing development, with an hour commute (one way), totally dependent on a freeway route.

Risks

.... Bet $10,000 on a gambling wager.

.... Put $10,000 into a new and uncertain business venture.

.... Go into business for yourself, with minimum resources.

.... Without an assured job, move to a place where you always wanted to live.

.... Risk arrest in a public demonstration for something about which you feel strongly.

3.4 Top five

List five things you want in life. Examine each of these to see what is most important to you. What have you done to support or express these values? What actions have you taken or do you need to take to move toward what you most want in life? What you say is important and what you are actually willing to do deserve close examination.

1. ....
2. ....
3. ....
4. ....
5. ....

3.5 Values related to careers

List below your top five values and three job descriptions (from Exercise 3.2) that you believe would allow you to fulfill many of those values. For example, creativity, variety, money, and independence might all be associated with a career as a lawyer, writer, or sales representative. Which job description best describes your values? What job title would you give to this job description?

Values

1. ....
2. ....
3. ....
4. ....
5. ....

Job descriptions

1. ....
2. ....
3. ....

3.6 Values related to ethics

a. In a class or group setting, discuss how values affect ethical behavior. Consider current events and prominent figures in the worlds of

athletics

business

education

entertainment

government

law enforcement

military

science

b. Choose one example from a newspaper or magazine article, and explain how you would have acted if you were in the same situation—for example, an athlete takes steroids to be competitive. What values are reflected in your actions?

3.7 Exercise summary

a. List the values that are most frequently reflected in your answers to this chapter's exercises.

1. ....

2. ....

3. ....

4. ....

5. ....

b. Rank the values listed above into your top five.

1. ....

2. ....

3. ....

4. ....

5. ....

c. List the top values that could most likely be satisfied by a future career.

....

....

....

....

d. What I have learned from reading and answering the exercises:

....

....

....

e. I feel .... after completing this chapter (e.g., more aware, confused, satisfied).

f. I am energized by the following types of activities (use values grid, past jobs, or hobbies):

1. ....

2. ....

3. ....

Job description answers

(for Exercise 3.2)

Job Number	Value	Job Title (examples)
1	Helping others	Social worker, Teacher, Counselor
2	Creativity	Writer, Artist, Graphic designer
3	Prestige	Executive, Politician, Doctor, Police officer
4	Security	Education administrator, Administrative assistant
5	Intellect	Researcher, Mathematician, Scientist
6	Adventure	Archaeologist, CIA investigator, Firefighter
7	Association	Educator, Restaurant worker, Tour guide
8	Advancement	Assistant sales manager, Engineer
9	Independence	Landscape artist, Contract worker, Marketing representative
10	Productivity	Sales representative, Clerk, Bookkeeper
11	Power	Manager, Team leader, Company president, Coach
12	Money	Stockbroker, Accountant, Real estate developer
13	Variety	Electrician, Plumber, Lawyer, Freelance editor
14	Physical activity	Game warden, Physical trainer, Physical education teacher
15	Lifestyle	Minister, Guidance counselor, Consultant

Go to page 158, of the Part One Chapter Summaries, and fill out the Chapter Three exercise summary now.

FOUR

Focusing on You: Personality and Interests

LEARNING OBJECTIVES

At the end of the chapter you will be able to . . .

Understand differences in personality types

Understand more about your own personality type

Recognize how personality type relates to career planning

Identify college majors that interest you

Match your interests to occupations, using the Worker Trait Groups and other inventories

The more you know about your natural tendencies and preferences, the easier it will be for you to identify a career path that enables you to maximize what comes naturally. If you take your personality and interests into account when starting down your career path, you are much more likely to enjoy your work and be fulfilled by it.

Many of us dismiss the notion that we can have careers based on who we are and what we like to do. Somewhere along the line, we lose track of early dreams inspired by our true selves and begin focusing on more practical matters: what degrees are offered and what classes are needed? What occupation offers security and good pay? In many cases, we might have been able to explore careers much more closely aligned with our interests than we thought possible. For example, a young man who loves baseball might not enjoy the many hours of practice needed to become a professional ball player and might abandon the field altogether. Yet he might have been able to pursue a career related to his interests, perhaps an athletic trainer for a team, a facility manager at a ballpark, or a park recreation leader. These careers might have been more congruous with his personality and interests than that of ball player or a completely unrelated position.

This chapter will help you explore some aspects of your own personality and interests. You will learn how to interpret this

knowledge and apply it to your career decisions. Perhaps you will identify a career path you hadn't before considered, based on who you are and what you really like to do.

EXPLORING PERSONALITY

Have you ever said to a friend, "That's not like you"? Has anyone ever said to you, "You're not acting like yourself today"? These are common ways for us to talk about the complex set of tendencies, behaviors, attitudes, and characteristics that makes each of us unique. The sum total of these qualities is called your *personality*.

The more you know about yourself and your personal preferences, the better able you will be to identify work and outside activities that complement your personality type. Several different assessment instruments are available to help you learn about yourself. Like the following activity, some of these instruments are based on the work of noted Swiss psychologist Carl Jung (1923), who developed a way to help us understand and categorize our inborn tendencies. Katherine Briggs and Isabel Briggs Myers (1962) later expanded upon Jung's theory to develop an assessment tool that helps identify personality preferences. This widely used survey is called the Myers–Briggs Type Indicator® (MBTI).* It might be possible for you to arrange through your instructor or career center to take this or some other survey to learn more about your personality type than is possible here.

The following activity is not intended to give you an exact description of your personality, nor to indicate that a certain personality fits exactly within a certain career. In fact, there is debate about the extent to which personality relates to career choice or satisfaction. Instead, this discussion and the accompanying exercise are intended to make you aware of some characteristics of your personality and give you some insight into what types of interactions and activities might be more comfortable and satisfying for you than others.

The information you gain about your personality can help you make practical decisions about the types of classes to take and the career you pursue. Career success is based on a knowledge of self. The more you know, understand, and accept your unique self, the better able you will be to make appropriate life and career choices. Learning about personality will also make you better able to understand and accept differences in others.

Next, identify your personal preferences from the four parts in the following activity.

What lies behind us and what lies before us are tiny matters compared to what lies within us.
Ralph Waldo Emerson

---

*Myers-Briggs Type Indicator and MBTI are registered trademarks of Consulting Psychologists Press, Inc., Palo Alto, CA.

ACTIVITY

IDENTIFYING YOUR PERSONAL PREFERENCES

The work of Jung, Myers, and Briggs provides us with a four-part framework in which to examine our inborn tendencies; thus the following exercise consists of four parts. In each part, you will determine which of two characteristics or preferences better describes you. Briefly, in Parts 1 through 4 you will select items that indicate personality tendencies toward (1) extroversion or introversion; (2) sensing or intuition; (3) thinking or feeling; and (4) judging or perceiving. Each of these characteristics will be explained below.

Instructions: Read the following pairs of descriptions and check the item in each pair that is like you *most of the time.* (All of us have aspects of all of these qualities to some degree.)* To help you decide, think of your most natural self, your behavior as if no one were looking.

PART 1 In describing your *flow of energy*, which pattern more closely resembles you, E or I?

E	**I**
.... Likes action and variety	.... Likes quiet and time to consider things
.... Likes to do mental work by talking to people	.... Likes to do mental work privately before talking
.... Acts quickly, sometimes without much reflection	.... May be slow to try something without understanding it first
.... Likes to see how other people do a job, and to see results	.... Likes to understand the idea of a job and to work alone or with just a few people
.... Wants to know what other people expect of him or her	.... Wants to set his or her own standards

E's interest turns mostly outward to the world of action, people, and things. I's interest turns more often to the inner world of ideas and personal concerns. Of course, everyone turns outward to act and inward to reflect. You too must do both, but you are more comfortable doing one or the other and rely on one more often than the other, just as right-handers are more comfortable using their right hands.

E stands for extroversion, which means outward turning.
I stands for introversion, which means inward turning.

Go on to next page

---

*The checklists in this exercise are adapted from *People Types and Tiger Stripes: A Practical Guide to Learning Styles*, 3rd edition, 1993, by Dr. Gordon Lawrence (Gainesville, FL: Center for Applications of Psychological Type). The exercise "Thinking About Mental Habits" from *People Types and Tiger Stripes* is NOT a type indicator, nor does it replicate the Myers-Briggs Type Indicator, which is a validated instrument. Used with permission. Parts of this exercise are also based on an exercise in *Building Self-Esteem: Strategies for Success in School and Beyond*, 2nd edition, 1997, by Bonnie Golden and Kay Lesh (Upper Saddle River, NJ: Prentice Hall).

ACTIVITY (Continued)

Typical extroversion type

Jesse is a computer consultant. He thrives on attending meetings at which several people at a company explain their computer needs, and he loves providing training for clients on their upgraded systems. His hobbies include attending conferences and serving as a Boy Scout leader for his son's troop, which he has also taken on weekend outings. Jesse gets energy from being around groups of people.

Typical introversion type

Jennifer is a computer consultant. She works in computer system design. She meets individually with a company's computer networking specialist who provides her with a list of company needs, and then she manipulates the company's system until it is operating as requested. She lets others train the staff. Jennifer gets her energy from working intensively with a technical system. She also gets recharged by spending time alone. Her hobbies include reading and exploring new ways of learning through the Internet and other distance learning programs.

In describing the ways in which you *take in information*, which pattern resembles you more closely, S or N?   **PART 2**

S

.... Pays most attention to experience as it is

.... Likes to use eyes, ears, and other senses to find out things

.... Dislikes new problems unless there are standard ways to solve them

.... Enjoys using skills already learned more than learning new ones

.... Is patient with details but impatient when the situation gets complicated

N

.... Pays most attention to the meanings of facts and how they fit together

.... Likes to use imagination to come up with new ways to do things, new possibilities

.... Likes solving new problems, and dislikes doing the same thing over and over

.... Likes using new skills more than practicing old ones

.... Is impatient with details but doesn't mind complicated situations

S and N represent two kinds of perception, that is, two ways of finding out or giving attention to experiences. Everyone uses both sensing and intuition, but we are likely to use one more than the other. S pays most attention to the facts that come from personal experience. S can more easily see the details, while N can more easily see the "big picture." N pays most attention to meanings behind the facts.

S stands for Sensing.
N stands for iNtuition.

Go on to next page

This exercise is NOT a type indicator, nor does it replicate the Myers-Briggs Type Indicator, which is a validated instrument.

ACTIVITY (Continued)

Typical sensing type

Georgette has a good memory for numbers and has been a bookkeeper at a car dealership for several years. One day, she commented to her boss that spoilers and dash covers were selling well. Upon reviewing the sales figures, the boss confirmed Georgette's observations and promoted her to work with inventory management. The boss found it helpful that Georgette enjoyed keeping track of materials.

Typical intuitive type

Santos is a freelance writer and teaches scriptwriting at a community college. He uses his creative and real-life experiences to assist others in creating scripts for independent producers. He often gets ideas while daydreaming or exercising at the gym. Santos keeps a journal in his car to jot down his thoughts and he teaches others how to keep track of their ideas for writing assignments.

PART 3 In describing your ways of *making decisions*, which pattern resembles you more closely, T or F?

T	F
.... Likes to decide things logically	.... Likes to decide things with personal feelings and human values, even if they aren't logical
.... Wants to be treated with justice and fair play	.... Likes praise, and likes to please people, even in unimportant things
.... May neglect and hurt other people's feelings without knowing it	.... Is aware of other people's feelings
.... Gives more attention to ideas or things than to human relationships	.... Can predict how others will feel
.... Doesn't need harmony	.... Gets upset by arguments and conflicts; values harmony

T makes decisions by examining data, staying less personally involved with the decision. F makes decisions by paying attention to personal values and feelings. Each of us uses both T and F judgments every day, but we tend to use one kind of judgment more than the other.

T stands for Thinking judgment.
F stands for Feeling judgment.

Go on to next page

This exercise is NOT a type indicator, nor does it replicate the Myers-Briggs Type Indicator, which is a validated instrument.

ACTIVITY (Continued)

Typical thinking type

Malcolm is a student trying to decide if he wants to major in business. He is basing his decision on the facts that he has collected: he has talked to a college counselor, researched his interests in the career center, taken classes related to business, and visited workplaces that hire people with such majors. He has even investigated graduate degrees related to the types of business specialties that employers have suggested they need.

Typical feeling type

Shareen has always wanted to be a model, but was influenced by her husband and adult children to get a college degree. She stays in shape and is taking modeling classes in the community while also attending college full-time. After meeting with a college counselor, she's decided that majoring in fashion merchandising will allow her to study something related to her ideal job as well as please her family.

In describing your *day-to-day lifestyle*, which pattern resembles you more closely, J or P?

PART 4

J

.... Likes to have a plan, to have things settled and decided in advance

.... Tries to make things come out the way they "ought to be"

.... Likes to finish one project before starting another

.... Usually has mind made up about situations, people

.... May decide things too quickly

.... Wants to be right in forming opinions, making decisions

.... Lives by standards and schedules that are not easily changed

P

.... Likes to stay flexible and avoid fixed plans

.... Deals easily with unplanned and unexpected happenings

.... Likes to start many projects but may have trouble finishing them

.... Usually looks for additional information about situations, people

.... May decide things too slowly

.... Wants to miss nothing before forming opinions, making decisions

.... Lives by making changes to deal with problems as they come along

J people show to others their thinking or feeling judgment more easily than they show their sensing and intuitive perception. The opposite is true of P people; they show their sensing or intuition rather than judgment in dealing with the world outside themselves.

J stands for Judgment.
P stands for Perception.

Go on to next page

This exercise is NOT a type indicator, nor does it replicate the Myers-Briggs Type Indicator, which is a validated instrument.

ACTIVITY (Continued)

Typical judging type

Marion is a film editor. He has a computerized appointment calendar programmed with alarm beeps to remind him about important dates. All of his clients know that when he makes a deadline to finish a project, the project will be delivered on time. He lets nothing interrupt his plans. Rush jobs, given to his department by higher-level management, drive him crazy; he doesn't want to start a new project before he finishes his current obligations.

Typical perceiving type

Cathy is also a film editor. Some colleagues think that Cathy is scattered. She works on several projects at the same time. Even though her office is a mess, she seems to be able to find the tapes, telephone numbers, and accessories she needs. She often takes on new assignments before she is finished with old ones because she doesn't want to miss out. She gets irritated when her supervisor reminds her that a project should have been completed yesterday and tends to get projects done just in time.

Reviewing each of the four areas, which do you resemble most closely in each pair? (Circle the appropriate letters.)

E or **I**

S or **N**

T or **F**

J or **P**   Your 4-letter preferences are: _____ _____ _____ _____

You now have a four-letter personality preference based primarily on the work of Jung and of Myers and Briggs. This preliminary self-assessment offers one way to appreciate and value your natural individuality. Although we all represent combinations of each characteristic described, we have natural preferences, revealed in our type, that have implications for our career choices. To understand your preferences further, arrange to take the Myers–Briggs Type Indicator® (MBTI) at your college counseling center.

This exercise is NOT a type indicator, nor does it replicate the Myers-Briggs Type Indicator, which is a validated instrument.

Your career choices may be based in part on your temperament or personality preferences. If you enjoy detail and structure, such fields as accounting, engineering, math, sciences, law, and the health sciences might interest you. If you prefer unstructured, global thinking, then majors and fields such as the creative arts and social sciences may better suit your temperament. It is essential to note, however, that all types are found in all fields. In order to truly do well, you must stretch yourself in areas that do not come as naturally for you. This stretching takes extra effort above and beyond the demands of the occupation. Keep this in mind as you experience yourself responding to various work settings and demands.

Be aware that a major or career choice that does not mesh with your personality preferences most of the time takes more energy and concentration than one that more closely matches your preferences. The purpose of understanding personality type in relation to your classes and major is not to discourage you from pursuing a specific career, but to help you become more aware of why you might master certain subjects more easily than others and be attracted to certain careers over others.

IDENTIFYING FIELDS OF INTEREST

The rest of this chapter explores the ways that interests can be grouped into job categories or "clusters" so that you can begin to select specific fields of interest to investigate.

We will be highlighting three different approaches to identify interests. The first refers to the *Holland Interest Environments* (or categories) (Holland, 1985), which are Realistic, Investigative, Artistic, Social, Enterprising, and Conventional. The second system is an *interest inventory* from the Department of Labor organized around *"Worker Trait Groups,"* which are described in the *Guide for Occupational Exploration (GOE)*. Interest inventories ask if you like or dislike a variety of subjects and offer you a profile of the results. The results from the GOE are clustered into interest categories such as Artistic, Scientific, Nature, Mechanical, Industrial, Business Detail, Persuasive, Accommodating, Humanitarian, Social-Business, and Physical Performing. This inventory is provided especially for readers who do not have access to other interest assessments. The third system is provided by the *American College Testing (ACT) Program*. ACT clusters, as well as the "tech-prep" and "school to career" clusters listed later in this chapter, have been used in secondary school career centers.

Although many readers have access to career inventories, it is important to remember the information gathered by printed or electronic assessments is not magic. Assessments simply provide a quick, efficient way of gathering and organizing the information that you know about yourself. Remember that the answers come from you. In the absence of an inventory, you are still able to collect the same information by completing the exercises and activities provided throughout this book.

Interest clusters, known as *personality types* or *environments*, are based on the following assumptions: (1) People express their personalities through their vocational choices; (2) People are attracted to occupations that they feel will provide experiences suitable to their personalities; (3) People who choose the same vocation have similar personalities and react to many situations in similar ways. On the following page, select the category that best describes you.

If you review Chapter One, Exercise 1.4, you will notice the adjectives are grouped by the six types described on the next page. Most interest inventories relate your interests to these six types and provide a list of jobs related to these interests. If you are in a class that uses the Self-Directed Search® or the Strong Interest Inventory®, your instructor will explain which jobs are related to these six environments. If you don't have access to separate inventories, the interest inventory developed by the U.S. Department of Labor (see pages 62–65) should give you a general idea of how your interests relate to potential jobs.

RIASEC (Holland Interest Environments)

Doers *(Realistic–R)* These types like jobs such as automobile mechanic, air traffic controller, surveyor, farmer, electrician. They like to work outdoors and to work with tools. They prefer to deal with things rather than with people. They are described as:

conforming	humble	natural	shy
frank	materialistic	persistent	stable
honest	modest	practical	thrifty

Problem Solvers *(Investigative–I)* These types like jobs such as biologist, chemist, physicist, anthropologist, geologist, medical technologist. They are task-oriented and prefer to work alone. They enjoy solving abstract problems and understanding the physical world. They are described as:

analytical	curious	introverted	precise
cautious	independent	methodical	rational
critical	intellectual	modest	reserved

Creators *(Artistic–A)* These types like jobs such as composer, musician, stage director, writer, interior designer, actor/actress. They like to work in artistic settings that offer opportunities for self-expression. They are described as:

complicated	idealistic	impulsive	nonconforming
emotional	imaginative	independent	original
expressive	impractical	intuitive	unordered

Helpers *(Social–S)* These types like jobs such as teacher, clergy, counselor, nurse, personnel director, speech therapist. They are sociable, responsible, and concerned with the welfare of others. They have little interest in machinery or physical skills. They are described as:

convincing	generous	insightful	sociable
cooperative	helpful	kind	tactful
friendly	idealistic	responsible	understanding

Persuaders *(Enterprising–E)* These types like jobs such as salesperson, manager, business executive, television producer, sports promoter, buyer. They enjoy leading, speaking, and selling. They are impatient with precise work. They are described as:

adventurous	domineering	optimistic	risk-taking
ambitious	energetic	pleasure-seeking	self-confident
attention-getting	impulsive	popular	sociable

Organizers *(Conventional–C)* These types like jobs such as bookkeeper, word processing technician, banker, cost estimator, tax expert. They prefer highly ordered activities, both verbal and numerical, that characterize office work. They have little interest in artistic or physical skills. They are described as:

careful	conservative	orderly	reserved
conforming	efficient	persistent	self-controlled
conscientious	obedient	practical	structured

ACTIVITY

SAMPLE MAJORS RELATED TO HOLLAND TYPES

Now that you are familiar with Holland interest environments, the following chart will help you review some sample majors that may be of interest to you. Underline or circle those areas that seem to fit you. Not all possible majors are listed, of course.

Realistic

architectural/ mechanical drafting technology	civil engineering	criminal justice technology	industrial engineering
	civil engineering technology	dietitian	mechanical engineering
architectural construc- tion technology		forestry	medical technology

Investigative

biological science	dental hygiene	electronics	materials science
biology	earth sciences	environmental sciences	mathematics
chemical engineering	economics	geography	paralegal
chemistry	electrical engineering	geology	physics
computer sciences	electrical engineering technology	law	psychology

Artistic

advertising art	computer animation	English	music
art	computer graphics	graphic technology	studio art
art history	design drafting	instructional media	theater
commercial art	design technology	multi-media technology	

Social

American studies	elementary & secondary education	history	political science
anthropology		home economics	pre-law
child care		medical assistant	religious studies
classical studies	English	nursing	sociology
communications	foreign languages	nutrition	special education
dental hygiene	health	physical education	speech

Enterprising

advertising technology	finance	marketing	marketing technology
business administration	industrial & transporta- tion management	law enforcement administration	public administration
business education	industrial, manage- ment, & retail	management engineering	real estate
business management			

Conventional

accounting	computer technology	legal/medical office management	transportation man- agement technology
administrative assistant	court reporting		
computer information systems	executive technology	library science	word processing

*Holland Interest Environments and hobbies, abilities, and careers**

	Realistic "Doers"	Investigative "Thinkers"	Artistic "Creators"
Hobbies	Refinishing Growing Tinker Use hands Build things	Book clubs Computers Do puzzles Visit museums Collect rocks, stamps, etc.	Photography Performing Writing stories, poems Sewing Playing music
Abilities or Interests	Repair Plant Operate tools Play a sport	Think abstractly Solve math problems Do complex calculations Use a microscope Interpret formulas	Sketch, draw, paint, etc. Sing, dance, act Design fashions or interiors Play a musical instrument Write stories, poems, music
Sample Careers	Air conditioning mechanic (RIE) Archaeologist (IRE) Architectural drafter (RCI) Athletic trainer (SRE) Automotive engineer (RIE) Automotive mechanic (RIE) Baker/chef (RSE) Carpenter (RCI) Commercial airline pilot (RIE) Construction worker (REC) Dental assistant (RES) Electrical engineer (RIE) Fiber optics technician (RSE) Floral designer (RAE) Forester (RIS) Industrial arts teacher (IER) Optician (REI) Petroleum engineer (RIE) Police officer (SER) Radio/T.V. repair (REI) Software technician (RCI) Truck driver (RSE) Ultrasound technologist (RSI)	Actuary (ISE) Anesthesiologist (IRS) Anthropologist (IRE) Archaeologist (IRE) Biochemist (IRS) Biologist (ISR) Chemical engineer (IRE) Chemical technician (IRE) Computer analyst (IER) Computer programmer Dentist (ISR) Ecologist (IRE) Economist (IAS) Geologist (IRE) Hazardous waste technician Medical technologist (ISA) Nurse practitioner (ISA) Physician (ISE) Psychologist (IES) Statistician (IRE) Technical writer (IRS) Veterinarian (IRS) Webmaster	Actor (AES) Advertising (AES) Artist Broadcasting executive (EAS) Camera operator Clothing designer (ASR) Copywriter (ASI) Dancer (AES) Drama/music/art teacher (ASE) English teacher (ASE) Fashion designer (ASR) Fashion illustrator (ASR) Furniture designer (AES) Graphic designer (AES) Interior designer (AES) Journalist (ASE) Landscape architect (AIR) Librarian (SAI) Medical illustrator (AIE) Museum curator (AES) Musician Photographer (AES) Writer (ASI)

*Compiled from on-line career search sources.

(continued)

Holland Interest Environments and hobbies, abilities, and careers, continued

	Social "Helpers"	Enterprising "Persuaders"	Conventional "Organizers"
Hobbies	Volunteering Organizations Caring for children Religious activities Playing team sports	Start own service or business Campaign Lead organizations Promote ideas	Collecting memorabilia Arranging and organizing household Playing computer or card games Studying tax laws Writing family history
Abilities or Interests	Teach/train others Express yourself Lead a group discussion Mediate disputes Cooperate well	Initiate projects Persuade people Sell things or promote ideas Organize activities Lead a group	Work within a system Be organized Keep accurate records Use a computer Write effective business letters
Sample Careers	Air traffic controller (SER) Athletic coach (SRE) Chaplain (SAI) College faculty (SEI) Consumer affairs director (SER) Counselor (SAE) Cosmetologist (SAE) Dental hygienist (SAI) Historian (SEI) Homemaker (S) Hospital administrator (SER) Mail carrier (SRC) Medical record administrator (SIE) Nurse (SIR) Occupational therapist (SRE) Paralegal (SCE) Police officer (SER) Radiological technologist (SRI) Real estate appraiser (SCE) School teacher (SEC) Social worker (SEA) Speech pathologist (SAI) Youth services worker (SEC)	Advertising executive (ESA) Automobile sales worker (ESR) Banker/financial planner (ESR) Buyer (ESA) Claims adjuster (ESR) Computer operator (ESI) Credit manager (ERS) Dental assistant (E) Financial planner (ESR) Flight attendant (ESA) Food service manager (ESI) Funeral director (ESR) Hotel manager (ESR) Industrial engineer (EIR) Insurance agent (ECS) Journalism (EAS) Lawyer (ESA) Office manager (ESR) Politician (ESA) Public relations representative (EAS) Real estate agent (ESR) Stockbroker (ESI) Urban planner (ESI)	Accountant (CSE) Administrative assistant (ESC) Bank teller (CSE) Budget analyst (CER) Building inspector (CSE) Business teacher (CSE) Catalog librarian (CSE) Claims adjuster (SEC) Clerk (CSE) Computer operator (CSR) Congressional-district aide (CES) Cost accountant (CES) Court reporter (CSE) Customer inspector (CEI) Elementary school teacher (SEC) Financial analyst (CSI) Insurance underwriter (CSE) Internal auditor (ICR) Legal secretary (CSA) Medical records technician (CSE) Paralegal (SCE) Tax consultant (CSE) Travel agent (ECS)

ACTIVITY

INTEREST CHECKLIST FOR WORKER TRAIT GROUPS*

It is important to each of us that we like our job; doing so will increase our chances of success.

This Interest Checklist may help you decide what kinds of work you would like to do. It lists activities that are found in a broad range of industries and occupations in the United States today.

Read each of the statements carefully. If you think you would *like* to do this kind of activity, make a check (✓) under the *L;* if you *wouldn't like* the activity, make a check under the *D;* if you are not certain whether you would like the activity, make a check under the *?.* After you have checked each activity, go back and circle at least five activities that you think you would enjoy most.

You may check an activity even if you do not have training or experience in it, if you think you would enjoy the work. Check the *?* only when you cannot decide whether you would like or dislike the activity, or when you do not know what the activity is. There are no right or wrong answers. Check each activity according to how you feel about it.

L (Like)			? (Uncertain)			D (Dislike)		
L	**?**	**D**				**L**	**?**	**D**

01.01
Write short stories or articles ___ ___ ___
Edit work of writers ___ ___ ___
Write review of books or plays ___ ___ ___

01.02
Teach classes in oil painting ___ ___ ___
Carve figures of people or animals ___ ___ ___
Design artwork for magazines ___ ___ ___

01.03
Direct plays ___ ___ ___
Perform magic tricks in a theater ___ ___ ___
Announce radio or television programs ___ ___ ___

01.04
Conduct a symphony orchestra ___ ___ ___
Compose or arrange music ___ ___ ___
Play a musical instrument ___ ___ ___

01.05
Create routines for professional dancers ___ ___ ___
Dance in a variety show ___ ___ ___
Teach modern dance ___ ___ ___

01.06
Restore damaged works of art ___ ___ ___
Carve designs in wooden blocks for printing greeting cards ___ ___ ___
Design, cartooning, or animation ___ ___ ___

01.07
Analyze handwriting and appraise personality ___ ___ ___
Introduce acts in a circus ___ ___ ___
Guess weight of people at a carnival ___ ___ ___

01.08
Model clothing for customers ___ ___ ___
Pose for a fashion photographer ___ ___ ___
Be a stand-in for a television star ___ ___ ___

02.01
Develop chemical processes to solve technical problems ___ ___ ___
Analyze data on weather conditions ___ ___ ___
Develop methods to control air or water pollution ___ ___ ___

02.02
Study causes of animal diseases ___ ___ ___
Develop methods for growing better crops ___ ___ ___
Develop new techniques to process foods ___ ___ ___

02.03
Examine teeth and treat dental problems ___ ___ ___
Diagnose and treat sick animals ___ ___ ___
Give medical treatment to people ___ ___ ___

Go on to next page

*Source: U.S. Dept. of Labor, Employment and Training Administration, U.S. Employment Service.

ACTIVITY (Continued)

L (Like)			? (Uncertain)			D (Dislike)		
	L	?	D		L	?	D

02.04
Prepare medicines according to prescription ___ ___ ___
Study blood samples using a microscope ___ ___ ___
Test ore samples for gold or silver content ___ ___ ___

03.01
Manage a beef or dairy ranch ___ ___ ___
Operate a commercial fish farm ___ ___ ___
Manage the use and development of forest lands ___ ___ ___

03.02
Supervise farm workers ___ ___ ___
Supervise a logging crew ___ ___ ___
Supervise a park maintenance crew ___ ___ ___

03.03
Train horses for racing ___ ___ ___
Feed and care for animals in a zoo ___ ___ ___
Bathe and groom dogs ___ ___ ___

03.04
Pick vegetables on a farm ___ ___ ___
Catch fish as a member of a fishing crew ___ ___ ___
Trim branches and limbs from trees ___ ___ ___

04.01
Direct police activities ___ ___ ___
Issue tickets to speeding motorists ___ ___ ___
Enforce fish and game laws ___ ___ ___

04.02
Guard inmates in a prison ___ ___ ___
Guard money in an armored car ___ ___ ___
Fight fires to protect life and property ___ ___ ___

05.01
Plan and design roads and bridges ___ ___ ___
Design electrical equipment ___ ___ ___
Plan construction of a water treatment plant ___ ___ ___

05.02
Direct operations of a power plant ___ ___ ___
Direct construction of buildings ___ ___ ___
Supervise operations of a coal mine ___ ___ ___

05.03
Survey land to determine boundaries ___ ___ ___
Make drawings of equipment for technical manuals ___ ___ ___
Operate a radio transmitter ___ ___ ___
Design and draft master drawings of automobiles ___ ___ ___
Direct air traffic from an airport control tower ___ ___ ___
Conduct water pollution tests ___ ___ ___

05.04
Pilot a commercial aircraft ___ ___ ___
Operate a ferry boat ___ ___ ___
Captain an oil tanker ___ ___ ___

05.05
Build frame houses ___ ___ ___
Make and repair dentures ___ ___ ___
Prepare and cook food in a restaurant ___ ___ ___
Plan, install, and repair electrical wiring ___ ___ ___
Repair and overhaul automobiles ___ ___ ___
Set up and operate printing equipment ___ ___ ___

05.06
Operate generators at an electric plant ___ ___ ___
Operate boilers to heat a building ___ ___ ___
Operate water purification equipment ___ ___ ___

05.07
Inspect fire-fighting equipment ___ ___ ___
Inspect aircraft for mechanical safety ___ ___ ___
Inspect cruise control in automobiles ___ ___ ___
Grade logs for size and quality ___ ___ ___

05.08
Drive a tractor-trailer truck ___ ___ ___
Operate a train ___ ___ ___
Operate a motorboat to carry passengers ___ ___ ___

05.09
Prepare items for shipment and keep records ___ ___ ___
Receive, store, and issue merchandise ___ ___ ___
Record amount and kind of cargo on ships ___ ___ ___

05.10
Develop film to produce negatives or prints ___ ___ ___
Repair small electrical appliances ___ ___ ___
Paint houses ___ ___ ___

05.11
Operate a bulldozer ___ ___ ___
Operate a crane ___ ___ ___
Operate an oil drilling rig ___ ___ ___

05.12
Recap automobile tires ___ ___ ___
Operate a duplicating or copying machine ___ ___ ___
Clean and maintain office buildings ___ ___ ___

06.01
Set up and operate a lathe to cut and form metal ___ ___ ___
Drill tiny holes in industrial diamonds ___ ___ ___
Hand polish optical lenses ___ ___ ___

Go on to next page

ACTIVITY (Continued)

L (Like)	? (Uncertain)	D (Dislike)

		L	?	D
06.02	Operate a drill press	___	___	___
	Operate a power saw in a woodworking factory	___	___	___
	Assemble refrigerators and stoves in a factory	___	___	___
	Operate a power sewing machine to make clothing	___	___	___
	Operate a dough-mixing machine for making bread	___	___	___
	Assemble electronic components	___	___	___
06.03	Inspect bottles for defects	___	___	___
	Sort fruit according to size	___	___	___
	Test electronic parts before shipment	___	___	___
06.04	Work on a factory assembly line	___	___	___
	Operate a machine that fills containers	___	___	___
	Hand package materials and products	___	___	___
	Assemble parts to make computer components	___	___	___
	Drive a forklift truck to move materials in a factory	___	___	___
07.01	Take dictation, type, and handle business details	___	___	___
	Search records to verify land ownership	___	___	___
	Maintain records on real estate sales	___	___	___
07.02	Maintain spread sheets	___	___	___
	Keep time card records	___	___	___
	Compute average weekly production from daily records	___	___	___
07.03	Receive and pay out money in a bank	___	___	___
	Sell tickets at places of entertainment	___	___	___
	Operate a cash register in a grocery store	___	___	___
07.04	Answer questions at an information counter	___	___	___
	Interview persons opening checking accounts	___	___	___
07.05	Check typewritten material for errors	___	___	___
	Compile and maintain employee records	___	___	___
	Deliver mail to homes and businesses	___	___	___

		L	?	D
07.06	Input letters and reports	___	___	___
	Operate a computer keyboard to send or receive information	___	___	___
	Operate a billing system to prepare customer bills	___	___	___
07.07	File office correspondence	___	___	___
	Locate and replace library books on shelves	___	___	___
	Hand stamp return addresses on envelopes	___	___	___
08.01	Sell telephone and other communications equipment	___	___	___
	Sell newspaper ad space	___	___	___
	Select and buy fruits and vegetables for resale	___	___	___
08.02	Sell automobiles	___	___	___
	Demonstrate products at a trade exhibit	___	___	___
	Sell articles at auction to highest bidder	___	___	___
08.03	Sell merchandise from door to door	___	___	___
	Sell candy and popcorn at sports events	___	___	___
	Persuade nightclub customers to pose for pictures	___	___	___
09.01	Supervise activities of children at vacation camp	___	___	___
	Greet and seat customers in a restaurant	___	___	___
	Serve meals and beverages to airline passengers	___	___	___
09.02	Give haircuts	___	___	___
	Style, color, and treat hair	___	___	___
	Give scalp-conditioning treatments	___	___	___
09.03	Drive a bus	___	___	___
	Drive a taxicab	___	___	___
	Teach automobile driving skills	___	___	___
09.04	Wait on tables in a restaurant	___	___	___
	Park automobiles	___	___	___
	Cash checks and give information to customers	___	___	___
09.05	Check passenger baggage	___	___	___
	Help hotel guests get taxicabs	___	___	___
	Operate a carnival ride	___	___	___
10.01	Plan and carry out religious activities	___	___	___
	Work with juveniles on probation	___	___	___
	Help people with personal or emotional problems	___	___	___

Go on to next page

ACTIVITY (Continued)

L (Like)			? (Uncertain)			D (Dislike)		
	L	?	D				L	?	D

10.02
Provide nursing care to hospital patients ___ ___ ___
Plan and give physical therapy treatment to patients ___ ___ ___
Teach the blind to read Braille ___ ___ ___

10.03
Give hearing tests ___ ___ ___
Care for children in an institution ___ ___ ___
Prepare patients for examination by a physician ___ ___ ___

11.01
Plan and write computer programs to help solve scientific problems ___ ___ ___
Plan collection and analysis of statistical data ___ ___ ___
Apply knowledge of statistics to set insurance rates ___ ___ ___

11.02
Teach courses in high school ___ ___ ___
Teach vocational education courses ___ ___ ___
Manage the library program for a community ___ ___ ___

11.03
Conduct research to develop new teaching methods ___ ___ ___
Conduct research to understand social problems ___ ___ ___
Review and analyze economic data ___ ___ ___

11.04
Serve as a court judge ___ ___ ___
Advise clients on legal matters ___ ___ ___
Settle wage disputes between labor and management ___ ___ ___

11.05
Manage a department of a large company ___ ___ ___
Plan and direct work of a government office ___ ___ ___
Purchase supplies and equipment for a large firm ___ ___ ___

11.06
Examine financial records to determine tax owed ___ ___ ___
Approve or disapprove requests for bank loans ___ ___ ___
Buy and sell stocks and bonds for clients ___ ___ ___

11.07
Direct administration of a large hospital ___ ___ ___
Serve as principal of a school ___ ___ ___
Direct operations of a museum ___ ___ ___

11.08
Write news stories for publication or broadcast ___ ___ ___
Broadcast news over radio or television ___ ___ ___
Direct operations of a newspaper ___ ___ ___

11.09
Plan advertising programs for an organization ___ ___ ___
Direct fund-raising for a nonprofit organization ___ ___ ___
Lobby for or against proposed legislation ___ ___ ___

11.10
Direct investigations to enforce banking laws ___ ___ ___
Inspect work areas to detect unsafe working conditions ___ ___ ___
Inspect cargo to enforce customs laws ___ ___ ___

11.11
Manage a hotel or motel ___ ___ ___
Direct activities of a branch office of an insurance company ___ ___ ___
Manage a grocery, clothing, or other retail store ___ ___ ___

11.12
Investigate and settle insurance claims ___ ___ ___
Obtain leases for outdoor advertising sites ___ ___ ___
Sign entertainers to theater or concert contracts ___ ___ ___

12.01
Manage a professional baseball team ___ ___ ___
Referee sporting events ___ ___ ___
Drive in automobile races ___ ___ ___

12.02
Perform as a trapeze artist in a circus ___ ___ ___
Perform stunts for movie or television scenes ___ ___ ___
Perform juggling feats ___ ___ ___

Now go back and circle at least five activities that you would like most.

Worker Trait Groups

The number beside each group of activities in the Interest Checklist refers to a *Worker Trait Group*. The trait groups are broad, general categories of interest that describe many of the occupational functions and factors related to these areas of interest, such as physical requirements, necessary academic skills, and specific vocational preparation time. These descriptions then lead to a listing of some possible occupations that fall within the interest categories and trait groups. Look at each of the five activities that you would enjoy most (the ones you circled), note the number beside its group, and find the corresponding number in the following list. This gives you some idea of the kinds of occupations that are of greatest interest to you. **The boldface letter(s) to the left of each trait group title indicates the related Holland Environment Type(s).**

More complete and detailed descriptions may be found in the *Guide for Occupational Exploration (GOE)* and McKnight's *Worker Trait Group Guide* (1997), which can be found in college career centers, in libraries, and on the Internet.

A 01. Artistic
01.01 Literary Arts
01.02 Visual Arts
01.03 Performing Arts: Drama
01.04 Performing Arts: Music
01.05 Performing Arts: Dance
01.06 Technical Arts
01.07 Amusement
01.08 Modeling

I 02. Scientific
02.01 Physical Science
02.02 Life Science
02.03 Medical Science
02.04 Laboratory Technology

R 03. Nature
03.01 Managerial Work: Nature
03.02 General Supervision: Nature
03.03 Animal Training and Care
03.04 Elemental Work: Nature

R 04. Authority
04.01 Safety and Law Enforcement
04.02 Security Services

R 05. Mechanical
05.01 Engineering
05.02 Managerial Work: Mechanical
05.03 Engineering Technology
05.04 Air and Water Vehicle Operation
05.05 Craft Technology
05.06 Systems Operation
05.07 Quality Control
05.08 Land-Vehicle Operation
05.09 Materials Control
05.10 Skilled Hand and Machine Work
05.11 Equipment Operation
05.12 Elemental Work: Mechanical

R 06. Industrial
06.01 Production Technology
06.02 Production Work
06.03 Production Control
06.04 Elemental Work: Industrial

C 07. Business Detail
07.01 Administrative Detail
07.02 Mathematical Detail
07.03 Financial Detail
07.04 Information Processing: Speaking
07.05 Information Processing: Records
07.06 Clerical Machine Operation
07.07 Clerical Handling

E 08. Persuasive
08.01 Sales Technology
08.02 General Sales
08.03 Vending

09. Accommodating
09.01 Hospitality Services
09.02 Barbering and Beauty Services
09.03 Passenger Services
09.04 Customer Services
09.05 Attendant Services

S 10. Humanitarian
10.01 Social Services
10.02 Nursing and Therapy Services
10.03 Child and Adult Care

S/E 11. Social–Business
11.01 Mathematics and Statistics
11.02 Educational and Library Services
11.03 Social Research
11.04 Law
11.05 Business Administration
11.06 Finance
11.07 Services Administration
11.08 Communications
11.09 Promotion
11.10 Regulations Enforcement
11.11 Business Management
11.12 Contracts and Claims

R 12. Physical Performing
12.01 Sports
12.02 Physical Feats

ACTIVITY

IDENTIFYING OCCUPATIONAL INTEREST AREAS

Circle the areas or words in 1, 2, and 3 that you find most interesting. If you had two hours to research careers, which area(s) would you select? ....

1. What fields interest you?

Social	Do you like to work with people? Do you help others organize activities? Are you active in social events?
Sales–verbal	Do you like to sell, convince, persuade, influence, lead? Do you like to talk, write, read?
Mechanical	Do you like to fix things? Do you use and repair machines, appliances, equipment? Do you like to make or build things?
Scientific	Are you curious about ideas and abstract processes? Do you like to experiment and solve problems?
Clerical–computational	Do you like to keep things orderly? Do you like to keep records, use a keyboard, be accurate?
Artistic	Do you like music, dance, art, literature, photography, decorating? Do you like to express yourself creatively?

2. Occupational categories according to the six Holland types

Realistic (R)	Occupations include jobs in industry, trade, and service.
Investigative (I)	Occupations include jobs in the fields of science and technology.
Artistic (A)	Occupations include jobs in the fields of art, music, and literature.
Social (S)	Occupations include jobs in the fields of education and welfare.
Enterprising (E)	Occupations include jobs in sales and management.
Conventional (C)	Occupations include office and clerical jobs.

3. Occupational fields—Job families or job clusters (letters relate to Holland types described above)

Agriculture and Home Economics—R & I

Arts and Letters—A

Business—C

Education and Welfare—S

Engineering and Architecture—R & I

Government and Law—E & S

Health—I & S

Industry, Trade, and Service—R & C

Science—I & R

CAREER CLUSTERS

Career centers often organize their materials by the following career clusters (created by the U.S. Office of Career Education and used in "tech-prep" or "school to career" programs):

> Agriculture
> Arts/Communication/Human Services
> Business
> Consumer and Family Services
> Engineering Technology
> Health Services
> Industry and Technology

If you are attending school and have chosen a major, you might research the cluster in which your major falls. Otherwise, select the area that seems to relate to your interests, values, and skills, and explore it.

OCCUPATIONAL CLASSIFICATION SYSTEM

The American College Testing Program (ACT) has devised a useful system of organizing jobs into job clusters (Table 4.A). A valuable aspect of the ACT cluster system that differentiates it from the system of the U.S. Office of Career Education is its reference to the educational preparation needed by cluster. Table 4.B provides you with a further breakdown of the business, sales, and management cluster, including educational preparation information. At some point you will have to decide how much education you will need to enter the career of your choice. This example allows you to see which jobs require a high school education and which require higher education.

TABLE 4.A ACT job clusters.

There are more than 21,000 job titles in the world of work. This table illustrates how jobs can be clustered into related categories.

BUSINESS, SALES, AND MANAGEMENT JOB CLUSTER

A. Promotion and Direct Contact Sales
Public relations workers, fashion models, travel agents, sales workers who visit customers (for example, real estate brokers, insurance agents, wholesalers, office supplies sales workers)

B. Management and Planning
Hotel, store, and company managers, bankers, executive secretaries, buyers, purchasing agents, small business owners

C. Retail Sales and Services
Sales workers in stores and shops, auto salespersons, retail sales workers

BUSINESS OPERATIONS JOB CLUSTER

D. Clerical and Secretarial Work
Word processors, file clerks, mail clerks, office messengers, receptionists, secretaries

E. Paying, Receiving, and Bookkeeping
Bank tellers, accountants, payroll clerks, grocery check-out clerks, ticket sellers, cashiers, hotel clerks

(continued)

TABLE 4.A Continued.

F. **Office Machine Operation**
Adding, billing, and bookkeeping computer operators, data processing operators

G. **Storage, Dispatching, and Delivery**
Shipping and receiving clerks, stock clerks, truck and airplane dispatchers, delivery truck drivers, cab drivers, mail carriers

TECHNOLOGIES AND TRADES JOB CLUSTER

H. **Human Services Crafts**
Barbers, hairdressers, tailors, shoemakers, cooks, chefs, butchers, bakers

I. **Repairing and Servicing Home and Office Equipment**
Repair and service workers for TV sets, appliances, telephones, heating systems, photocopiers, computers

J. **Growing and Caring for Plants/Animals**
Farmers, foresters, ranchers, gardeners, yard workers, groundskeepers, plant nursery workers, animal caretakers, pet shop attendants

K. **Construction and Maintenance**
Carpenters, electricians, painters, custodians (janitors), bricklayers, sheet metal workers, construction laborers (buildings, roads, pipelines, etc.)

L. **Transport Equipment Operation**
Long-haul truck and bus drivers, bulldozer operators, crane operators, forklift operators

M. **Machine Operating, Servicing, and Repairing**
Auto mechanics, machinists, printing press operators, sewing machine operators, service station attendants, laborers and machine operators in factories, mines, lumber camps, etc.

N. **Engineering and Other Applied Technologies**
(For science and medical technicians, see Job Families O and P.) Engineers and engineering technicians, draftsmen and draftswomen, pilots, surveyors, computer programmers

NATURAL, SOCIAL, AND MEDICAL SCIENCES JOB CLUSTER

O. **Natural Sciences and Mathematics**
Biologists, chemists, lab technicians, physicists, geologists, statisticians, agricultural scientists, ecologists

P. **Medicine and Medical Technologies**
Dentists, doctors, veterinarians, medical technologists and lab workers, pharmacists, X-ray technicians, optometrists, dental hygienists, dietitians

Q. **Social Sciences and Legal Services**
Sociologists, lawyers, political scientists, historians, psychologists, home economists

CREATIVE AND APPLIED ARTS JOB CLUSTER

R. **Creative Arts**
Authors, concert singers, musicians, actresses and actors, dancers, artists

S. **Applied Arts (Verbal)**
Reporters, technical writers, interpreters, newscasters, newswriters, ad copy writers

T. **Applied Arts (Visual)**
Interior decorators, architects, commercial artists, photographers, fashion designers

U. **Popular Entertainment**
Nightclub entertainers, popular singers and musicians, disc jockeys, circus performers

SOCIAL, HEALTH, AND PERSONAL SERVICES JOB CLUSTER

V. **Education and Social Services**
Teachers,* counselors, social workers, librarians, athletic coaches, recreation workers, clergy

W. **Nursing and Human Care**
Child-care aides, nurses, dental assistants, physical therapists, hospital attendants

X. **Personal and Household Services**
Waiters and waitresses, airline flight attendants, housekeepers, porters, parking valets, butlers and maids

Y. **Law Enforcement and Protective Services**
Police officers; building, food, and postal inspectors; security guards; plant guards; firefighters

*NOTE—Teachers: Students thinking about high school or college teaching should consider whether their main goal is *teaching students* (mark Job Family V) or *doing work or research in the subject area*, for example—chemistry (mark Job Family O), art (mark R or T), economics (mark Q).

Source: Reprinted with permission from the American College Testing Program (American College Testing Program).

TABLE 4.B

Business, sales, and management cluster.

The left-facing arrow (←) for certain jobs means that workers may also enter that job with the type of preparation shown in the column at the left. The right-facing arrow (→) refers to the type of preparation shown in the column at the right.

TYPICAL FORMAL PREPARATION

	High School Graduation Desirable	Up to Two Years of Preparation Beyond High School	Three or More Years of Preparation Beyond High School	Related High School Courses
A. Promotion and direct contact sales	House-to-house salesperson Sample distributor Promotion worker Demonstrator Interviewer Survey worker Telemarketer Car rental clerk Sound-truck operator	Fashion model Travel clerk or agent Radio–TV time salesperson → Auctioneer ← Encyclopedia salesperson → Bridal consultant Wholesale workers ← who visit customers who sell products such as computers, medical supplies, office machines, food products	Fashion coordinator ← Lobbyist ← Public relations worker ← Advertising worker ← Business agent ← Salesworker who sells services to customers, for example, stocks and bonds salesperson, insurance agent, account executive, real estate agent, investment analyst	General business Speech Bookkeeping General math Economics Distributive education programs such as sales, marketing, product information
B. Management and planning	See note below (*)	Credit manager → Buyer → Import-export agent → Store or hotel manager → Sales manager → Automobile parts manager ← Apartment house manager ← Postmaster → City planning aide Funeral director ← Manager or owner of → small business such as skating rink, record shop, beauty shop, donut shop	Bank officer Assessor Controller Treasurer City manager Urban planner ← Purchasing agent Hospital administrator Personnel manager Athletic director	Business law Bookkeeping Speech Economics General business Distributive education programs such as business operation, product information
C. Retail sales and services	Concession attendant Newspaper carrier Will-call clerk Lost-and-found clerk Counter attendants in restaurants, dry cleaners, and snack bars Salesclerks and retail salesworkers, → in stores selling products such as shoes, clothing, flowers, garden equipment, books, pets	Sales clerks and retail salesworkers in stores selling such products as furniture, drapery, radios, televisions, gas and electric appliances, stereos, automobiles, sporting goods, hearing aids, photographic supplies, jewelry	See note below (*)	Economics General math General business Distributive education programs such as product information, sales, marketing

*Workers with this type of job preparation are sometimes employed in jobs listed in the other columns of this chart. Jobs in another column might have arrows pointing toward this column. Check with your counselor if you want to know about other jobs with this type of preparation. Remember that the jobs on these charts are listed under the type of preparation typical of most, but not all, workers entering the jobs.

Source: Reprinted by permission of American College Testing Program.

Understanding your interests will be a great aid to you in making satisfying educational and career choices. The more you are able to incorporate your interests into your work, the more you will enjoy your work. Once you have completed an interest inventory, plan to explore those occupations associated with your interests. Find out what people actually do and compare these jobs to your interests.

SUMMARY

Now that you have completed this chapter, you are aware that your satisfaction in a career is related to how much you can incorporate your unique personality and interests into your work.

In the next chapter, we will focus on skills: you will learn how to identify the skills you possess and you will get ideas about the types of skills you may need in the future. With this information, you will be well into your career fitness program!

The following exercises serve to help you summarize information. Exercise 4.1 asks you to record your personality type as determined earlier. Exercise 4.2 is a review of the Holland Interest Environments as they describe you. Exercises 4.3 and 4.4 ask you to list information about your interests, and Exercise 4.5 asks you to record the results of any additional assessments you have taken. The exercise summary encourages you to put this information together and describe an ideal job or set of activities that best reflects who you are.

4.1 Your personality type

Check your four-letter personality preference (pages 52–56).

.... Extroversion   .... Introversion

.... Sensing   .... Intuition

.... Thinking   .... Feeling

.... Judging   .... Perception

4.2 Your Holland Interest Environment

a. Check your top three Holland Environments (page 58).

.... Realistic   .... Investigative   .... Artistic

.... Social   .... Enterprising   .... Conventional

b. What adjectives best describe you from these environments (page 58)?

....

....

....

c. List three interesting majors from your top categories (page 59).

....

....

....

d. List three interesting jobs/careers from your top categories (pages 60–61).

....

....

....

4.3 Your occupational interests

List the occupational interest areas you have circled in this chapter (page 67).

....

....

....

....

4.4 Job clusters

List three ACT job clusters that are most interesting to you (pages 68–70).

1. ....

2. ....

3. ....

4.5 Interest inventories

Record below the results of any other interest or personality inventories you have taken (e.g., top three career choices).

....

....

....

4.6 Exercise summary

What kinds of activities or job description would your ideal job reflect, based on what you have learned about your personality and interests?

*Go to page 159,
of the Part One Chapter Summaries,
and fill out the Chapter Four exercise summary now.*

FIVE

Skills Assessment

LEARNING OBJECTIVES

At the end of the chapter you will be able to . . .

Understand the importance of skills in your career search

Define and identify your skills

Recognize the power of the transferability of your skills

Use the language of skills in writing your resume and preparing for an interview

Skills are the currency of the job market

The next step in the career-planning process is to identify your skills. Skills are the building blocks of your future career just as muscles are the building blocks of your future body shape. A career fitness program helps you to identify your current skills and the skills you want to develop. A thorough skills analysis is a critical component of the career-planning process.

Skills are the currency used by job seekers. In the job market you receive pay in exchange for skills. Individuals who can describe themselves to a potential employer in terms of their skills are the people most likely to enjoy their careers, because they are the most likely to obtain jobs that use their particular skills. People who enjoy their work tend to be more productive and healthy. After completing this chapter, you will be able to analyze a potential job on the basis of how the skills required by the job compare with both the skills you possess and enjoy using and the skills you want to develop. Furthermore, you will have a broader vocabulary to use in describing your strengths when you prepare your resume and when you are interviewed for jobs.

DEFINING "SKILLS"

Skills include the specific attributes, talents, and personal qualities that we bring to a job as well as the tasks we learn on the job. Every job requires skills. We also develop skills simply through the process of living, by interacting with others and going through our daily routines. Our personal preferences often affect our skills and abilities. We tend to be motivated to repeatedly use skills that are part of enjoyable activities. Our repeated use of and success with certain preferred skills identifies them as our *self-motivators*. Self-motivators are skills we enjoy and do well.

By learning the vocabulary of skills you can recognize the hundreds of skills that may be within your grasp. Skills are generally divided into three types: functional, work-content, and adaptive. All of these can be considered transferable. *Functional skills* are those that may or may not be associated with a specific job, such as maintaining schedules, collecting data, and diagnosing and responding to problems. They are called functional skills because they are used to accomplish general tasks or functions of a job. *Work-content skills* are specific and specialized to one job, e.g., bookkeeping is done by bookkeepers, assigning grades is done by teachers, interpreting an electrocardiogram is done by specific medical practitioners. *Adaptive* or *self-management skills* are personal attributes; they might also be described as personality traits. The ability to learn quickly, the ability to pay close attention to detail, task orientation, self-direction, congeniality, and cooperativeness are some examples of adaptive skills.

IDENTIFYING YOUR SKILLS

If you were asked right now to list your skills, what would your list look like? It might be a short list, not because you do not have skills, but simply because you have never been asked to identify them and are not accustomed to thinking and talking about them. Reflecting on your skills may also be difficult because most of us have been taught to be modest and not to brag. We often feel that something we do well doesn't take any special skills, that is, we discount our own special talents. We may also feel that if we are not currently using a skill, we can no longer claim it—that some-how it has escaped us. Or, if we haven't been paid to use the skill, we may not recognize its value.

All of these false assumptions make it difficult to list our skills honestly and accurately. Your goal now will be to recognize the many skills you possess that make you valuable in the job market. You have acquired hundreds of skills just by virtue of your life experiences and, paid or not, they are part of your portfolio!

To find out what one is fitted to do and to secure an opportunity to do it is the key to happiness.
John Dewey

Once you begin to recognize your skills, you will become more aware of your identity as extending beyond the narrow limits you tend to apply to yourself. We all unconsciously tend to categorize ourselves too narrowly. For instance, you might typically answer the question "Who are you?" with statements like "I am a student," "I am a history major," "I am a graphic artist," "I am a conservative," or "I am a homemaker." The problem with these labels is that they tend to stereotype you. This is especially true when you are interviewing for a job. If you say you are a student, the interviewer might stereotype you as not having enough experience. If you say you are a secretary, the interviewer may consider you only for a secretarial job or may insist that you start as a secretary. But suppose you say your experience has involved public speaking, organizational work, coordinating schedules, managing budgets, researching needs, problem solving, following through with details, motivating others, resolving problems caused by low morale and lack of cooperation, and establishing priorities for allocation of available time, resources, and funds. Not only does this sound impressive, but you appear eligible for many positions that require these skills.

A particular challenge may be faced by homemakers who feel that, because they have been out of the job market, they have no transferable or marketable skills. To the contrary, homemaking is a full-time job requiring a wide range of skills that can translate into paid employment. (Review the creative functional resume in Chapter Ten for ideas on skills in the areas of management, office procedures, personnel, finances, and purchasing that might be included in a homemaker's list of transferable skills.)

Can you talk about your skills?

Employers look for employees who are task-oriented and who think and talk in terms of what they as employees can do to make the employer's operation easier, better, and more efficient. The best way to describe what you can do for an employer is to talk about your skills and how they apply to the job. Unfortunately, we tend to discount our accomplishments and the related skill development. While climbing a mountain and running a four-minute mile are noteworthy accomplishments, so are the following:

Sample accomplishments

raising a child	raising funds
getting into college	giving a speech
delivering papers on a route	writing a term paper
using a software program	getting a job
repairing a car	consoling a child
designing a costume	graduating from high school
completing a computer course	planning a trip and traveling
planning a surprise party	working as a food server
surfing the Internet	mastering a sport
completing a degree	overcoming a bad habit

In reviewing this list, you may be thinking that some of these activities are simple, "no big deal." Some are activities that you can do without much thought or preparation. However, just because they don't take much preparation does not mean they aren't accomplishments. Start thinking of goals that you have set and then later met as accomplishments!

Analyze Your Accomplishments

You can begin to recognize your skills by identifying and examining your most satisfying accomplishments, because your skills led you to these accomplishments. By analyzing these accomplishments, you are likely to discover a pattern of skills (your self-motivators) that you repeatedly use and enjoy using. Again, accomplishments are simply completed activities, goals, projects, or jobs held.

There are several ways to analyze accomplishments. One way is to describe something that you are proud of having completed, and then list the skills that were required to complete it. Let's look at John as an example.

John, an 18-year-old freshman, planned a surprise party for his girlfriend by persuading several friends to contribute decorations and assist in decorating her house. Then he had a few other friends divert his girlfriend from arriving home until everything was in place. Additionally, he arranged for entertainment and party food. In discussing his completed goal (to surprise his girlfriend), he discounted his efforts, saying, "Anyone could do it." However, in analyzing this accomplishment, he identified the following skills: organization, persuasiveness, thoroughness, leadership, creativity, communication skills, determination, drive, persistence, dependability, courage, attentiveness to detail, and supervisory ability.

Can you think of any that he missed? We all have many more skills than we credit ourselves with having.

Another method used to identify skills is to write a story about one of your accomplishments and then list the skills used. Richard Bolles has popularized this approach in his *Quick Job Hunting Map (1996)*, a booklet that lists hundreds of skills. Following is an example of one student's story and the skills involved. The student's classmates listened to her story and helped her identify eighteen skills.

Writing my Term Paper on the Computer

It was necessary for me to learn how to use the computer at a simple level to complete my term paper. I knew the traditional keyboard and could type. I went to our campus computer center for instruction on how to use all the additional keys. I wrote down on paper all the key functions I had to use in order to give the correct commands to the computer. I got a mini-operations course. I learned to do the following:

1. find any page
2. enter the file
3. transfer material to different pages
4. type simple graphs
5. print out on printer
6. make corrections
7. delete and insert characters

I proofread, corrected, and typed 60 pages in three weeks, then edited it down to 35 pages. The paper received an A. I'm now taking a class in Windows 97 and computer graphics!

List of Skills

1. learns quickly
2. displays flexibility
3. meets challenges
4. directs self
5. follows through
6. faces new situations
7. proofs and edits
8. translates concepts
9. word processes
10. organizes
11. gets the job done
12. displays patience
13. attends to detail
14. overcomes obstacles
15. communicates clearly
16. works under stress
17. displays persistence
18. asks questions

Sample job descriptions from the DOT

131.067.014 COPYWRITER (Profess. & Kin.) Writes advertising copy for use by publication or broadcast media to promote sale of goods and services: consults with sales media and marketing representatives to obtain information on product or service and discuss style and length of advertising copy. Obtains additional background and current development information through research and interview. Reviews advertising trends, consumer surveys, and other data regarding marketing of specific and related goods and services to formulate presentation approach. Writes preliminary draft of copy and sends to supervisor for approval. Corrects and revises copy as necessary. May write articles, bulletins, sales letters, speeches, and other related informative and promotional material.

241.267.030 INVESTIGATOR (Clerical) Investigates persons or business establishments applying for credit, employment, insurance, loans, or settlement of claims: Contacts former employers, neighbors, trade associations, and others by telephone to verify employment record and to obtain health history and history of moral and social behavior. Examines city directories and public records to verify residence history, convictions and arrests, property ownership, bankruptcies, liens, and unpaid taxes of applicant. Obtains credit rating from banks and credit concerns. Analyzes information gathered by investigation and prepares reports of findings and recommendations. May interview applicant on telephone or in person to obtain other financial and personal data for completeness of report. When specializing in certain types of investigations, may be designated CREDIT REPORTER (bus. ser.); INSURANCE-APPLICATION INVESTIGATOR (insurance).

Use the *DOT* to Identify Skills

If you have had one or more jobs, you can research the skills associated with these jobs by reading their job descriptions, often located in the employer's personnel office, or by researching the jobs in the *Dictionary of Occupational Titles* (referred to as "the *DOT*"). The *DOT* is an excellent reference source for identifying tasks required in over 21,000 different occupations.

In addition to identifying specific tasks in each job, the *DOT* identifies the primary skills required for each job according to the three broad categories of *data* (instructions and information), *people* (supervisors, coworkers, or the public), and *things* (materials, equipment, or products). The 9-digit number that precedes each job title (refer to the two sample job descriptions) includes an indication of how the job is related to data (the fourth digit), people (the fifth digit), and things (the sixth digit). For example, by finding the middle three digits for *Investigator*—2, 6, 7—in their appropriate columns in Table 5.A, we know that the position involves *analyzing* data, *speaking to and signaling* people, and *handling* things. For a teacher, the fifth digit would likely be 2, signifying *instruction*. For a crane operator, the sixth digit would probably be 3, representing *driving and operating*.

The *DOT* can be of great use to you in identifying types of skills involved in jobs. Perhaps more important, it can alert you to the existence of thousands of jobs and careers you never knew existed. In Chapter Seven, the *DOT* will be discussed as one of many sources of career information.

If your local career center or One Stop Career Center has access to O*NET, you may find it easier to discover the relationship between occupations and skills. O*NET is the acronym for the Occupational Information Network developed by the U.S. Department of Labor. The program is an easy-to-use, interactive computer database that collects, analyzes, and disseminates skill and occupational information in over 1,100 occupational areas. Simply type three skills and the computer will bring out various occupations that use them. O*NET has crosswalks with the DOT. Therefore, knowing your DOT code allows you to find several related occupations using O*NET.

Skills relationships of jobs to data, people, and things, as identified in the *Dictionary of Occupational Titles (DOT)*.

TABLE 5.A

DATA (4TH DIGIT)	PEOPLE (5TH DIGIT)	THINGS (6TH DIGIT)
0 Synthesizing	0 Mentoring	0 Setting up
1 Coordinating	1 Negotiating	1 Precision working
2 Analyzing	2 Instructing	2 Operating-controlling
3 Compiling	3 Supervising	3 Driving-operating
4 Computing	4 Diverting	4 Manipulating
5 Copying	5 Persuading	5 Tending
6 Comparing	6 Speaking-signaling	6 Feeding-offbearing
7 No significant relationship	7 Serving	7 Handling
	8 No significant relationship	8 No significant relationship

Move now to the next page and complete the activity checklist. This list includes over 200 skills in 13 different categories. These categories are useful because they're familiar to employers and often show up in job announcements. As you complete the checklist, carefully consider how each skill applies specifically to you.

If you are currently working, think of ways to use those skills you identify in the activity checklist as your motivated skills as often as possible to give you job satisfaction. Talk to your supervisor and identify additional ways to use these skills now or in the future; for example, if you were hired because of your word processing skills, you might suggest that you become the company expert on formatting documents and reports to give them a consistent look! If your people skills are one of your strengths, make sure your boss keeps you in mind for office supervisor, or as a member of a committee, or as the company liaison with an important client. Don't take your skills for granted and don't let others do so!

Identify your skills

The "Portfolio" Employee

As we have discussed, your skills are your most valuable asset in the job market because they are transferable. For example, the word processing and data management skills you use in your current job as administrative assistant or insurance claims processor will be equally valuable in other jobs that you seek in the future, such as journalist or lawyer. The more skills you develop, the more valuable and versatile you are in the job market. In his book *The Age of Paradox (1994)*, Charles Handy proposes that in the next decade the number of "portfolio" workers will grow dramatically. Such workers would not be a full-time part of one organization, but instead will sell their portfolio of skills to several employers on a freelance basis. Thus, the person who has word processing and data management skills may work for more than one firm

(text continues on page 85)

ACTIVITY

ASSESSING YOUR SKILLS

For each item in this table, mark an *X* next to each skill you enjoy using (even if you aren't expert at it!). Then go back over the list and place a check (✔) next to each skill that you perform particularly well. Underline any skills that you have never used. Finally, place an *O* next to any skills that you would like to develop or acquire. Under personal qualities, check all that apply to you.

Once you have completed these steps, review those skills that are marked with both an *X and* a check. These are your *motivated* or preferred skills. These skills represent your areas of mastery and probably your areas of greatest satisfaction as well. If you use these skills on the job whenever possible, and look for additional ways to use them, you will increase the enjoyment and satisfaction you derive from your job.

Review your list and identify five skills that interest you and that you would like to develop. Think of ways you can develop these skills, such as taking a course or class, getting on-the-job training, joining a club, volunteering, or asking a friend, associate, colleague, or mentor for help. To further clarify your responses, complete Exercise 5.7 at the end of the chapter.

CLERICAL SKILLS

_____ Examining
_____ Evaluating
_____ Filing
_____ Developing
_____ Improving
_____ Recording
_____ Collating
_____ Computing
_____ Recommending
_____ Following
_____ Bookkeeping
_____ Keyboarding
_____ Transcribing
_____ Indexing
_____ Arranging
_____ Systematizing
_____ Tabulating
_____ Photocopying
_____ Collaborating
_____ Sorting
_____ Retrieving
_____ Organizing
_____ Purchasing
_____ Handling people
_____ Problem solving

TECHNICAL SKILLS

_____ Financing

_____ Evaluating
_____ Calculating
_____ Adjusting
_____ Aligning
_____ Observing
_____ Verifying
_____ Drafting
_____ Designing
_____ Cataloguing
_____ Examining
_____ Adjusting
_____ Problem-solving
_____ Creating
_____ Detailing
_____ Restructuring
_____ Reviewing
_____ Revising
_____ Synthesizing
_____ Structuring
_____ Solving
_____ Refining
_____ Reviewing
_____ Following
        specifications

PUBLIC RELATIONS SKILLS

_____ Planning
_____ Conducting

_____ Informing
_____ Consulting
_____ Writing
_____ Researching
_____ Representing
_____ Negotiating
_____ Collaborating
_____ Communicating
_____ Promoting
_____ Convincing
_____ Hosting
_____ Entertaining
_____ Mediating
_____ Performing
_____ Endorsing
_____ Recruiting
_____ Demonstrating
_____ Creating
_____ Problem solving

AGRICULTURAL SKILLS

_____ Inspecting
_____ Costing
_____ Lifting
_____ Cultivating
_____ Assembling
_____ Problem solving
_____ Devising
_____ Scheduling

_____ Demonstrating
_____ Inspecting
_____ Evaluating
_____ Estimating
_____ Diagnosing
_____ Repairing
_____ Maintaining
_____ Replacing
_____ Constructing
_____ Operating

SELLING SKILLS

_____ Contacting
_____ Persuading
_____ Reviewing
_____ Inspecting
_____ Informing
_____ Promoting
_____ Positioning
_____ Influencing
_____ Convincing
_____ Comparing
_____ Differentiating
_____ Representing
_____ Asking
_____ Closing
_____ Costing
_____ Negotiating
_____ Communicating

x = skills you enjoy using
✔ = skills you perform especially well

o = skills you would like to develop or acquire
underlining = skills you have never used

Go on to next page

ACTIVITY (Continued)

_____ Calculating
_____ Advising
_____ Contracting
_____ Recommending
_____ Problem solving

MAINTENANCE SKILLS

_____ Operating
_____ Repairing
_____ Maintaining
_____ Dismantling
_____ Adjusting
_____ Cleaning
_____ Purchasing
_____ Climbing
_____ Lifting
_____ Assembling
_____ Problem solving
_____ Devising
_____ Scheduling
_____ Demonstrating
_____ Inspecting
_____ Evaluating
_____ Estimating

MANAGEMENT SKILLS

_____ Planning
_____ Organizing
_____ Scheduling
_____ Assigning
_____ Delegating
_____ Directing
_____ Hiring
_____ Measuring
_____ Administering
_____ Conducting
_____ Controlling
_____ Coordinating
_____ Enabling
_____ Empowering
_____ Initiating
_____ Formulating
_____ Supervising
_____ Sponsoring
_____ Modeling
_____ Supporting
_____ Negotiating
_____ Decision making
_____ Team building
_____ Conceptualizing
_____ Problem solving

COMMUNICATION SKILLS

_____ Reasoning

_____ Organizing
_____ Defining
_____ Writing
_____ Listening
_____ Explaining
_____ Interpreting
_____ Reading
_____ Speaking
_____ Editing
_____ Instructing
_____ Interviewing
_____ Collaborating
_____ Presenting
_____ Formulating
_____ Proposing
_____ Synthesizing
_____ Integrating
_____ Connecting
_____ Summarizing
_____ Articulating
_____ Interpreting
_____ Translating
_____ Problem solving

RESEARCH SKILLS

_____ Recognizing
_____ Interviewing
_____ Questioning
_____ Synthesizing
_____ Writing
_____ Diagnosing
_____ Compiling
_____ Reviewing
_____ Designing
_____ Theorizing
_____ Testing
_____ Equating
_____ Evaluating
_____ Investigating
_____ Summarizing
_____ Communicating
_____ Collaborating
_____ Demonstrating
_____ Analyzing
_____ Refining
_____ Problem solving

FINANCIAL SKILLS

_____ Calculating
_____ Projecting
_____ Budgeting
_____ Recognizing
_____ Accounting

_____ Processing
_____ Computing
_____ Correlating
_____ Costing
_____ Forecasting
_____ Comparing
_____ Compiling
_____ Examining
_____ Leveraging
_____ Verifying
_____ Problem solving

MANUAL SKILLS

_____ Operating
_____ Monitoring
_____ Controlling
_____ Setting up
_____ Driving
_____ Cutting
_____ Assembling
_____ Drafting
_____ Drawing
_____ Inspecting
_____ Programming
_____ Tabulating
_____ Constructing
_____ Creating
_____ Repairing
_____ Problem solving

SERVICE SKILLS

_____ Counseling
_____ Guiding
_____ Leading
_____ Listening
_____ Coordinating
_____ Teaching
_____ Responding
_____ Collaborating
_____ Facilitating
_____ Monitoring
_____ Integrating
_____ Motivating
_____ Persuading
_____ Evaluating
_____ Summarizing
_____ Planning
_____ Correcting
_____ Mediating
_____ Encouraging
_____ Contracting
_____ Demonstrating
_____ Problem solving

PERSONAL QUALITIES

_____ Adaptable
_____ Aggressive
_____ Assertive
_____ Alert
_____ Adventuresome
_____ Ambitious
_____ Calm
_____ Capable
_____ Confident
_____ Conscientious
_____ Creative
_____ Cooperative
_____ Candid
_____ Dependable
_____ Determined
_____ Diplomatic
_____ Dominant
_____ Discreet
_____ Enthusiastic
_____ Efficient
_____ Energetic
_____ Enterprising
_____ Flexible
_____ Forceful
_____ Frank
_____ Idealistic
_____ Initiating
_____ Innovative
_____ Logical
_____ Loyal
_____ Methodical
_____ Optimistic
_____ Objective
_____ Organized
_____ Patient
_____ Persistent
_____ Practical
_____ Precise
_____ Quiet
_____ Realistic
_____ Resourceful
_____ Risk taking
_____ Reliable
_____ Serious
_____ Sensitive
_____ Sincere
_____ Self-starter
_____ Tactful
_____ Tenacious
_____ Versatile

x = skills you enjoy using
✓ = skills you perform especially well

o = skills you would like to develop or acquire
underlining = skills you have never used

Identifying the basic skills required by employers: The SCANS Report

In 1991, the U. S. Department of Labor issued the *SCANS* (Secretary's Commission on Achieving Necessary Skills) *Report*. The goal of this report was to sum up the competencies and skills that form the basis of solid job performance. The results are based on extensive questioning of employers and educators.

Review the core competencies, qualities, and skills identified by the *SCANS Report* below. These are considered *essential skills* that workers must possess to be competitive in the 21st-century job market. In how many of these areas do you currently feel you have adequate skill levels? If an employer asked you to prove your competencies, could you identify an area of accomplishment in which you demonstrated your use of these skills?

Workplace know-how

The know-how identified by the *SCANS Report* is made up of a three-part foundation of skills and personal qualities along with five competencies; both the foundation and the competencies are needed for solid job performance.

THE FOUNDATION

Basic skills: Reading, writing, arithmetic and mathematics, speaking, and listening. These are the *minimum* skills needed by today's workers. If you are unsure about your skills in these basic areas, now is the time to take steps to improve them. Don't shy away from basic testing and coursework or assume that, as an adult, you naturally have these abilities. Begin thinking in terms of doing all of these things *well* and taking steps to achieve this level of proficiency.

Thinking skills: Thinking creatively, making decisions, solving problems, seeing things in the mind's eye, knowing how to learn, and reasoning. Thinking skills allow you to identify your strengths and weaknesses and take steps to remedy the latter. They allow you to acquire new skills, think creatively, and identify problems and solutions. Once again, if you are unsure of your abilities in these areas, talk to your career counselor or instructor about testing and coursework that can help.

Personal qualities: Individual responsibility, self-esteem, sociability, self-management, and integrity. Included are the personality characteristics described in Chapter Two and the adaptive skills described in this chapter.

THE COMPETENCIES

Effective workers can productively use:

Resources: Allocating time, money, materials, space, and personnel.

Interpersonal skills: Working on teams, teaching others, serving customers, leading, negotiating, and working well with people from culturally diverse backgrounds.

Information: Acquiring and evaluating data, organizing and maintaining files, interpreting and communicating, and using computers to process information.

Systems: Understanding social, organizational, and technological systems, monitoring and correcting performance, and designing or improving systems.

Technology: Selecting equipment and tools, applying technology to specific tasks, and maintaining and troubleshooting technologies.

TABLE 5.B

Tasks from diverse occupations representative of level of performance in SCANS know-how required for entry into jobs with career ladder.

POSITION AND TASK

Resources	**Travel Agents:** Sets priorities for work tasks on a daily basis so that travel arrangements are completed in a timely manner.	**Restaurant Manager:** Prepares weekly sales projections—conducts inventory of food supplies; calculates the costs of purchased and on-hand food; determines sales.	**Medical Assistant:** Acquires, maintains, and tracks supplies on hand—inventories supplies and equipment, fills out reorder forms, and obtains extra supplies when merchandise is on sale.	**Quality Control Inspector:** Establishes a system for inspecting elevators within a given area and time frame while allowing for other contingencies.	**Chef:** Performs a cost analysis on menu items in order to turn a profit.
Interpersonal Skills	**Child-Care Aide:** Works as a member of a team in the classroom.	**Outside Equipment Technician:** Coordinates with a peer technician to install a point-to-point data circuit in two different cities.	**Carpenter:** Shares experiences and knowledge with other workers, and cooperates with others on a variety of tasks to accomplish project goals.	**Accounting/ Financial Analyst:** Teaches a co-worker the procedure for sending bimonthly memos.	**Customer Service Representative:** Assists customers in selecting merchandise or resolving complaints.
Information	**Travel Agents:** Uses on-line computer terminal to retrieve information relating to customer requests, plans itinerary, and books airline tickets.	**Blue-Collar Worker Supervisor:** Records and maintains purchase requests, purchase invoices, and cost information on raw material.	**Child-care Aide:** Compiles accurate written records including all facets of the child's play for the office and the parents.	**Order-Filler:** Communicates a down-time situation to co-workers, and explains the situation so that everyone can visualize and understand it.	**Cosmetologist:** Keeps abreast of new and emerging styles and techniques through magazines and attendance at fashion shows.
Systems	**Medical Assistant:** Understands the systems of the organization and the organization's ultimate goal (i.e., excellent patient care).	**Accounting/ Financial Analyst:** Performs analysis comparing current expenditures with projected needs and revenues.	**Shipping and Receiving Clerk:** Unloads and directs material throughout the plant to storage and the assembly line in accordance with company policy.	**Food Service Worker:** Evaluates the performance of workers and adjusts work assignments to increase staff efficiency.	**Plastic Molding Machine Operator:** Monitors gauges and dials to ensure that the machine operates at the proper rate of speed.

(continued)

TABLE 5.B Continued.

POSITION AND TASK

Technology	**Travel Agent:** Uses the on-line computer terminal to retrieve information relating to the customer's request, plan the itinerary, and book the airline ticket.	**Accounting/ Financial Analyst:** Prepares the monthly debt schedule, including reviews of financial statements.	**Expeditor/ Purchasing Agent:** Accesses the computer to retrieve required forms used to request bids and to place purchase orders.	**Industry Training Specialist:** Uses available computer and video technology to enhance the realism of training and to conserve time.	**Order Filler:** Operates a forklift and ensures that it is in proper operating condition.
Basic Skills	**Dental Hygienist:** Reads professional manuals to understand issues related to new techniques and equipment.	**Sales Representative, Hotel Services:** Assesses client accounts to determine adherence to company standards.	**Optician:** Measures a customer's facial features to calculate bifocal segment height.	**Law Enforcement Officer:** Prepares written reports of incidents and crimes.	**Contractor:** Prepares a letter to a subcontractor delineating responsibilities for completion of an earth-grading contract.
Thinking Skills	**Expeditor/ Purchasing Agent:** Decides what supplier to use during a bid evaluation based on supplier information stored in the computer.	**Blue-Collar Worker Supervisor:** Sets priorities for processing orders to resolve a conflict in scheduling.	**Truck Delivery Salesperson/ Outside Sales:** Collects money from delinquent customers and uses judgment on extending credit.	**Contractor:** Analyzes and corrects the problem when timber piles break before reaching specified bearing loads.	**Travel Agent:** Compensates a customer who is dissatisfied with his or her travel experience.
Personal Qualities	**Optician:** Responds appropriately to customer requests, demonstrates understanding of customer needs, and exhibits friendliness and politeness to customers.	**Quality Control Inspector:** Performs independent research to assess compliance.	**Computer Operator:** Assumes responsibility for the arrangement and completion of jobs run on the mainframe.	**Telemarketing Representative:** Displays a sense of concern and interest in customers' business and company.	**Sales Representative, Hotel Services:** Asserts self and networks with people at conventions in order to obtain hotel business.

Source: *School to Career Handbook* (California Community Colleges, Chancellor's office, 1995).

Using SCANS Skills

Resume Writing	Career Info Search	Informational Interview	Making a Budget	SCANS FOUNDATION
				BASIC SKILLS
X	X		X	Reading
X				Writing
			X	Arithmetic
		X	X	Listening
	X	X		Speaking
				THINKING SKILLS
X	X	X	X	Creating thinking
			X	Decision making
		X	X	Problem solving
	X	X		Seeing things in the mind's eye
X	X	X	X	Knowing how to learn
	X		X	Reasoning
				PERSONAL QUALITIES
X			X	Responsibility
X	X	X		Self-esteem
X		X		Sociability
X	X	X	X	Self management
X	X	X	X	Integrity/honesty
				SCANS COMPETENCIES
				RESOURCES
X	X	X		Time
	X		X	Money
	X	X		Material and facilities
X	X	X		Human resources
				INTERPERSONAL
	X	X		Participates as member of a team
	X	X		Teaches others new skills
			X	Serves clients/customers
	X	X	X	Exercises leadership
		X	X	Negotiates
X	X	X		Works with diversity
				INFORMATION
	X	X	X	Acquires and evaluates info
	X	X	X	Organizes and maintains info
	X	X		Interprets and communicates info
	X	X		Uses computers to process info
				SYSTEMS
	X		X	Understands systems
X				Monitors and corrects performance
	X	X	X	Improves designs systems
				TECHNOLOGY
X	X		X	Selects technology
X	X	X	X	Applied technology to task
	X			Maintains and troubleshoots equipment

Source: *School to Career Handbook* (VATEA funded project through the California Community Colleges, Chancellor's office, 1995).

in various capacities. A greater number of workers in the future will be self-employed, and their job security will come not from the traditional employer–employee relationship, but from their ability to offer needed skills to many employers. This increased trend toward self-employed, portfolio employees means that each of us will benefit from being able to identify our skills and from determining which skills we want to use, improve, and develop to stay competitive in the job market.

IDENTIFYING TRANSFERABLE SKILLS

As we've discussed throughout this chapter, transferable skills are those skills that you carry from one job to another and can utilize in performing many jobs. Perhaps you are concerned about a lack of paid job experience; or you may have chosen a liberal arts major and are concerned that you will not learn specific job skills or be trained for a job when you graduate.

Note how many SCANS skills you are using by completing exercises in this book related to resume writing, career information search, information interviewing, and making a budget (see the box "Using SCANS Skills").

Let's examine the possible transferable skills that a liberal arts major can and should develop while in school. We will also explore the notion that your *personal, natural abilities* and *attitude* are perhaps the most important set of skills you have for selling yourself and your talents to a potential employer.

The Transferable Skills of a Liberal Arts Major

A liberal arts degree is preparation for a variety of careers. In fact, the majority of those who graduate with a liberal arts degree do not find employment in fields

Identifying the transferable skills of a teacher

Do you think a teacher would have the skills necessary to find employment in the business world? If you know or have read about anyone working in sales, marketing, or management, you may notice that similar skills are involved in all these jobs.

Assessment of teacher skills

Teaching. Training, coordinating, communicating, arbitrating, coaching, group facilitating, accessing the Internet, using computers.

Making lesson plans. Designing curricula, incorporating learning strategies, problem solving, creating visual aids.

Assigning grades. Evaluating, examining, assessing performance, interpreting test results, determining potential of individuals, monitoring progress.

Writing proposals. Assessing needs, identifying targets, setting priorities, designing evaluation models, identifying relevant information, making hypotheses about unknown phenomena, designing a process, estimating costs of a project, researching funding sources.

Advising the yearbook staff. Planning, promoting, fund-raising, group facilitating, handling detail work, meeting deadlines, assembling items of information into a coherent whole, classifying information, coordinating, creating, dealing with pressure, delegating tasks, displaying ideas in artistic form, editing, making layouts.

Supervising interns. Training, evaluating, mentoring, monitoring progress, diagnosing problem areas, inspiring, counseling, guiding.

Interpreting diagnostic tests. Screening, placing, identifying needs, diagnosing.

Interacting with students, parents, and administration. Confronting, resolving conflicts, establishing rapport, conveying warmth and caring, drawing out people, offering support, motivating, negotiating, persuading, handling complaints, mediating, organizing, questioning, troubleshooting.

Chairing a committee or department. Administering, anticipating needs or issues, arranging meetings, creating and implementing committee structures, coordinating, delegating tasks, guiding activities of a team, having responsibility for meeting objectives of a department, negotiating, organizing, promoting.

related to their major (e.g., history majors do not necessarily become historians).

Whether you are an anthropology, English, or history major, you have (or will develop) transferable skills that are useful in the workplace as a result of being a successful college student. As you read the following clusters of skills, think about which skills you have gained while being a student. The *cluster* approach to skills will be further explained in Chapter Ten when we discuss the *functional resume*. Do you have research skills? Do you have organizational skills? Chances are, you do!

Examples of the skills learned in a typical college liberal arts degree program include the following (note how these resemble the skills identified by the SCANS report):

Communication skills.

Listening effectively, writing essays and reports, convincing individuals and groups of the importance of your ideas, negotiating disputes and differences.

Problem-solving or critical thinking skills.

Analytical thinking, thinking abstractly, determining broader issues, defining an issue, identifying several solutions to the same problem, creating new ways to handle an issue, persuading others to act in the best interests of the group.

Human relations skills.

Speaking with colleagues, advising people, helping people resolve problems, communicating ideas effectively, cooperating with others to solve problems and to complete projects, working well with diverse groups of people, teaching or coaching others.

Organizational skills.

Assessing needs, planning or arranging presentations or social events, designing programs, coordinating events, delegating responsibility, evaluating programs, managing the implementation of projects.

Research skills.

Searching computerized databases and published reference materials, identifying themes, analyzing data, classifying data, handling detail work, investigating problems, recording data, writing reports and term papers.

These skills are the critical competencies that employers look for when hiring new employees. Your ability to prove you have developed these skills as a successful college student will set you apart in the interview process and will make you the successful candidate for a job. Start to think about specific ways in which you have demonstrated these skills in school, during your leisure activities, and in any jobs or volunteer experiences you have had.

By now, it should be apparent that you carry many skills from one job to another. Once you are able to describe a job by its skills, you can use these skills in your own letters of application, in your resumes, and during job interviews to reinforce the fact that you have what it takes to do the job, even if you have never had the exact job title.

YOUR MOST VALUABLE ASSETS: YOUR PERSONALITY TRAITS

We've talked about transferable skills that were learned or acquired at school, work or home, or through leisure and volunteer activities. Many of your skills may have come to you naturally, without training or education. We call these skills *natural abilities*—we're referring here to aspects of your personality such as the ability to stay calm in a crisis, the ability to manage many things at once, a natural ability with math and numbers, a natural ability with words, and so forth. More important, we're referring to personal characteristics such as enthusiasm, a good attitude, persistence, confidence, a sense of humor, and many other qualities of success that we discussed in Chapter Two.

These abilities will help you *sell yourself and your talents*. It is often these personal characteristics, called adaptive skills, that in the end separate you from many other qualified applicants and enable you to get the job, top evaluations, raises, and promotions. They may even help you keep your job in tough times.

We don't mean to imply that an employer will look at your enthusiastic, smiling face and say, "It doesn't matter that you have no experience—we want you because you're cheerful!" However, once you have learned to identify your many job-specific skills and to summarize your experience in such a way as to make certain it relates closely to the job being discussed, you will have a much greater chance of succeeding if you are aware of and express your "best self" with interest, enthusiasm, and friendliness. Know and use your personal skills!

SUMMARY

We each have our own special excellence. This excellence is most likely to be demonstrated in experiences that you consider to be achievements or life satisfactions. Your most memorable achievements usually indicate where your greatest concentration of self-motivator ("motivated") skills exists. Analyzing several such achievements is likely to reveal a pattern of skills used repeatedly in making them occur. The more you know about your motivated skills, the better you will be able to choose careers that require the use of these skills. Using these skills gives you a sense of mastery and satisfaction. You will be happier, more productive, and more successful if you can incorporate your motivated skills into your chosen work. You will also find that your skills transfer to many different jobs.

Past accomplishments reveal skills

If you have started reading about occupations by visiting a local library or college career center, you may find that some occupational information sources list the skills related to the specific career described. There are also computer programs such as EUREKA in California, SIGI Plus (System of Interactive Guidance and Information), CIS (Career Information System), and other systems that include lists of skills correlated with job descriptions. Check with your local college or computer store to learn about other skill analysis software. Be certain to review Tables 5.B and 5.C to identify how the SCANS skills relate to a variety of entry-level jobs. Now, complete the exercises that follow.

The following exercises will assist you in identifying your personal constellation of skills. Exercise 5.1 asks you to write about several major experiences in your life with enough detail so that you will be able to analyze each experience for the particular skills utilized. Exercises 5.2 and 5.3 ask you to list ten accomplishments and then to describe them in detail. Exercise 5.4 allows you to identify the skills used in the accomplishments described in the two previous exercises. Exercise 5.5 identifies your cluster of favorite skills. Exercise 5.6 helps you identify the extent of your experience related to the responsibilities of your ideal jobs. Exercises 5.7 and 5.8 serve to review and summarize your preferred and most often used skills.

5.1 Experiography

To explore your past experiences and relate them to your career plan, write an account of the significant experiences in your life; in other words, write an *experiography*. The best way to go about this task is to think of three or four major experiences in each of the following categories and then describe each of them in writing in as much detail as you can. It is important to describe not only what happened but also your feelings (good or bad) about the experience or person and what you learned from the experience. The categories to include are:

a. work experience
b. activity experience—school, clubs, etc.
c. life events
d. leisure time
e. people in your life
f. life's frustrations
g. life's rewards

Remember, neither the chronology nor the order of significance is important. What is important is that you describe people or events that have had an impact on who you are right now. Keep in mind that the writing needs to be specific enough for you to be able to analyze these experiences for particular skills you have demonstrated.

5.2 Accomplishments

Make a list of up to ten accomplishments. You may wish to look back at the ones you have already listed in the Values Grid in Chapter Three, but you do not necessarily have to include them in this list.

1. ....
2. ....
3. ....
4. ....

5. ....
6. ....
7. ....
8. ....
9. ....
10. ....

5.3 Description of accomplishments

Select one or two of the accomplishments listed above, and describe each of them. Use one sheet of paper for each. To be as detailed as possible in your description of the event, try to elaborate on *who* influenced you, *what* you did, *where* it happened, *when* it occurred, *why* you did it, and *how* you did it.

5.4 The skills

List the skills you used in the accomplishments described in Exercise 5.3. ....

....

....

....

5.5 Your favorite skills

Rank the following skills categories as they reflect your favorite skills. (1 = favorite; 6 = least favorite.)

.... a. Help people, be of service, be kind

.... b. Write, read, talk, speak, teach

.... c. Analyze, systemize, research

.... d. Invent, create, develop, imagine

.... e. Persuade, sell, influence, negotiate

.... f. Build, plant crops, use hand-eye coordination, operate machinery

5.6 Ideal jobs

Write five ideal job responsibilities. Next to each one write two or more examples of your experience in each of these areas (e.g., "writing—I wrote a ten-page report that was used to justify a grant application"). In areas where you have not developed extensive experience, you may want to create additional learning experiences to make yourself eligible for your ideal jobs. You can create learning experiences or gain experience by taking classes, by volunteering for extra work in your present job, or by finding another job closely related to your ideal jobs.

....

....

....

....

....

....

5.7 SCANS

Review the SCANS skills description on page 82. Identify up to eight volunteer, job, or homework activities.

1. ....

2. ....

3. ....

4. ....

5. ....

6. ....

7. ....

8. ....

On the Exercise 5.7 worksheet on the next page, check the skills you used in these activities. Use the box on page 85 as an example.

Exercise 5.7 Worksheet: Identify up to eight volunteer, job, or homework activities here and check off which skills were used in each activity.

1.	2.	3.	4.	5.	6.	7.	8.	SCANS FOUNDATION
								BASIC SKILLS
								Reading
								Writing
								Arithmetic
								Listening
								Speaking
								THINKING SKILLS
								Creating thinking
								Decision making
								Problem solving
								Seeing things in the mind's eye
								Knowing how to learn
								Reasoning
								PERSONAL QUALITIES
								Responsibility
								Self-esteem
								Sociability
								Self management
								Integrity/honesty
								SCANS COMPETENCIES
								RESOURCES
								Time
								Money
								Material and facilities
								Human resources
								INTERPERSONAL
								Participates as member of a team
								Teaches others new skills
								Serves clients/customers
								Exercises leadership
								Negotiates
								Works with diversity
								INFORMATION
								Acquires and evaluates info
								Organizes and maintains info
								Interprets and communicates info
								Uses computers to process info
								SYSTEMS
								Understands systems
								Monitors and corrects performance
								Improves designs systems
								TECHNOLOGY
								Selects technology
								Applied technology to task
								Maintains and troubleshoots equipment

Source: *School to Career Handbook* (VATEA funded project through the California Community Colleges, Chancellor's office, 1995).

5.8   Skills review

List the skills that you have at present. ....
....
....
....
....

Review your responses in the *Assessing Your Skills* activity on pages 80–81. What skills would you most like to use in your future career? ....
....
....

Which of the above skills do you need to develop? ....
....
....

How will you develop these skills? ....
....
....
....

You have now identified your foundation—the areas in which you have been most effective and successful in your life. By examining these successes or achievements, you now know what you can do and what motivates you. It is especially important that you focus on skills you use and enjoy.

5.9   Exercise summary

Write a brief paragraph answering these questions

What did you learn about yourself? How does this knowledge relate to your career/life planning? How do you feel?

*Go to page 160,
of the Part One Chapter Summaries,
and fill out the Chapter Five exercise summary now.*

SIX

The World and You

LEARNING OBJECTIVES

At the end of the chapter you will be able to . . .

Identify personal beliefs and assumptions that will affect your career

Recognize how social and cultural conditioning influences your career choice

Identify trends that will affect your career planning through the next decade

Your assumptions, limitations, aspirations, dreams, and fantasies are all influenced by the spoken and unspoken rules and norms of the society in which you live.

In every society, even one as free as that of the United States, social and cultural traditions influence career choice. For example, it may still seem a little strange to us to hear the word *nurse* applied to a male healthcare worker, even though both men and women are found in this profession. Old associations and stereotypes linger because of the many years during which societal limitations and expectations played a much greater role in determining career choices for men and women.

The next step in the career-planning process is to examine the societal and cultural factors that directly or indirectly affect your career choice. The goal is to heighten your awareness of the trends, beliefs, and assumptions that influence your choice of possible occupations and will continue to influence you as you follow your career path. These cultural norms may be limiting, as in the cases of (1) pay inequities between men and women, and (2) racial discrimination. Other cultural norms may facilitate your career success; for example, our society encourages the entrepreneurial spirit that may help you start a small business. Although further changes are needed, social and legislative action of the past

two decades has made the career playing field more level for all participants. The ultimate goal is to assure women and men—of all ages, lifestyles, races, religions, social groups, and ethnicities—equal treatment and opportunities.

The first part of this chapter will explore cultural norms, gender equity issues, cultural diversity, and ageism. The latter part of the chapter will explore trends in the workforce as they relate to possible career choices. Finally, we provide some written exercises to assist you in identifying your own barriers, attitudes, and biases and in better planning your own future.

SOCIETAL INFLUENCES ON CAREER CHOICES

Career planning does not happen in a vacuum. Your life situation influences the decisions you make and how you make them. The society in which you grow up, your background, your family, your peers, and the way you feel about yourself are all influences on the decisions you make. Sometimes these factors make it easier to choose and follow a career path. For instance, a friend or family member who encourages you in school and work efforts may help to build your confidence and therefore improve your chances of success in whatever field you choose. Or family support may allow you to devote full-time effort to schooling and thus more quickly complete your chosen degree.

However, social and cultural considerations, family, peers, and feelings about yourself can also act as obstacles to making and following through on decisions. For example, your time available for school may be limited due to family responsibilities, or you may feel that the career you would like to pursue requires an advanced degree, or that it would not pay enough to support your family. Consider the following statements.

One way to increase your chances of getting something is to ask for it.
Ashleigh Brilliant

> *"I'm too old* [or perhaps too far along in school] *to start thinking about changing careers now."*
>
> *"What I would really like to be is an engineer, but I've given up on that because I can't go to school full-time to get that kind of degree."*
>
> *"I don't know whether I'm going to apply for that job or not. Besides, they're not going to hire a Latino."*
>
> *"I'm not really qualified to do that kind of job, and my high school grades were weak. I was never good at schoolwork."*
>
> *"Sure, I'd like to go back to school, but how could I get all the housework done, and who would look after the kids? There's no money for day care."*

Do any of the preceding statements sound like some you have heard people say, or maybe even some you yourself have said or felt? They represent some of the most common obstacles that people face when making academic and career decisions. An obstacle to a satisfactory decision is anything or anyone that prevents you from adequately considering all the possible alternatives. For example, the people who say, "I'm too old to start something new" when looking for a job will miss out by not even considering some positions for which they may be well-qualified. Age stereotyping prevents these people from considering all the possible alternatives.

STRIVING FOR EQUALITY IN THE WORKFORCE

Gender Roles

As recently as 30 years ago, female students seeking career advice from school counselors were frequently encouraged to choose fields such as teaching and nursing. These choices were recommended both because they were "women's jobs" and because they fit best with the traditional female family role of mothering. It wasn't until the 1970s that newspapers no longer divided the classified employment ads into the categories of "men" and "women."

Within the past 25 years, school counselors began to recognize that female roles in society were expanding and that women could be doctors, engineers, and members of, in fact, any profession. Today, academic counselors are more aware of gender fairness issues (see "equity definitions") and more often attempt to treat men and women similarly, without making judgments or assumptions about marriage, and family roles.

As suggested above, many of our career and pay biases were based on the social norm of a "typical" four-member family in which the husband was the principal wage earner and the wife was primarily responsible for raising the children. Societal changes and evolutions have moved us away from these traditional roles and toward gender equity. Because many couples find it difficult if not impossible to manage a home and family on one income, both partners in today's "typical" marriage work outside the home. This major change has forced us (or permitted us) to rethink traditional male and female roles. Partners in a relationship are more likely to share home and child rearing responsibilities.

Just as women's roles have changed over the past few decades, so too have men's roles undergone change. For example, some men may choose careers that don't require extensive travel or long work hours because they want and expect to assume an equal parenting role. And despite ongoing pay inequities, many women now play the role of primary breadwinner in a family. In some families, men are choosing to

Equity definitions

Affirmative action: Programs, policies, or procedures that attempt to overcome the effects of past discrimination, bias, and/or stereotyping.

Ageism: Any action or policy that discriminates on the basis of age, affecting employment, advancement, privileges, or rewards.

Americans with Disabilities Act (ADA): Legislation passed July 26, 1990, that prohibits discrimination on the basis of a disability.

Barriers: Anything that prevents a person from equal access to the use of goods, services, facilities, and so on. There are physical and architectural barriers (such as stairs) and there are attitudinal barriers (such as stereotyping).

(continued)

work or stay at home and take care of the children. Both traditional and nontraditional types of families face new challenges with each passing year. Finding reliable, affordable child care is a struggle for many parents, and this concern may influence career decisions and directions. Today, a great many families are single-parent households, in which the adult must combine the full-time job of earning a living with the all-consuming task of raising a family.

In an ideally unbiased society composed of 50 percent men and 50 percent women, it can be expected that most occupations would employ approximately 50 percent of each gender and would pay them like salaries for like work. However, in our society such equity is being achieved gradually. Table 6.A (later in the chapter) illustrates ongoing inequities in the types of jobs held by women and men.

Although you cannot predict the exact course of your life or your career, you can begin considering possible choices and how they relate to *you*. Take time now to anticipate challenges you may encounter in the future. Now is the time to plan. By setting objectives that lead toward accomplishment of a career goal, you may later avoid having to take a job just to pay the bills. It is now more important than ever to choose a career that truly reflects your interests and abilities, your values, your personality, and your life plan. The concept of gender equity means that everyone is free to explore a career of their choice.

Age and Opportunity

Ten years ago, there were 20 million people over age 65 in the United States. As we approach the year 2000, the figure is nearly 35 million, or 14 percent of the population. By 2020, the over–65 population could go as high as 53 million, or 15 percent. There will be more single people older than 65, particularly women. Currently, 38 percent of seniors are over 75; by 2000, 45 percent will be over 75.

It should be noted that the number of people retiring at age 65 continues to decrease. Many victims of corporate downsizing are let go before becoming eligible for retirement pensions. And due to no-fault divorce laws and lack of retirement plans in the traditionally female occupations, many divorced women must continue to work long after their male counterparts have retired.

Discrimination: Practices, policies, or procedures that are specifically prohibited by law; any action that limits or denies a person or group of persons opportunities, privileges, roles, or rewards on such prohibited bases as their sex, race, age, and so on.

Feminist: Any person (male or female) who believes that women should have political, economic, and social rights equal to those of men.

Gender bias: An attitude or behavior that reflects adversely upon a person or group because of gender but may not be covered under present legislation; behavior resulting from the assumption that one sex is superior to the other.

Gender fair: Practices and behaviors that treat males and females similarly; may imply separate but equal.

Gender role: Social behavior that is prescribed and defined for males and females according to tradition, as contrasted with actual biological differences.

Gender stereotyping: Attributing behaviors, abilities, interests, values, and roles to a person or group of persons on the basis of gender.

Nontraditional job: Working in a field or an occupation that typically employs 80 percent or more of the opposite gender; e.g., nursing employs only 5 percent males, while construction work employs only 1 percent females.

Sexism: Any attitude, action, or institution that subordinates or assigns roles to a person or group of persons based on their gender. Sexism may be individual, cultural, or institutional; intentional or unintentional; effected by omission or commission.

Facts and figures: Women in the workplace

- In 1970 only 1 in every 4 women age 16 and over was in the labor force. Today, 1 out of every 2 women work outside the home. Approximately 80 percent of women between 25 and 44 are in the workforce.

- In 1970, 30 percent of all mothers with children under 6 years old had paid employment. That figure has now increased to over 50 percent and is expected to rise to 75 percent by the year 2000. Since 1970, households headed by women have increased 70 percent. Women are the sole earners in more than 18 percent of families.

- Currently, a women earns, on average, 75 cents for every dollar earned by a man.

- While percentages of women in nontraditional areas have increased, often the increase has occurred in the lower-paying jobs. About 25 percent of women work in what the U.S. Census labels "professional and technical jobs"; however, women are employed in only eight of the fifty job titles that comprise that area. *Two-thirds* of employed women hold clerical, service, nursing, and education jobs; these are traditionally low-paying occupations.

- Women make up over 48 percent of managers and 53 percent of professionals, including teachers and registered nurses. In the professions, women have made gains in the last ten years and now comprise 21.8 percent of doctors and 10.5 percent of dentists. In such traditionally male jobs as pilots and navigators, women now make up 3.9 percent, up from 1.5 percent; among firefighters, women comprise 3.3 percent, up from .5 percent. Although women constitute 46 percent of the workforce, they fill only 10 percent of the top corporate positions.

- Woman-owned businesses number approximately 8 million and employ over 16 million people (35 percent more than all Fortune 500 companies employ worldwide). An estimated 40 to 50 percent of all woman-owned firms in this country are based in homes.

If present trends continue, retirement-age single women will be the poorest segment of society.

Accentuate your assets

Older workers competing in the workforce may face discrimination and the perception by employers that they are "out of date" or "too old to learn." Although such ageism is illegal, it occurs. Young workers are valued for their energy, flexibility, and entry-level salaries. Some employers, however, may choose an older, more mature job candidate over a recent college graduate, in the belief that anyone, at any age, can display high energy and flexibility, but with age come maturity, reliability, problem-solving abilities, and a wealth of experience. As a prospective employee, it is your responsibility to know your assets, whether those of youth or maturity, and to highlight them at the right times with the right decision makers. The most effective way to deal with ageism (whether it's directed against your youth or lack of it) is to sell your present or prospective employer on how your age and particular experience are an asset to the job.

Many of today's retirement-age workers are finding satisfaction in the entry-level jobs once dominated by teenage workers, such as in fast-food and

retail outlets. For some seniors, this work offers a social outlet, and the minimal pay is sufficient for workers whose income is supplemented by social security benefits.

People who live long, healthy lives may change careers frequently during their lifetimes, and their most satisfying and perhaps most financially rewarding career may come later in life. Novelist James Michener was first published after the age of 40; Colonel Sanders started Kentucky Fried Chicken after he was 50; "Dr. Ruth" became a celebrity talk show sex therapist when she was 48; Sam Walton opened his first Wal-Mart at age 44; and Ted Turner started Cable News Network (CNN) at 42. Don't forget Margaret Mitchell who won her first Pulitzer Prize, for *Gone With the Wind*, when she was 37; Senator Margaret Chase Smith, elected to the Senate for the first time when she was 49; Shirley Temple Black, named ambassador to Ghana at age 47; and Grandma Moses, who began a painting career at the age of 76!

Affirmative Action

Affirmative action has become a highly controversial and much-debated issue. Its advocates support policies and programs that increase opportunities for women, minorities, and other underrepresented groups. These policies involve special consideration or "set aside positions" for candidates who would, if hired, admitted, or promoted, increase the percentage of diverse members in a professional, academic, social, or business group. Many people oppose preferences or quota selection criteria and would prefer to see impartial screening of all candidates, regardless of gender, ethnicity, or socioeconomic status. A wide range of feelings and opinions exists on this issue. Compounding the controversy is a high demand for scarce resources that is pervasive in the fields of education, health and welfare services, and employment opportunities. Immigration, both legal and illegal, also complicates affirmative action decision making.

Recent decisions by state and federal courts have narrowed the scope of affirmative action by rejecting quotas or preferential formulas in favor of open and competitive criteria. These courts, however, have reversed unjustified discrimination in hiring, firing, and admissions and have also rejected forced early retirements due to age. Affirmative action remains a challenge as we enter the next century.

Other Cultural Considerations: Valuing Diversity

Today's workforce is more culturally diverse than ever, and this diversity will increase as the next wave of workers joins the workforce. To remain globally competitive, companies in the United States must improve training and advancement opportunities and use each employee's talent to the fullest. Stereotypes about and prejudices against particular ethnic or racial groups must be diminished and opportunities expanded for all workers.

Hispanics, African Americans, and Asian Americans are projected to make up approximately 27 percent of the workforce by the year 2005, with Caucasians declining from 78.6 percent to 73 percent. Moreover, projections for new workers entering the workplace indicate that in most urban centers, all minority group members will together make up the majority of the entering workforce by the year 2000.

Legislation has also been enacted to eliminate discrimination against persons who have a disability. The Americans with Disabilities Act prohibits discrimination on the basis of a disability and calls for the elimination of barriers, that is, anything that prevents a person or group of persons equal access to goods, services, and facilities. All places of employment must make reasonable accommodations for such otherwise qualified employees, including access to rooms and buildings, use of auxiliary aids, and services such as interpreters and hearing devices. Persons with disabilities should enjoy the same freedom of choice in making career decisions as those without disabilities, and this becomes more of a reality each year.

Companies are learning to respect diversity as an important component of the workplace. Just as many college campuses now require a course in diversity, firms are offering employee training in diversity to enable workers of differing backgrounds, educational levels, physical abilities, and cultures to accept and value one another. Whether in a social, political, academic, or economic context, we have begun to realize that our society will benefit from the fullest utilization of all its citizens and their many different talents.

THE CHANGING WORKPLACE

Ten years ago terms such as the knowledge worker, global economy, computer literacy, learning organization, virtual workplace, small entrepreneurial business, woman-owned business, meeting customer needs, and temporary/leasing agencies would have been irrelevant in a book on career planning. But these terms represent trends, and the trends affect a large percentage of new entrants to the workforce. Therefore, it is to your advantage to understand the shifting nature of the workplace.

Manufacturing used to be the mainstay of the U.S. economy, but we are increasingly becoming a service-based economy, in which the majority of workers provide services (e.g., health care, retail, food preparation) instead of producing a commodity.

The Need for "Knowledge" Workers

An employee becomes more valuable as he or she accumulates new skills. The challenge is to remain an outstanding contributor on the job (i.e., as a specialist) while learning new skills. As organizations downsize or flatten, employees must possess multiple skills, such as the ability to learn, use new technology, or sell a product. These people have an edge. They may, for example, be able to transfer from the training division if it is reduced in size to the sales division—and therefore remain employed.

There is still opportunity to move up. For example, Courtney got a job straight out of high school as a file clerk in a firm making shoulder pads. Learning new skills on the job, she began to manage the computer system and handle most payroll and personnel duties.

Sometimes it is necessary to spend time after work taking classes and studying job-related materials at home to get a head start. LaTricia was a public relations manager at a computer firm and had to spend as many as five hours a week on her own time becoming familiar with the company's new products. She also took a class in teaching English as a Second Language to

become more sensitive to cultural diversity at a time when her business was becoming increasingly international.

Courtney and LaTricia are examples of workers continually learning new skills so they can be available for openings within their organizations and elsewhere. Remember, *luck* is *preparation* meeting *opportunity!*

The Global Economy

A decade ago the U.S. was generating 75 percent of the world's technology; today that figure is closer to only 50 percent. The United States is striving to develop a more global economy by establishing trade agreements with other countries, such as the North American Free Trade Agreement (NAFTA). Global competition and multinational corporations will continue to influence the business world and our economy. Today it is not just the Fortune 500 companies, such as General Electric, IBM, and AT&T, that conduct business and have offices throughout the world. Employees wishing to advance in this new international economy must have the ability to speak more than one language and understand the cultural customs of other countries.

In today's global economy, NAFTA has created a need for multilingual talents. Asian investments in Latin America and Mexico are expanding. Many of the "maquiladora" (border) factories in Tijuana, for example, are run by Japanese, Chinese, and Korean corporations. It is estimated that Asian companies invested over $1 billion in Mexico in 1996 alone. Nissan of Japan will spend over $80 million in Mexican facilities. Obviously, the ability to converse in several languages is an asset in the job hunt.

Computer Literacy

No more than one in eight jobs is directly related to a field of high technology. However, it is necessary to be computer literate even in a nontechnical job. Many jobs will be affected by advances in technology, and those who are comfortable with and knowledgeable about computers may be the best job candidates.

The Changing Corporate Structure

The corporate world is changing its organization. The one-time hierarchical structure in which young professionals could look forward to "climbing the ladder" at the same company for the rest of their lives has given way to a flattened organization. The traditional pyramid structure of companies with a "top down" management style (the boss at the top with employees subordinate) has given way to two new structures:

1. The diamond: "thick" in the middle with service providers and other self-supervising workers who produce revenue—and "thin" on support staff and executives;
2. The virtual corporation: a group of experts (joined together by computer networks throughout the world) working specifically on temporary projects and then disbanding.

The diamond-shaped corporation gives its employees opportunities for advancement after showing they have learned a variety of technical and people-oriented skills such as those described in Chapter 5. A software engineer at a telecommunications company might find herself marketing to customers all over the world the products she created. Thus your career may evolve based on the skills you contribute to the bottom line. To become more competitive and productive, large companies are eliminating layers of middle management and striving to improve worker productivity, teamwork, and responsibility.

Telecommuting: The Virtual Workplace

Technological advancements will continue to shape the modern workplace. In the near future, more employees will be able to perform their jobs via telecommunications, thus cutting down on pollution caused by commuting. Some cities are creating telecommuting centers, where employees from many companies can use computers, modems, and fax machines without driving far from home. Many small businesses, too, are being operated from home with the aid of phones, modems, and fax machines.

Small Businesses

More jobs are created by small businesses than by large corporations. During the 1970s, 9.6 million jobs were generated by firms with fewer than 20 employees; in contrast, the 1,000 largest firms created only 75,000 jobs. Between 1981 and 1990, small firms created over 20 million new jobs. If you want variety and responsibility and are results-oriented, a small business might be the place for you.

It is estimated nearly 50 million people have a home office with a personal computer. According to IDC/Link, a New York market research firm, nearly 13 million Americans operated full-time businesses from their homes in the mid-1990s. They estimated 14 million more have part-time home businesses and 8 million telecommute from home. The rest use their home office for work they bring from the outside office or for freelancing. See Exhibit 6.C for a list of occupations (some of which can be operated from home) that are projected to grow quickly.

Meeting customer needs

Every day, small businesses are created to serve consumer needs. Did you know that the Home Shopping Network was created when a company that could not pay its bills instead gave its inventory to a TV executive? The executive needed to get rid of the inventory and announced the availability of the materials on his network. Everything sold within two hours!

Woman-Owned Businesses

In 1995, nearly eight million companies were owned by women. It is estimated that one in four American workers is employed in a woman-owned business. Forty to 50 percent of these companies are home-based, according to a 1995 study by the National Foundation for Women Business Owners.

Temporary Agencies/Leasing Companies

Temporary employment agencies, in addition to their traditional business of providing secretarial and clerical professionals on a contract basis, now provide employees in such areas as accounting, health care, telemarketing, the paralegal field, and computers. Technical service contracting firms place a range of engineering and computer professionals as well as technicians and draftspeople in temporary positions. If this trend toward growing numbers of temporary employees continues as predicted, many people will find themselves working for an employee-leasing firm. Kelly Services, one of the largest temporary service agencies, expanded 800% in one five-year period.

Temporary employment is also a method of obtaining permanent employment. One multimedia graphic artist took temporary work through an agency and changed jobs four times in his first year, with a typical contract lasting about two months. Once he developed a reputation, however, potential clients began seeking him out, so he worked less through temporary agencies and agents.

TRENDS: MOVING INTO THE TWENTY-FIRST CENTURY

It helps to have a picture of tomorrow's opportunities when defining a reasonable job target. For example, you might guess that now is not the time to prepare for a lifelong job in an automotive assembly plant. Such positions will likely be phased out in the next decade by computerized robots. In fact, 80 percent of General Motors employees now work at jobs other than assembly.

Getting the right skills and education now will give you an advantage tomorrow. Over 80 percent of jobs require some postsecondary education or training. Computer literacy will continue to be a necessity in a great majority of jobs. As discussed earlier in connection with the government's *SCANS* report, employers will seek individuals with strong reading, writing, and communications skills, the ability to reason and to solve problems, and the ability and willingness to keep learning. *Transferable skills*

More important than knowing what jobs will be available is being *flexible*—having the ability to adapt to this changing world of work. It is estimated that forty percent of the jobs that will be available in the year 2005 are yet to be created. Thus you cannot obtain training specifically for every career change you may encounter, but you can develop learning skills that will prepare you for training in new job skills and applications. It is also possible that, due to advancing technology and other factors, you may change careers not just once but many times during your life. Even if this is not the case and you move along one career path throughout your life, you will need to continue educating yourself just to keep up with technological change. The trend *Lifelong learning* toward lifelong learning is evidenced by the fact that 1.6 million people over age 40 were in college in 1993, compared to only 477,000 in 1970. Additionally, an increasing number of people are enrolled in "corporate universities." Corporate universities and colleges range from company-run classes designed primarily for that company's employees to programs run by companies that confer credible degrees such as an associate's degree or a bachelor's degree.

The multimedia revolution ignites creative industries

Film, animation, entertainment, fashion, graphic design, publishing, architecture, and other media-related fields are creating a new surge of employment opportunities. The evolution of this trend is closely related to the development of computer software and hardware.

Digital Domain, which produced special effects for *Apollo 13*, employs artists, digital designers, and technicians. From film special effects, this firm has expanded to commercials, music videos, CD-ROM games, and theme park attractions—with additional plans to be involved in high resolution, interactive programming delivered over cable.

While multimedia may best be known for the CD-ROMs that combine text, sound, pictures, and video, the technology is advancing into new forms. One form is "virtual reality" where special glasses or headsets allow a person to perceive an experience as if it were real. Another form of multimedia technology created "smart cameras" that recognize faces and facial expressions in order to identify people for security systems. Another application of the technology is evident in incorporating animation into real-life film. The film industry labels this animation "digital effects." It can be seen regularly in commercials (e.g., cola drinking polar bears, flirtatious M & Ms, and an athletic Pillsbury doughboy). Employers emphasize they are looking for good technicians who have developed artistic talents and technological skills. The digital designer must understand lighting, texture, and motion. Such professionals are rewarded with salaries ranging from $40,000 to over $150,000.

Disney University is an example of the former type of "university," although it also has an "external" program for employees from the automotive and health care industries related to customer and quality service. The MGH Institute of Health Professions Corporation (originally initiated by the Massachusetts General Hospital Corporation) is an example of the latter type of "university," granting a Master's degree in health-related professions. This program is open to anyone working in a health-related field. The number of corporate universities has increased from 400 in the 1970s to more than 1,000 now.

It is estimated that 90 percent of all scientific knowledge has been generated in the last forty years. The extent of scientific knowledge will again double in the next ten to fifteen years! (Engineers, computer scientists, and others in fast-changing technical fields must constantly update their knowledge. According to one estimate, an engineer's knowledge either becomes obsolete or is incorporated into computers every three years.) Since information is accumulating at such a fast pace, it is highly useful to know how to retrieve and manage information and to perceive common threads and patterns in the information. Thus, information management and interpersonal communications will be especially important skill areas in the future.

Many of the best job opportunities during the next decade will demand that applicants have cross-functional training to broaden their qualifications. Dual majors, interdisciplinary programs, and studying foreign languages can make a difference in the competitive, increasingly global job market. Job applicants are also being informed they need both "people skills" and "technical skills" in order to be competitive. Today's college graduates are finding that, to compete for the best jobs, they must commit to lifelong continuing education to bolster their job skills and prepare for career changes.

If you aren't interested in a career that requires a four-year degree, there will always be a need in society for people selling merchandise, running businesses, maintaining homes, caring for children, working in restaurants, attending to health and fitness needs, and working in a variety of trades that may or may not require training beyond high school. Many of these fields are experiencing greater demand due to the important sociological changes mentioned previously in this chapter and the increase in the number of

Job growth throughout the next decade

- *Health services.* Demand will be especially great for primary-care workers such as nurse practitioners, nutrition counselors, gerontological social workers, radiology technicians, home health-care aides, and health service administrators.

- *Hotel management and recreation.* This category includes restaurants, resorts, and travel services, as well as opportunities in conference planning.

- *Food service.* Managers and chefs will be in demand for all those restaurants and hotel kitchens, as well as for food processing plants and labs. Specialty restaurants will continue to expand.

- *Engineering.* Specializations in high demand will include robotics, aviation, biotechnology, and manufacturing technology.

- *Environmental sciences.* Specializations include hazardous waste management, environmental impact research, conservation and environmental preservation, and alternative fuels.

- *Basic science.* Biogenetic engineering will be an important field in the next decade, as will chemistry (especially food science) and fiber optics.

- *Computer science, information systems.* Opportunities will continue to be strong in design, engineering, programming, networking, and maintenance.

- *Business services.* Growing fields will be accounting, statistical analysis, and payroll management. Many jobs will be filled by temporary workers. In management, managers of telecommunication and environmental protection will be in demand.

- *Human resources and personnel.* The field of employee management continues to grow as a result of legislation concerning employee rights, new payroll requirements and new compensation options. Specialists are needed to handle such responsibilities as job evaluation, hiring and firing, benefits planning, and training.

- *Financial services.* This field includes financial planning and portfolio management. An increased demand for "temp" employees and employees specializing in retirement planning is expected.

- *Educational services and products.* Demand is growing in the school system, where both teachers and administrators will be needed to meet the changing needs of immigrants and the baby boomers' children (and grandchildren!). Corporate America will be hiring educators and trainers to teach literacy skills such as English. High demand subjects include math, science, computer software, interactive learning modalities, and foreign languages, such as Spanish, Japanese, and Chinese. The latest need for educational products is on the Internet, where new interactive products are being introduced daily.

- *Maintenance and repair.* These are the people who will take care of all the equipment that will keep tomorrow's world running.

- *Artistic/Multimedia.* Writers, entertainers, party planners, artists, digital designers, animators, and graphic designers will have good prospects but must be entrepreneurial types.

For specific predictions regarding growing job fields, see Tables 6.D to 6.G at the end of this chapter. Since data are presented from several sources, figures may differ from table to table for the same profession and are meant to be representative.

Internet related growth areas

1. Web Master, Web page designers
2. Internet security
3. Cybrarians (or cyber-librarians)
4. Geographic Information Systems (GIS)
5. Multimedia designers (art and computer backgrounds)
6. Intellectual property lawyers
7. On-line content developers

Top 10 high-income home businesses

Money Magazine listed these as the top 10 high-income home businesses in its March 1996 issue:

- Export agent
- Employer trainer
- Management consultant
- Commercial debt negotiator
- Business plan writer
- Desktop video publisher
- Computer tutor and trainer
- Mailing list service provider
- Home inspector
- Temporary-help provider

The magazine cited the following sources: American Home Business Association, *The Best Home Businesses for the 90s* by Paul Edwards; *Home Business News*; *Export Sales and Marketing Manual*, Gene Fairbrother; National Association of the Self-Employed; Small Office Home Office; IEEE; IDC Link.

two–wage earner households. Many of the jobs listed on the previous page in the box titled "Job growth throughout the next decade" and later in Exhibit 6.A and Table 6.E, do not require a bachelor's degree.

Although it is helpful to take growth trends into consideration as you explore your options, it is not necessary to choose a career path only in the areas most likely to have openings. In fact, as will be discussed in the job search strategy section of this book, the best direction to follow is most often *directly toward what you really want to do.* The key is *desire.* Desire plus talent and perseverance get people jobs in even the tightest job markets.

FINDING YOUR PLACE IN A CHANGING WORLD

How do all these social and cultural changes affect you? Your expectations about your future are influenced by your early socialization and by the culture that surrounds you. (Look back at Super's theory in Chapter One.) Career opportunities can be discovered and pursued through family, childhood play, school experiences, volunteer work, and early work activities. *The degree of satisfaction you find in work and in life depends upon your finding opportunities to develop and use your abilities, interests, values, and personality traits.*

Unfortunately, opportunity is not distributed equally throughout society. You may feel limited economically, academically, or by family responsibilities. Opportunities may be limited by gender stereotyping, by educational requirements, by discrimination, or by the changing economy. However, as perceptions change, as laws change, as the economy becomes more global and requires employers to appreciate and utilize diverse human talents, all women and men should feel free to choose and train for the type of career that best suits their interests and talents.

If you are experiencing (or worrying about) limitations of one type or another, seek help in overcoming them. Talk to a career or academic counselor, or seek help from a support group or your family. As you read this book, you are preparing for the career that best fits you. Don't let the world set unnecessary limitations on your plans and goals. Instead, use this opportunity to reach beyond those limitations and take

advantage of all possible opportunities. You will find that as you form definite plans and objectives, it becomes easier to move forward and to anticipate and avoid obstacles.

TABLES, FACTS, AND FIGURES

The tables and exhibits that follow provide a cross-section of information about salaries, including pay equity across gender and race, and about occupations projected to experience good job growth. The tables and exhibits are intended to provide general information of interest to you as you consider various career options. Although numerical data gives the impression of being "hard facts," remember that such information should be considered approximate. The future is only partially predictable, but it's a good idea to be informed!

TABLE 6.A

Percentages of specified groups in selected occupations in the United States.

OCCUPATION	TOTAL EMPLOYED (THOUSANDS)	PERCENTAGE OF WOMEN	PERCENTAGE OF AFRICAN AMERICANS	PERCENTAGE OF LATINOS
Law				
Lawyers	777	22.9	2.7	2.1
Legal Assistants	254	79.6	8.6	4.9
Education				
Teachers, College and University	772	42.5	4.8	3.1
Elementary School Teachers	1,668	85.9	9.3	3.9
Secondary School Teachers	1,237	57.5	6.9	3.1
Special Education	286	84.0	10.1	2.3
Health				
Physicians	605	21.8	3.7	4.6
Dentists	152	10.5	1.9	3.0
Radiologic Technicians	146	70.2	8.3	7.0
Registered Nurses	1,859	94.4	8.4	3.2
Health Administrators	450	70.5	6.5	4.2
Health Records Technicians	63	88.8	20.4	5.7
Social Science				
Economists	117	47.1	4.8	3.5
Psychologists	241	64.1	7.1	3.1
Engineering and Science				
Electrical and Electronics Engineers	533	7.6	4.5	3.4
Civil Engineers	221	9.4	4.7	3.8
Industrial Engineers	201	16.4	3.4	4.4
Mechanical Engineers	296	5.2	4.4	3.3
Chemists	133	28.8	4.3	3.0
Arts				
Writers, Artists, Entertainers, and Athletes	2,026	46.6	5.3	4.7
Designers	541	52.6	3.7	4.4
Musicians and Composers	174	32.8	8.8	5.8
Photographers	135	26.2	6.5	7.1
Protective Service				
Firefighters	188	3.3	7.5	5.0
Police and Detectives	923	16.0	18.0	5.4
Sheriffs and Bailiffs	117	19.5	13.4	4.6
"Traditional" Female Occupations				
Bank Tellers	446	88.4	6.9	6.2
Billing Clerks	160	88.5	8.4	6.6
Bookkeepers	1,806	90.9	4.5	4.9
Office Clerks	731	82.0	11.4	9.6
Secretaries	4,174	98.2	8.9	5.9
"Nontraditional" Female Occupations				
Airplane Pilots	101	3.9	5.5	2.4
Electricians	666	1.1	6.1	5.1
Auto Mechanics	854	.6	6.4	10.8
Truck Drivers (Heavy)	2,786	4.5	12.3	8.8

Source: *Employment and Earnings,* U.S. Department of Labor, Bureau of Labor Statistics, Washington, DC, January 1994.

1996 Median weekly earnings of the nation's 88.7 million full-time workers.

TABLE 6.B

TYPE OF WORKER	WEEKLY MEDIAN INCOME
CAUCASIANS	
Women	$419.00
Men	580.00
AFRICAN AMERICANS	
Women	372.00
Men	417.00
HISPANICS	
Women	315.00
Men	344.00
MEDIAN WEEKLY EARNINGS OF ALL WORKERS:	$489.00

Source: U.S. Department of Labor, Bureau of Labor Statistics, Washington DC, January 1997.

Cap and gown = $$$$$$: Higher education continues to be the ticket to higher earnings. Mean annual earnings for persons aged 18 and over, by level of education

TABLE 6.C

EDUCATION LEVEL	MEAN ANNUAL EARNINGS
Doctorate (Ph.D., Ed.D.)	$54,904.00
Master's (MA, MS)	$40,368.00
Bachelor's (BA, BS)	$32,629.00
Associate (AA, AS)	$24,398.00
Some College, No Degree	$19,666.00
High School Graduate	$18,737.00
Not a High School Graduate	$12,809.00

From: U.S. Bureau of the Census, August 1994.

TABLE 6.D   Starting salaries for college graduates.

	1995	1996–97
ENGINEERING		
Industrial	$35,244	$37,536
Electrical	$35,943	$39,811
Computer	$34,914	$39,047
Mechanical	$36,025	$39,852
Civil	$30,348	$32,770
Chemical	$39,863	$42,450
BUSINESS/COMPUTER SCIENCE		
MIS	$30,654	$34,799
Computer Science	$32,607	$36,964
Business Administration	$25,142	$28,506
Marketing	$24,726	$28,658
Accounting	$27,873	$30,393
Economics/Finance	$26,597	$30,000
HUMANITIES/SOCIAL SCIENCE/HEALTHCARE		
Nursing	$31,798	$32,927
Allied Health	$33,810	$35,000
English/Liberal Arts	$22,520	$24,081
Sociology	$22,298	$24,232
Psychology	$20,487	$22,232
Political Science/Government	$23,812	$26,924

Source: NACE (National Association of Colleges and Employers).

EXHIBIT 6.A

High-paying, fast-growing occupations.

Of the 500 occupations for which the Bureau of Labor Statistics projects employment, 21 are growing faster or much faster than average, will add at least 100,000 jobs between 1994 and 2005, and have earnings higher than average. The chart shows them sorted by average weekly earnings for full-time workers.

While most of these occupations require at least a college degree, about a third do not. The jobs also have a great deal of variety with regard to the skills and aptitudes of workers, working conditions, and the nature of the work.

OCCUPATIONS	AVERAGE WEEKLY WAGES OF FULL-TIME WORKERS	TOTAL JOB OPENINGS 1994–2005 (THOUSANDS)	PERCENT CHANGE 1994–2005
Lawyers	$1,131	268	28
Physicians	1,040	205	22
Systems analysts	845	481	92
Computer engineers	845	191	90
Management analysts	789	109	35
Residential counselors	694	158	76
Teachers, secondary school	690	782	29
Registered nurses	685	740	25
Teachers, special education	647	262	53
Writers and editors, including technical writers	633	111	22
Police patrol officers	632	271	28
Personnel, training, and labor relations specialists	611	129	22
Designers, except interior	590	113	32
Artists and commercial artists	575	117	23
Instructors and coaches, sports and physical training	530	119	35
Instructors, adult (nonvocational) education	530	104	27
Teachers and instructors, vocational education	530	104	27
Social workers	506	288	34
Heating, air-conditioning and refrigeration mechanics	497	125	29
Correctional officers	485	194	51
Licensed practical nurses	450	341	28

Usual training required

- Bachelor's degree or higher
- Associate's degree
- Postsecondary vocational training

0   200   400   600   800   1,000   1,200

Source: Bureau of Labor Statistics. (Projected job openings and percent change are from the BLS industry-occupation matrix; earnings, from the Current Population Survey; training, from research conducted for the *Occupational Outlook Handbook*.) *Occupational Outlook Quarterly*/Spring 1996.

TABLE 6.E

Fastest-growing occupations, by education level required, projected through 2005.*

OCCUPATIONS REQUIRING HIGH SCHOOL EDUCATION OR LESS

(Service occupations account for nearly half of the twenty fastest-growing occupations at this education level)

Occupation

Home health aides
Personal home-care aides
Human services workers
Medical secretaries
Subway and public transportation operators
Travel agents
Corrections officers
Flight attendants
Child-care workers
Receptionists and information clerks
Nursing aides, orderlies, attendants
Detectives, except public
Gardeners and groundskeepers
Interviewing clerks
Animal caretakers
Manicurists
Bakers, bread and pastry
Camera operators, television and motion pictures
Bus drivers, school
Teacher aides and educational assistants

OCCUPATIONS REQUIRING SOME POSTSECONDARY TRAINING OR EXTENSIVE EMPLOYER TRAINING

(Health services occupations are a sizable portion of these occupations)

Occupation

Paralegals
Medical assistants
Radiologic technologists and technicians
Physical and corrective therapy assistants
Data processing equipment repairers
EEG technologists
Occupational therapy assistants and aides
Surgical technologists
Medical records technicians
Nuclear medicine technologists
Respiratory therapists
Electromedical and biomedical equipment repairers
Legal secretaries
Registered nurses
Cooks, restaurant
Licensed practical nurses
Dental hygienists
Producers, directors, actors, entertainers
Dancers and choreographers
Opticians, dispensing

OCCUPATIONS REQUIRING A COLLEGE DEGREE OR HIGHER LEVEL OF EDUCATION

(The top seven are tied to the health services industry or computer technology)

Occupation

Systems analysts and computer scientists
Physical therapists
Operations research analysts
Medical scientists
Psychologists
Computer programmers
Occupational therapists
Management analysts
Marketing, advertising, and public relations managers
Podiatrists
Teachers, preschool and kindergarten
Securities and financial services sales representatives
Teachers, special education
Recreational therapists
Lawyers
Accountants and auditors
Aircraft pilots and flight engineers
Engineering, mathematics, and natural science managers
Social workers
Teachers, secondary school

*Keep in mind that the term *fast-growing* may be misleading in the sense that if the occupation employs small numbers of people to begin with, even a 100 percent growth would still mean few overall employment opportunities. See Exhibit 6.A for occupations with largest overall job growth; in other words, the occupations that employ large numbers of people and have good job growth.

Source: *Occupational Outlook Quarterly,* U.S. Department of Labor, Bureau of Labor Statistics.

EXHIBIT 6.B

Job growth according to educational level.

For each educational or training level, occupations with the largest numerical increase in employment from 1994 to 2005. They are in descending order within each category. For instance, there will be more jobs for lawyers than physicians.

Professional Degree
Lawyers
Physicians
Clergy
Chiropractors
Dentists

Doctoral Degree
College and university faculty
Biological scientists
Medical scientists
Mathematicians

Master's Degree
Management analysts
Counselors
Speech-language pathologists and audiologists
Psychologists
Operations research analysts

Work Experience Plus Bachelor's Degree
General managers and top executives
Financial managers
Marketing, advertising, and public relations managers
Engineering, mathematics, and natural science managers
Education administrators

Bachelor's Degree
Systems analysts
Teachers, secondary school
Teachers, elementary school
Teachers, special education
Social workers

Associate Degree
Registered nurses
Paralegals
Radiologic technologists and technicians
Dental hygienists
Medical records technicians

Postsecondary Vocational Training
Secretaries, except legal and medical
Licensed practical nurses
Hairdressers, hairstylists and cosmetologists
Legal secretaries
Medical secretaries

Work Experience
Marketing and sales worker supervisors
Clerical supervisors and managers
Food service and lodging managers
Instructors, adult education

Long-Term Training and Experience (more than 12 months of on-the-job training)
Maintenance repairers, general utility
Correction officers
Automotive mechanics
Cooks, restaurant
Police patrol officers

Moderate-Length Training and Experience (1 to 12 months of on-the-job experience and informal training)
Human services workers
Medical assistants
Instructors and coaches, sports and physical training
Dental assistants
Painters and paper hangers, construction and maintenance

Short-Term Training and Experience (up to one month of on-the-job experience)
Cashiers
Janitors and cleaners, including maids and housekeepers
Salespersons, retail
Waiters and waitresses
Home health aides

Sources: Bureau of Labor Statistics, *Occupational Outlook Handbook*, 1996–97.

EXHIBIT 6.C

Occupations projected to grow the fastest, 1994–2005.

Occupation	Percent Growth
Personal and home care aides	~108
Home health aides	~100
Systems analysts	~85
Computer engineers	~85
Physical corrective therapy assistants and aides	~78
Graphic designers	~70
Occupational therapy assistants and aides	~70
Physical therapists	~68
Residential counselors	~64
Human services workers	~62
Occupational therapists	~62
Manicurists	~60
Medical assistants	~58
Paralegals	~58
Medical records technicians	~54
Teachers, special education	~54
Amusement and recreation attendants	~54
Correction officers	~52
Operations research analysts	~50
Guards	~48

Percent Growth (axis: 0, 20, 40, 60, 80, 100, 120)

Source: *Occupational Outlook Handbook, 1996–97.*

It is our hope that you will develop your own personal objectives, believe in yourself, acknowledge stereotypes pertaining to life and work, and develop a clear strategy for entering the career of your choice. Whether you have directly experienced bias or other barriers to employment, or have had the good fortune not to, we would like you to use the following written exercises to reflect upon your personal, social, and cultural opinions and biases.

EXERCISES

Exercise 6.1 helps you become aware of how you may react to roles and events that differ from those to which you are accustomed. Exercise 6.2 asks you to explore your own stereotypes. Be spontaneous with your answers; do not censor yourself because you fear your answer is "wrong." Exercise 6.3 asks you to list the advantages and disadvantages of belonging to one or more distinct groups. Exercise 6.4 helps you become aware of your knowledge of various groups of people. The more difficult it is for you to identify names for this exercise, the more likely it is that you have led a life that excludes other cultures. Stereotypes and barriers tend to develop when we stick to our own "groups." Exercise 6.5 asks you to think about the small businesses you use regularly. Exercise 6.6 asks you to consider how stereotypes about you might affect your ability to get a job.

6.1 First impressions

Think about each of the following situations. What are your first impressions?

a. You are applying for a job. A male receptionist ushers you into an office where you are greeted by a female vice-president who will conduct the interview.

b. You are flying to Chicago. A male flight attendant welcomes you aboard the plane; later a female voice says, "This is your captain speaking."

c. You go to enroll your 4-year-old in a nearby nursery school and discover all three teachers at the school are male.

d. You are introduced to a new couple in the neighborhood and discover the man stays home all day with two small children while the wife works outside the home.

e. You are African American and live in a neighborhood that is all Caucasian.

f. You have a conference with your child's teacher, who grew up in Taiwan.

g. You are in a class with many students who speak a different language.

h. You move into an apartment and learn your neighbors are homosexual.

i. You are temporarily disabled, must use a wheelchair, and have found a wonderful job opening. You haven't yet told the interviewer about your disability (and the room is on the second floor, with no elevator).

j. You arrive at your new dentist's office and find she has green and orange spiked hair.

k. You are referred to a hospital known for excellence in surgery, and your team of doctors is all Latino.

l. You go to court and find every jury member is African American.

m. You go to a job interview and find yourself facing a panel of younger men and women.

n. You find yourself in a statistics class in which all the students are Asian American.

o. You are on an airplane and the flight attendant is older than your grandmother.

6.2 Gender roles questionnaire

In order to explore your own stereotypes, complete these sentences with the first thought that comes to mind. Don't "censor" yourself.

Complete these sentences.

a. Women are happiest in careers when ....

b. Men are happiest in careers when ....

c. The most difficult emotion for a man to display is..

d. The most difficult emotion for a woman to display is...

e. Women tend to be better than men at ....

f. Men tend to be better than women at ....

g. Men get depressed about..

h. Women get depressed about ....

i. Men are most likely to compete over ....

j. Women are most likely to compete over..

k. Men tend to get angry about ....

l. Women tend to get angry about ....

m. As a man/woman, I was always taught to...

n. Men feel pressured on the job when ....

o. Women feel pressured on the job when...

6.3 Pros and cons

List advantages and disadvantages of being any of the following.

a. *Female*

advantage..

disadvantage...

b. *Male*

advantage..

disadvantage...

c. *Caucasian*

advantage ....

disadvantage ....

d. *African American*

advantage ....

disadvantage ....

e. *Latino*

advantage ....

disadvantage ....

f. *Asian American*

advantage ....

disadvantage ....

g. *Native American*

advantage ....

disadvantage ....

6.4 Famous people

For each of the groups listed above, name five famous people (may be currently living or a historical figure).

6.5 Small businesses

List three small businesses whose services or products you use.

1. ....

2. ....

3. ....

Name one business that is operated out of a home:

....

6.6 What about you?

How do you think gender, race, age, sexual orientation, or physical disability could affect your ability to get a job? While doing these exercises, did you discover anything about your stereotypes of people? Have affirmative action policies affected you or anyone you know in applying for college or a job? Summarize your feelings about what you have learned.

*Go to page 160,
of the Part One Chapter Summaries,
and fill out the Chapter Six exercise summary now.*

SEVEN

Information Integration

LEARNING OBJECTIVES

At the end of the chapter you will be able to . . .

Familiarize yourself with printed sources of information to use in further clarifying your career choices

Use your skills to gather information about specific occupations and career-related opportunities by using library materials

Confirm or revise your first impressions about your top career choices

By now you probably have one or several career areas in mind. This chapter will help you get more specific. It will enable you to review, clarify, and integrate the information you've collected about your needs, desires, values, interests, skills, and personal attributes. It is important to put these pieces together to identify some specific occupational areas that you can begin to research.

This chapter will introduce you to the written and electronic resources available in libraries and college career centers. By using these references, you will have the information necessary to further clarify and confirm your tentative career choices. Then, in Chapter 8, you will be encouraged to make a tentative career decision.

In case you get stuck or blocked in listing specific occupations, try using the guided fantasy (Exercise 7.4). Start by quickly reviewing all the written information that you've recorded (in the Part One Chapter Summaries section, beginning on page 157). Then close your eyes and visualize yourself in your perfect career. "Mental visualization" can sometimes focus your thoughts on areas that suit you perfectly. This technique helps you tap into and integrate the wealth of information, intuition, and wisdom that you already have about yourself. It is only natural to feel hesitant and even fearful about committing yourself to a career decision.

These are the feelings that block you from making a decision and getting specific. Mental visualization is a technique to help your mind "wander" into a career choice.

UNDERSTANDING CAREER PATHS AND COMMON ORGANIZATIONAL DIVISIONS

Sometimes a greater awareness of the job market can be gained by researching career paths or career ladders in a specific industry. Most career centers and libraries have books that outline career paths; for example, Exhibit 7.A illustrates related jobs within the business field. Once you've assessed where you currently fit in, you can start preparing to move up the ladder. If you are currently working, your immediate supervisor and the human resources department can provide information about routes for advancement, for example, in-house workshops, institutes, on-the-job training, community college associate degrees, and bachelor's degrees.

Although the world of work includes a number of broad fields such as business, education, government (including the military), health care, and nonprofit agencies, all of these fields share certain common functional needs and have some common organizational units. As an example, all five of the fields mentioned above need the accounting functions of payroll computation and disbursement, budgeting, and servicing of accounts payable and receivable. Administration, finance, human resources, marketing, public relations, management information systems, and research and development are departmental functions common to almost all work fields. The following list explains the general functions of these and other departments in typical businesses; however, you will find identical or very similar organizational units performing very similar functions in the fields of education, government, nonprofit agencies, or health care.

If you have been concentrating on specific industries in your search for job possibilities, you can gain a fresh perspective by selecting functions that may be interesting to you and then researching jobs within those functions, but among various industries.

You may be on the right track, but if you just sit there you'll get run over.
Will Rogers

Administration. An organization's top executive officers and other managers; secretarial and word processing personnel; and human resources staff are also included in this function.

Corporate relations. Responsible for advertising, public relations, community relations.

Distribution.   Sometimes called the transportation department; oversees warehousing and shipping of the company's products.

Engineering.   Product design and modification; often oversees manufacturing of product (process engineers).

Finance.   Accounting functions, including payroll, budgets, accounts payable and receivable.

Sales.   Responsible for initiating and maintaining customer accounts, selling the company's product; sometimes includes marketing function.

Remember that some companies are restructuring so that "jobs" may not be part of "career paths." They hire a "coordinator" with cross-functional skills: that person develops and tracks the project, motivates the team, assists the team in marketing the project/product, and also keeps track of the budget. The project may last six months or so, and then the coordinator is assigned to a different project with either similar or different duties. This type of organization is called the "web." Another type of web is a situation in which a specialist works for *several* companies, such as an accountant who does the books for a designer, publisher, educational consultant, and marketing specialist.

Web organization

Your research should reflect the location of your chosen path(s). Do you hope to work somewhere as a *generalist* and be adept in many areas in the web? Or do you prefer to be part of an organization as a *specialist*, such as an accountant? (See Exhibit 7.A for a diagram of sample career paths in the business field.)

Now that you have a clearer idea of the jobs that best suit your personality, it is necessary to research the actual requirements of the job. There are two primary ways to obtain job information: searching through written or computerized materials in the library, or contacting people who already work in your area of interest. This chapter focuses on written and computerized materials, whereas Chapter Nine focuses on people and contacts. Your local library or college career development and placement center should be able to provide you with some or all of the following resources.

GOVERNMENT EMPLOYMENT OPPORTUNITIES

Government listings offer opportunities

State and local governments hire the majority of people in public work. Local government alone hires over 50 percent of all public employees. In addition, the federal government hires hundreds of people each day across the United States.

Information regarding employment with local and state government offices is typically available at state or local One Stop Career Centers. Federal and state employment information is often available on the Internet's World Wide Web on computers at colleges and One Stop Career Centers. (For more information about "surfing the web," see the section of this chapter: Internet.) For those who don't have access to these locations, state personnel offices offer applications, tests, job descriptions, and occupational outlook data for that state. For example, California publishes "A Guide to the Use of Labor Market Publications" to help prospective employees research job opportunities. It is important to consider that it may take six to nine months to complete

Sample career paths, using business as an example.

EXHIBIT 7.A

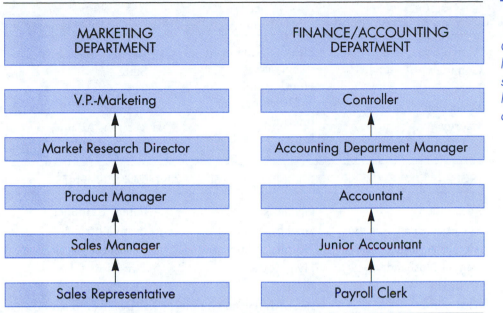

Organization charts listing career paths are sometimes found in human research department files.

the application, test, interview, and hiring process for state government jobs. This is not a good option for someone who needs immediate employment; however, many people find it possible to complete the process while employed elsewhere. Also, many college students begin the application and testing process during their senior year in college, enabling them to interview for jobs before they graduate.

No one in the federal government knows all the positions vacant on a particular day, week, or month, and you must contact the personnel office of each agency for a complete listing of vacancies in that agency. If you have access, however, to an on-line service (connection to the Internet), you may want to check out *America's Job Bank* (http://www.ajb.dni.us) or *Fed World Information Network* (http://www.fedworld.gov). These services are updated daily and have links to many other employment options. *FedWorld* lists federal jobs by state. At the end of this chapter, several other career information services available on the Internet are listed. These sources link to federal and state employment information.

You can also find information about federal jobs in publications such as the *Congressional Yellow Book*, a volume on congressional agencies, as well as personal and committee staff in the House and Senate. The *Federal Yellow Book* (Monitor Publishing), published twice yearly, lists who's who in the executive branch. Two newer resources for developing federal government career plans are *Career America Connection* and *Career Opportunities for the College Graduate in the Federal Government*. Both are available from the Government Printing Office or at your nearest branch of the Office of Personnel Management. Table 7.A lists some of the many federal employment opportunities.

Federal Job Information Centers may also have access to a national computerized job bank. This is especially useful for people who want to know about job opportunities located some distance away.

TABLE 7.A   Federal employment opportunities.

EXECUTIVE DEPARTMENTS

Agriculture
Commerce
Defense
Education
Energy

Health and Human
    Services
Housing and Urban
    Development
Interior
Justice

Labor
State
Transportation
Treasury
Veterans Affairs

FEDERAL EMPLOYMENT POSITIONS COVERED BY ANNOUNCEMENTS

Accountant
Aerospace Technologist
Air Traffic Controller
Animal Husbandry
Architect
Astronomer
Attorney
Bacteriologist
Biologist
Cartographer
Chemist
Dietitian
Education Officer
Engineer
Entomologist
Equipment Specialist
Estate Tax Examiner
Forester

Geodesist
Geophysicist
Hospital Administrator
Hydrologist
Illustrator
Internal Revenue Agent
Landscape Architect
Librarian
Manual Arts Therapist
Mathematician
Medical Record
    Librarian
Metallurgist
Meteorologist
Microbiologist
Nurse
Occupational Therapist
Oceanographer

Patent Examiner
Pest Controller
Pharmacist
Physicist
Plant Scientist
Prison Administrator
Range Conservationist
Refuge Manager
Social Worker
Soil Conservationist
Special Agent
Speech Pathologist
Teacher
Therapist
Urban Planner
Veterinarian

MAJOR INDEPENDENT AGENCIES

Central Intelligence
    Agency
Environmental
    Protection Agency
Equal Employment
    Opportunity
    Commission
Federal Deposit
    Insurance
    Corporation
Federal Emergency
    Management Agency
Foreign Service of the
    United States

General Services
    Administration
International Monetary
    Fund
National Aeronautics
    and Space
    Administration
National Archives and
    Records
    Administration
Nuclear Regulatory
    Commission
Office of Personnel
    Management

Panama Canal
    Commission
Small Business
    Administration
Smithsonian Institution
Tennessee Valley
    Authority
U.S. Information Agency
U.S. International
    Development
    Cooperative Agency
U.S. Postal Service

U.S. DEPARTMENT OF LABOR PUBLICATIONS

The Occupational Information Network (O*NET) is a relatively new interactive tool devised by the U.S. Department of Labor. The program is an easy-to-use computer database that collects, analyzes, and disseminates skill and job requirement information. It is designed to replace the *Dictionary of Occupational Titles (DOT)* and *Occupational Outlook Handbook (OOH)*.

Most libraries, college career and placement centers, One Stop Career Centers, and high school career centers have copies of the *DOT* and *OOH*. You may use the on-line services, CD-ROM copies, or hard copy publications.

The *Dictionary of Occupational Titles (DOT)* lists over 35,000 job titles and over 21,000 different occupations. This resource has been mentioned in previous chapters and will be referred to in Chapter Ten as a tool to use in writing a resume. It is especially useful because it lists specific tasks to be done on a job, as in the entry for COPYWRITER.

The *Occupational Outlook Handbook (OOH)* includes information on job descriptions, skills, places of employment, training, educational requirements, personality traits and values that might be important in a particular field, and salary ranges. It is updated every other year and represents a national survey of occupations. Salary information should be compared with local salaries and local cost-of-living factors. For example, Los Angeles employers tend to pay $1,000 to $2,000 more per year than many of the generalized estimates shown in the *OOH*.

Between editions of the *OOH*, the *Occupational Outlook Quarterly* provides updates of occupational projections as well as compensation ranges and cost-of-living comparisons throughout the United States.

The *Guide for Occupational Exploration (GOE)* provides detailed information about the interests, aptitudes, skills, and job activities of various occupational groups. The data in this publication are organized into 12 interest areas, 66 Worker Trait Groups, and 348 subgroupings. More detailed information regarding the *GOE* was provided in Chapter Four.

DOT entry for copywriter

Writes advertising copy for use by publication or broadcast media to promote sale of goods and services: Consults with sales media and marketing representatives to obtain information on product or service and discuss style and length of advertising copy. Obtains additional background and current development information through research and interview. Reviews advertising trends, consumer surveys, and other data regarding marketing of specific and related goods and services to formulate presentation approach. Writes preliminary draft of copy and sends to supervisor for approval. Corrects and revises copy as necessary. May write articles, bulletins, sales letters, speeches, and other related informative and promotional material.

EMPLOYER DIRECTORIES

Employer directories provide information about specific companies, such as those in your field with current job openings.

Information about a variety of enterprises, from foundations to corporations, can be found in directories. Directories list an employer's name and address, product, and geographic location, as well as other information including size in terms of volume of sales, number of employees, and names of top-level executives. Don't forget to use your local telephone directory. The white

Let your fingers do the researching

pages list government agencies and departments, and the yellow pages list other places of employment.

The Yellow Pages are available on the Internet. A benefit of this resource is that small businesses are listed. At the address line, simply type "yellow pages" and then key words pertaining to your job interest. If you are thinking about starting a landscape business, determine the competition in a specific geographic area by typing "yellow pages landscape businesses." At the prompt, click on "yellow pages." If you would like to work in a certain city, for instance, to get experience before opening your own business, a phone call to the businesses listed in the Yellow Pages may provide you with information about a job or when one might be available.

A list of commonly used directories can be found on the next page. Consider what to look for:

- a geographical list of companies in a specified field
- small, growing companies
- a company with international positions
- names and addresses of corporate officers

Note which directories give information about trade publications. These offer "insider" information about companies doing well, job openings in specific fields, and firms that may not be listed in any other directory. Again, a simple phone call will provide you with valuable information.

OTHER WRITTEN SOURCES OF INFORMATION

Newspapers

Want ads = only 15% of job openings

Check out all the newspapers in the geographical area in which you are interested in working. Read the help-wanted section for openings as well as for local wage and fringe benefit information. There may be a separate business section that advertises professional jobs. Read everything in terms of your own job target and keep a file, but be aware that only 15 percent of job openings are listed in want ads. Therefore, note other areas of the paper, such as articles that announce business expansions, personnel changes, and new ideas. Planning commission announcements usually mention new industrial parks and the expected number of employers to be located there. Marriage announcements usually list the bride's and groom's occupations and may give you the name of an important executive of a firm that interests you. "Lifestyle sections" may profile leaders in the community; gossip columns may suggest where to find trendsetters.

Trade Journals

Almost every trade and profession has at least one regularly published journal. The business section of your library should have references. A book or pamphlet on your chosen career may list names of related associations and trade journals. Your library or career center may also have computerized retrieval systems (see Computerized Information Sources later in this chapter) to

EXHIBIT 7.B

Directories useful to career explorers.

The Almanac of American Employers. Lists 500 companies with one page per firm, including the following information: recent financial performance, salaries and benefits, regional offices, brands, and divisions.

California Manufacturers Directory. Lists companies by location and product with an additional section on companies that have import/export business.

Directory of American Firms Operating in Foreign Countries. Lists about 3,000 American corporations with factories and branch offices covering over 36 countries. Also lists key personnel, but since it is not published annually, such information may be out-of-date.

Dun and Bradstreet Million Dollar Directory. Lists 160,000 companies in five volumes. Largest directory of its kind, indexed in a variety of ways. Includes subsidiaries not mentioned in other directories and is especially useful for direct mail campaigns (see Chapter 9).

Dun's Employment Opportunities Directory. Lists 11,000 companies throughout the U.S. Includes information about educational specialties the company values, most promising areas of employment, and a brief description of the company's insurance plans. Index is divided into geographical and industry sections.

Encyclopedia of Associations. Lists 15,000 associations in every field with names of officers, telephone numbers, and brief descriptions of orientation and activities.

Encyclopedia of Business Information Services. Lists source materials on businesses.

Gale Directory of Publications and Broadcast Media. Lists every newspaper, magazine, and radio station in the U.S. Information found by region or industry groups (e.g., retailing, restaurants). Excellent source of information about trade publications.

Guide to American Directories. Describes 3,300 directories subdivided into 400 topical areas.

Hoover's Handbook of American Business. Lists 200 companies, very thoroughly, including an overview of what the company owns, how it is structured, key personnel, and company performance. Lists show how employment prospects compare (i.e., top 100 companies in employment opportunities).

INFOTRAC. Computer-based program providing up-to-date directory information.

Regional and community magazines. Most large cities and metropolitan areas have community magazines that focus on business, industry, education, the arts, and politics; states and regions also have their own magazines.

Standard Periodical Directory. Describes 50,000 periodicals and directories.

Standard and Poor's Register of Corporations, Directors, and Executives. Lists about 55,000 public and private companies in three volumes. Volume one covers basic information; volume two includes summaries about key executives; volume three indexes companies according to industry classification.

Standard Rate and Data Business Publications Directory. Lists names and addresses of thousands of trade publications.

State directories. Each state has a directory of trade and industry. If one is not in your library, contact the local or state chamber of commerce, or write to U.S. Chamber of Commerce, 1615 H Street NW, Washington, DC 20006.

Thomas's Register of American Manufacturers. Lists 100,000 manufacturers by location and product.

Who's Who in Commerce and Industry. Gives names and biographical sketches of top executives.

access trade journal information. The following resources are useful in tracking down particular trade journals: *Ulrich's International Periodical Directory*, the *Encyclopedia of Business Information Services*, the *Gale Directory of Publications and Broadcast Media*, and the *Encyclopedia of Associations*. Use these trade journals to locate job ads and to familiarize yourself with the people, products, current trends, and specific vocabulary of a field.

Magazines

The *Reader's Guide to Periodicals*, available at any library in either printed or electronic form, can be used both to locate names of magazines and to find titles of informative and useful articles about any field you wish to research. Do you want to learn the latest in animation careers, the outlook for engineers in the western United States, opportunities for liberal arts graduates? It's been covered in some magazine recently! Business magazines also provide profiles of both businesses and their executive officers, which is information you might use in comparing companies.

Ask the librarian for the *Business Periodicals Index*. It accesses trade journal articles and has citations for hundreds of publications. The articles are arranged according to subject; broad subjects are divided into more specific categories. University business/management libraries are more likely to access publications listed in the *Business Periodicals Index:* they are less likely to be found in local libraries. Additional resources are listed at the end of this chapter under "Internet."

Sample useful magazines for business information

Black Entrepreneur	*High Technology Careers*
Business Week	*Inc.*
Entrepreneur	*National Business Employment Weekly*
Executive Female	*Success*
Forbes	*Wall Street Journal*
Fortune	*Working Woman*

Specialized magazines for college students and graduates

Black Collegian
Business World, a career magazine for college students
College Placement Annual; check with college placement office
Business Week's Guide to Careers
Hispanic Times Magazine
Women's Careers
Saludos Hispanos

In-House Bulletins and Announcements

Personnel offices in virtually every business, agency, school, and hospital post jobs as they become available. Job posting best serves the people already employed at such places; however, some of the job listings may be open to anyone.

Large corporations such as Bank of America and General Electric publish in-house job announcement newsletters monthly or quarterly. Most of these newsletters are not intended for public use but are circulated among all employees to encourage internal job mobility. The job announcements list required skills, degrees, and relevant experience. Such in-house newsletters are an excellent way to explore current needs within large companies and to learn more about the types of job skills being sought.

COMPUTERIZED INFORMATION SOURCES

Computerized information can often be more quickly accessed, as well as more complete, than traditional sources. Contact your library for assistance in locating the sources described here—and for others.

Selected Computerized Sources

Probably the largest resource on occupational information is the Career Information Service (CIS; also known as EUREKA in California). This software provides occupational information specific to the state in which it is located, including occupational information, job descriptions, locations for training, such as vocational schools and colleges, and financial aid information. Another component of CIS, called QUEST, helps users identify the work characteristics that are common to certain occupations. A second program, SIGI (System of Interactive Guidance and Information), is designed to clarify your values and to match your values with occupations. A third program, GIS (Guidance Information System), acts as a source of national occupational information. The program, DISCOVER, identifies career sources and includes vital information on decision making. A commercial program available on CD-ROM, *Discovering Careers*, contains the *Occupational Outlook Handbook*, *Dictionary of Occupational Titles*, current trends, projected job growth, wages and salary information, licensing rules, related publications (e.g., trade journals), associations, and potential employers.

In many colleges, computers located in counselors' offices or in the career center use software to help students explore occupations related to their college major. For students seeking help in selecting a major, 3,000 college majors can be scanned by a computer in three to five seconds to locate the ones that match the student's interests. Often this software includes a file with information on all two- and four-year colleges in the United States, which can assist students in choosing a school, preparing for admission, and planning a course schedule.

Many college career-planning and placement offices have on-line or CD-ROM resources that provide employment information about some of the largest companies in the United States. For example, "Moody's Corporate Profiles" on Dialog lists more than 5,000 publicly held companies with information such as business analysis, annual earnings, and financial data. Lotus One Source's "CD/Corporate: U.S. Public Companies" lists the 10,000 largest companies registered with the Securities and Exchange Commission. Another place to find such information is the business section of your campus library or most city libraries. Finally, if your family or a friend subscribes to an on-line service such as Prodigy, CompuServe, or America Online, company/

job information can be obtained from the business/financial sections, the career sections, or various bulletin boards.

The Internet

The information superhighway offers immediate access to unlimited sources for both job descriptions and company information. If you don't own a computer or haven't subscribed to an Internet server, access may be possible through libraries, colleges, universities, quick print centers, and even some coffeehouses. The local library is a great place to "try out" the Internet.

The library resource center

Librarians, as information specialists, may be available to help conduct your search and use the library's information-retrieval tools to access indexes, abstracts, and in some cases, the full text of thousands of newspapers, magazines, and journals. The library's Internet connections (called T-lines) are significantly faster than the typical family modem, allowing users to search through hundreds of thousands of references.

Libraries subscribe to powerful research index services such as Nexus and Dialog and have access to databases containing hundreds of periodicals. Library Internet access can simplify the search for information and articles. You may be able to tap into its indexes through your home computer; however, you'll probably have to *order* copies of articles rather than download them. (It may be possible to retrieve your college library documents at home or in the office, if your school allows such an arrangement.)

Career sites

To explore careers and the job market, on-line resources are available for every phase of the job search: identifying opportunities, researching specific industries and companies, posting resumes on-line, and making contacts with potential employers. Information on job search and resume resources is located in Chapter 9, "Targeting Your Job Search," and Chapter 10, "Preparing a Winning Resume."

To begin searching, you may wish to check out *The Online Career Center* (OCC) at http://www.occ.com. This site provides access to the *Occupational Outlook Handbook*. You can search for jobs by title and geographic area and select a broad career interest, narrowing it to a specific field. OCC also has a section titled, "Cultural Diversity: Resources for Women and Minorities." Type the general category where you see the word "search" or "find." Each site offers links to related sites, such as professional organizations, job opportunities, and educational and training information.

E-Span (http://www.espan.com) is another popular site offering career and employment information, including employer and job databases that are updated frequently. *E-Span* has the capability to scan by category, region, and key words to search for information about jobs in specific companies. One useful section is "Career Briefcase." It connects to assessment tools, professional associations, business indexes, career fairs, industry sites, job searches, and resume-writing assistance.

America's Job Bank (www.ajb.dni.us) is a valuable site during a job search. If you are interested in federal government jobs, look at *Fed World* (http://www.fedworld.gov). You may find access to your state employment service most easily through *America's Job Bank*. At your state site, you will have access to skill requirements for many of the state's jobs.

About Work (http://www.aboutwork.com) provides helpful information on general job hunting and topics related to starting a business. It offers advice on developing effective resumes and cover letters.

Interested in working overseas? The following sites may help you locate a position:

Overseas Jobs (http://www.overseasjobs.com) contains 1,500 overseas job vacancies which can be searched by key word. It also offers hundreds of resources in over 40 countries. In addition, it has an on-line bookstore with titles such as *Finding a Job in Australia*.

The Overseas Jobs Express Bookshop (http://www.hiway.co.uk/expats/ojebk. html) is another on-line bookstore with titles such as *Work Your Way Around the World*.

Searching an industry

It's necessary to use a "search engine" or "browser" to reach a particular address or to "surf" the Web. Browsers include Netscape, Microsoft Network Explorer (MSN), Yahoo, and others. If you are interested in financial services such as investment banking and retail banking, use the following search method: go to the browser and type "financial services" where it says "search." Narrow your search by adding key words, such as "banks" to the search box. Now you can investigate specific companies. To learn more about the banking business, visit several banking sites on the Web and return periodically to follow developments in each business. Firms often announce new departments, services, and products first on the Web.

If you know the address of the site you wish to visit, simply type it. For example, classified ads from several major newspapers can be found at http://www.careerpath.com. Or, you may type "resume and interview advice," "labor market information," or "career information," and the browser will list a number of possible sites to visit.

Trade journals on the Internet

Earlier in the chapter we mentioned industry trade journals. Sometimes these journals have Web sites. For example, *Advertising Age* is located at http://www. adage.com. Journals such as this provide the latest information about trends in the industry. You may be able to add your name to an e-mail list, which will allow you to receive information about current advertising issues. Most magazines and trade journals print their e-mail and Web site addresses in the front of the publication.

The computer resources available to you will vary from location to location. Check with your local library, college career center, college adviser, and computer store to explore how computers can help you obtain information that will aid in your career planning.

The following written exercises will help you digest the contents of this chapter. They can be completed by using your local library or college career center to explore some of the resources

mentioned in this chapter. Exercise 7.1 requires that you investigate resources utilizing the local library, college library, and local newspaper. Exercise 7.2 asks that you learn what kinds of information and assistance are available from your college career center, local state employment office, and other employment offices. Exercise 7.3 gives you a format for gathering facts about three jobs. Exercise 7.4 is a guided fantasy to help you visualize yourself in your chosen career.

7.1 Job research

a. Which directories could be most helpful to you now, and what do you need to know? Where are these directories found?...
....

b. What are the names of three trade journals related to your field of interest? Where are they found?

   1. ....

   2. ....

   3. ....

c. What are some of the current trends reflected in these journals?..
....

d. Name one professional association related to your field. Also list where and when local meetings are held. (What about the national conference: can you attend or join as a student?) For example:

American Society of Women Accountants (ASWA)

Local contact: Joan Smith—phone: 805-555-1213

Meeting time & location: 3rd Thursday of each month, 7 P.M. (dinner), Colonial House Restaurant, Oxnard

Your field:...

Association:..

Contact:..

Meeting:...
....

e. Study a local daily newspaper for three weeks, and make a scrapbook of articles that relate to your field. (Include want ads, feature articles, meetings, networking groups, and names of executives in your field who were mentioned anywhere in the paper.)

7.2 Local and Internet resources

a. Investigate local career and placement centers. Ask if they place people in your field or if they can refer you to others.

b. Visit the state employment office as well as private employment or temporary agencies to find out how they place people and how long it may take to get a job.

c. Find a local job opportunity on the Internet.

7.3 Gathering the facts

Following the format below, research three jobs in a library or career center. You may select either three different jobs (e.g., public relations specialist, social worker, manager), three jobs that are related (e.g., lawyer, paralegal, legal secretary), or three that represent the same field but vary in the nature of the work (e.g., marketing executive, graphic artist, display assistant).

Once you identify job titles of interest to you, gather the following information:

a. Title of career ....

b. Salary ....

c. Hours ....

d. Benefits ....

e. Outlook (will there be jobs in the future?) ....
....

f. Educational requirements—minimum training necessary ....

   If college is necessary, what types of programs are available in the local area? ....
....

g. Schools or colleges offering the training ....
....

h. Personal requirements ....
....

i. Physical demands ....
....

j. Work description (attach a copy of the DOT description) ....
....

k. Working conditions ....
....

l. Location ....
....

m. Opportunities for advancement ....

....

n. Related occupations ....

No additional training needed: ....

Some college needed: ....

B.A. or B.S. degree needed: ....

Other training (e.g., master's degree or special license) ....

o. Sources (may include resources in the career center and names of local people working in this field; **include Internet addresses** where you might find related information) ....

....

....

....

p. After researching the specifics, are you still interested? How does this mesh with your vision of a lifestyle? ....

....

....

....

If, after reading about three different careers you are still confused about how to choose one, try Exercise 7.4, a guided fantasy. Visualize yourself in each career. Which one feels most comfortable, most consistent with who you are?

Chapter Eight will help you narrow your focus and decide between different careers.

7.4 Guided fantasy

Close your eyes, take a few deep breaths, and relax. Remove all feelings of tension from your body, and erase all previous thoughts and worries from your mind. . . .

Imagine that you are getting up on a typical workday about five years from now. You're sitting on the side of your bed trying to decide what you are going to wear. Take a moment and look over your wardrobe. . . What type of clothing do you finally decide to wear? . . .

Imagine yourself getting ready for work. Any thoughts about the day to come while you're getting ready? . . . What kind of feelings do you have as you look forward to your workday? . . . Do you feel excited? Bored? Apprehensive? . . . What gives you these feelings? . . .

It's time for breakfast now. Will you be sharing breakfast with someone, or will you be eating alone? . . .

You've completed your breakfast now and are headed out the door. Stop for a moment and look around your neighborhood. What does it look like? . . . What does your home look like? . . . What thoughts and feelings do you experience as you look around? . . .

Fantasize now that you're heading toward work. How are you getting there? . . . How far is it? . . . What new feelings or thoughts are you experiencing? . . .

You're entering your work situation now. Pause for a bit and try to get a mental picture of it. Think about where it is and what it looks like. Will you be spending most of your time indoors or outdoors? . . . How many people will you be working with? . . .

You are going to your specific job now. Who is the first person you encounter? . . . What does this person look like? . . . What is this person wearing? . . . What do you say to this person? . . .

Try to form an image of the particular tasks you perform on your job. Don't think about it as a specific job with a title such as nurse or accountant. Instead, think about what you are actually doing, such as working with your hands, adding figures, typing, talking to people, drawing, thinking, etc.

In your job, do you work primarily by yourself or mostly with others? . . . In your work with others, what do you do with them? . . . How old are the other people? . . . What do they look like?. . . How do you feel toward them? . . .

Where will you be going for lunch? . . . Will you be going with someone else? Whom? What will you talk about?. . .

How do the afternoon's activities differ from those of the morning?. . . How are you feeling as the day progresses?. . . Tired?. . . Alert?. . . Bored?. . . Excited?. . .

Your workday is coming to an end now. Has it been a satisfying day? . . . If so, what made it satisfying? . . . Was there anything about the day that made you less happy? . . . Will you be taking some of your work home with you? . . .

*Go to page 160,
of the Part One Chapter Summaries,
and fill out the Chapter Seven exercise summary* now.

EIGHT

Making Decisions

Career decisions are the Olympic trials of your career fitness program. They give you an opportunity to integrate and test out all the components of your career fitness program—your attitudes, values, skills, interests, and biases. For most of us it is safe to assume that whatever decisions we make are the best we can make given the information, circumstances, and feelings of the moment. However, we can all improve our decision-making performance by examining some of the assumptions and strategies that other people have used in the decision-making process.

This chapter will review decision-making strategies that are potentially limiting and those that are potentially empowering and success oriented. The primary focus of this chapter is devoted to explaining a decision-making model that involves setting *realistic goals*. To bring about change, you must *set specific goals with specific time frames*. They must be realistic for you, and you must maintain an attitude that you are deserving and capable of reaching these goals.

In most of the previous chapters, exercises have been completed at the end of the chapter. This was done to help you solidify and integrate what you had read in the entire chapter. In this chapter on decision making, you will be asked to complete some of the chapter-end exercises as you read. This is done so that you

can begin to test your aptitude for using various aspects of the decision-making model directly after they are presented in the chapter.

OVERCOMING BARRIERS TO DECISION MAKING

Take time right now to think about recent decisions you have made. Write down at least five, large or small, in the space provided below:

1. ....

2. ....

3. ....

4. ....

5. ....

Because you are reading this book, you undoubtedly want to improve your life and increase your career options. Attitude has already been identified as an important internal factor in making decisions. Essentially, your attitude controls your ability to use your skills and potential to the fullest. Our attitudes are "gut level" feelings that indicate what we expect of ourselves. If we are aware of our attitudes and habits, we can enhance our daily effectiveness. Again, if we believe we can, we can!

Much of human behavior is based on attitudes that are limiting. People often make decisions that involve limited conscious involvement or personal responsibility, sometimes in an effort to simplify or accelerate the decision-making process. As you read the following sections, think about the process you followed in making these decisions.

Whatever you dream, you can begin it. Boldness has genius, power, and magic in it.
Goethe

DECISION-MAKING STRATEGIES (GOOD AND BAD)

The box below describes some of the ways people go about making decisions.

Read the following story to determine what decision-making strategies Art used.

At 21, Art left his easy sun-and-surf lifestyle and Southern California roots to join a new product design and sales group in the

Ways to make decisions (Strategies)

- *Planning.* "Weighing the facts." Consideration of values, objectives, necessary information, alternatives, and consequences. A rational approach with a balance between thinking and feeling.

- *Impulsive.* "Don't look before you leap." Little thought or examination; taking the first alternative.

- *Intuitive.* "It feels right." Automatic, preconscious choice based on "inner harmony."

- *Compliant.* "Anything you say, sir." Nonassertive; let someone else decide; follow someone else's plans.

- *Delaying.* "Cross that bridge later." Procrastination, avoidance, hoping someone or something will happen so that you won't have to make a decision. Taking a moratorium; postponing thought and action.

- *Fatalistic.* "It's all in the cards." What will be will be. Letting the environment decide; leaving it up to fate.

- *Agonizing.* "What if? I don't know what to do." Worrying that a decision will be the wrong one. Getting lost in all the data; overwhelmed by analyzing alternatives.

- *Paralytic.* "Can't face up to it." One step further than "what if "—complete indecision and fear. Accepting responsibility but being unable to approach it.

midwest. He quickly adjusted to the new climate and exhausting work schedule, and he realized annual earnings of over $40,000 within two years. Art met and married Joan, a young woman enrolled in a three-year nursing education program to earn her credentials. Within a year, however, he lost his job; he searched unsuccessfully for employment for several months. The couple decided job prospects would be better if he returned to California, while she finished her nursing program. Initially, they were able to maintain their relationship through letters, phone calls, and occasional visits. After six months, Joan began to question their marriage and economic future. Despite Art's attempts to reinforce his wife's commitment to him, he felt his marriage slipping away. They are now separated and in divorce proceedings.

Were Art's decisions appropriate to his circumstances? What would you have decided, given similar circumstances? (Complete Exercise 8.1 at the end of this chapter.)

Choosing a career is a life development process. At different points during the process, different issues must be decided. Thus, planning (the first of the strategies listed above) is the key to reaching your goals. It implies gaining control of your life. You might glance back at the lifeline you completed in Chapter One. Analyze which strategy you used most often. Then note the other strategies used. Planning and intuitive strategies are the only two positive strategies listed. The others contain a hint of fear: fear of failure, fear of imperfection, fear of rejection, fear of ridicule.

Getting unstuck, gaining control   When you feel "stuck" or unable to make a decision, try asking yourself the following questions.

1. What are my assumptions (attitudes)?
2. What are my feelings?
3. Why am I clinging to this behavior? (What are the rewards or payoffs?)

There is no "right" decision   1. *What are my assumptions?* Many of us assume that if we could only make the one right decision about the matter at hand, everything else would fall into place and we'd be happy. In fact, most decisions do not have such power over our lives. Decisions are not typically black and white in terms of their consequences, but simply move you in one direction rather than another. Decisions open up some options and close off others. If you assume that most decisions can be changed or altered, that most decisions do not, in fact, signify life or

death, then you will not be so hesitant to make a decision, act on it, assess the implications as they occur, and make adjustments (or new decisions) as necessary.

2. *What are my feelings?* Some people create unnecessary stress about making decisions because they give themselves an "either/or" ultimatum. Neither option really feels right, but they panic and impulsively choose one just to ease the anxiety, or they become paralyzed and don't make any choice, allowing circumstances to decide for them. When you are feeling pressured or paralyzed about making a decision, stop, take several deep breaths, and begin to generate some additional alternatives. A friend, counselor, or skilled listener can often help with this process. As you gain more information about your options, you will realize which decision is best for you.

Avoid "either/or" ultimatums

Other people cry over spilled milk; in other words, they think back over past decisions and lament not having decided differently. This psychological stance wastes time and energy and can be destructive to the self-image. When you begin to feel self-doubt or regret about past decisions, remind yourself that you made the best decision you could, given the time, circumstances, and information available.

3. *Why am I clinging to this behavior?* Acknowledging that you are causing this indecisiveness may generate a different point of view. For example, sometimes people cling to old, nonproductive behaviors because they are the safe ways to act; they don't have to deal with the unknown or the possibility of making mistakes (also known as taking risks). However, without risk there is no challenge and no growth.

Old habits can limit you

We usually find it difficult to change habits because they have given us some form of positive payoff or reward. A person who enjoyed the status and praise gained by being an excellent and achieving student might find that superior achievement in a work environment alienates others on the job. It is important to recognize when the old, comfortable ways of doing things no longer provide the payoffs they once did.

Visualize yourself at your best

Are you a risk taker? Whether you consider yourself a risk taker or not, it is important to remember that you have, in fact, taken many risks, just as we all have. What has been your greatest risk? What risk have you taken in the last two weeks? In its most basic sense, risk taking means moving from the safe and familiar to the unknown and scary. Most of us are fairly conservative risk takers in that we want the odds to be at least 50–50 before we jump in. Yet millions of people play the lottery, start businesses, and get married even when the odds are clearly not in their favor. Why? Because regardless of the probability of success (the odds), people sometimes take risks based on the *desirability* of the successful outcome. In a lottery, the probabilities are a million to one against winning, yet people continue to gamble because of the high desirability of the positive outcome of winning. You are in the best position to take a calculated risk when you assess both the probability and desirability of an outcome and weigh it against other possible outcomes. Failure to consider outcomes in this fashion is the most common cause of unsuccessful risk taking. For example, most people are afraid to take the risk of changing careers or even changing jobs. They immediately think of the worst possible outcome: "I'll fail" or "I will never find another job if I quit this one." They don't ask themselves how probable or desirable the best possible outcome is. The probability of their worries actually materializing, that is, the likelihood of a highly

Calculated risk-taking

negative outcome, is very low. Many people paralyze themselves with this "worst possible consequence" thinking, decide not to risk it, and consequently feel trapped. What they haven't done is generate other possible outcomes that are more probable and more desirable. What are some of these? A new job that is more energizing and financially rewarding, a new career with an opportunity to grow and develop, a chance to get retraining. The probability and desirability of these outcomes are, in fact, much higher, and therefore the decision is less risky. Yet many people miss opportunities because they fail to generate and assess all possible outcomes. This process often takes the assistance of another person who can help identify negative or limiting thinking, as well as some realistic and positive outcomes.

Generate other possible outcomes

CONDITIONS FOR CHANGE

Decisions provide an opportunity to experience life in new ways, to learn and find out who you are and what you would like to do. Each path is filled with opportunities. Just imagine: by making good decisions, renewal and growth are within your reach. By engaging in affirming self-talk, positive change is possible.

Decisions = opportunities

It has been said that three conditions must be present to trigger change. First, there must be a real dissatisfaction with what is, then there must be a concept of what would be better, and, last, there must be a belief that there is a way to get there. This whole process rests on the premise that the benefits of the change outweigh the costs of making the change. Affirmations help you believe that change is possible.

The following questions relate to obstacles that may be interfering with the achievement of your desires.

1. How much determination do you really have?
2. What identity would be threatened by achieving your goal? For example, would a better job make you too independent or enable you to earn more than you mate? Would it demand more time, giving you less time as "mother," "husband," or "partner?"
3. Do you secretly feel you don't deserve to attain your desires?
4. Are you proving to anyone else that you can't change?
5. Is it worth it to you? (the work, concentration, time)
6. Are you following all the steps suggested?
7. Is it what you really want?

A DECISION-MAKING MODEL

Exhibit 8.A offers a model for making informed decisions. The five steps necessary to make an informed decision are the following: *defining your goal; knowing your alternatives; gathering information; considering the consequences (both probable and desirable); and determining your plan of action or the steps needed to achieve your goal.* Read through Exhibit 8.A now.

Choice, not chance: Decisions are in our power.

EXHIBIT 8.A

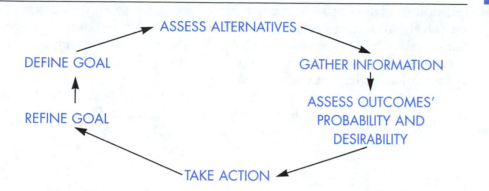

1. **Define goal or objective**
   - Can you change part of the problem into a definite goal?
   - What do you want to accomplish by what date?
   - Can you state your objective now?

2. **Assess alternatives**
   - What are your alternatives or options?
   - Are your alternative choices consistent with your important values?
   - Can you summarize your important values in writing?
   - What is a reasonable amount of time in which to accomplish your alternatives?

3. **Gather information**
   - What do you know about your alternatives?
   - What assumptions are you making that you should check out?
   - What more do you need to know about your alternatives?
   - What sources will help you gather more information about your alternatives?
   - What sources will help you discover further alternatives?

4. **Assess outcomes or consequences**
   - Probability:
     What is the probability of the success of each alternative?
     Are your highest values part of each alternative?
   - Desirability:
     Can you eliminate the least desirable alternatives first?
     When you consider the best possible alternative, how much do you want it?
     What are you willing to give up in order to get what you want?

5. **Establish a plan of action**
   - Weighing everything you now know about your decision, what is your plan of action?
   - What dates will you start and complete your plan of action?
   - Does your plan of action state a clear objective?
   - Does your plan of action specify the steps necessary to achieve its objective?
   - Does your plan of action specify the conditions necessary to achieve its objective?

Until you start your plan of action, you haven't really made a decision. So start now. Make systematic decision making an adventure!

RATIONAL/LINEAR DECISION MAKING

"Planning" is also known as the rational, or linear, approach to decision making. Decisions involve prediction. Prediction involves uncertainty. And uncertainty makes most people uncomfortable. Planning is one approach that decreases the amount of uncertainty and discomfort and increases your chances of achieving your designated goals.

Rational decision making uses the talents of the "left brain," which is analytical and logical and deals with deductive thinking. It ideally follows the sequential step-by-step procedure described in Exhibit 8.A.

INTUITIVE DECISION MAKING

Personality/temperament studies have estimated that up to 75 percent of the population prefer and use the "rational" decision-making approach. These studies also suggest, therefore, that 25 percent of the population prefer to use the strategy known as "intuitive." People who prefer the intuitive approach tend to be more creative and artistic. Intuitive decision makers look for the direction that "feels right." They use their "right brain," which thrives on imagination, creativity, and adapting to change spontaneously. They feel confined when asked to write out a step-by-step process.

When faced with career planning and job search, such individuals tend to engage in research to the point at which they have several alternatives that they believe would satisfy them equally. They like to get a feel for the overall, global picture and then to decide where they fit in. Once they have researched several options, talked to people in the field, and walked around the work environment, they tend to know if it's right for them. Call it an "intuitive hunch," but it is based on the cumulative insight that fits their personality. Intuitive decision makers are most apt to say they were "lucky" in finding the right job, the right major, or the right college. However, their luck is actually "preparation meeting opportunity." Intuitive decision makers are highly adept at finding opportunities. Thus it is very important that such people be truly familiar with their values, interests, skills, and personalities as they explore careers.

Luck = preparation meeting opportunity

Sometimes, the best approach for the intuitive decision maker is to fantasize and describe an ideal occupation, or to give examples of people who have an appealing career. Intuitives tend to be able to fantasize, daydream, and create verbal or written pictures of what they think is appealing. Thus a "collage" of images depicting a career plan may be as useful as the written action plan created by a rational decision maker. While intuitive decision making may work for some people, however, for the majority of us, a logical, step-by-step approach will yield better results.

GOAL SETTING

Your goals and objectives are the road signs that lead you to what you want to attain in life. It is important, therefore, that a goal be distinguished from an objective.

Goals are broad statements of purpose. They are general and long-range. They refer to an ongoing process, a challenge that's meant to stretch our

limits. If you have trouble defining your goals, try listing the dissatisfactions and problems in your life that are bothering you. Now ask yourself what you can do about them. You have just defined a goal. Thus, if you have been analyzing yourself while reading each chapter, you may have concluded that your problem is that you are not working in a field that utilizes your values, interests, attitudes, and skills. The goal would be to find a career that best allows you to utilize your talents. (At this point, complete Exercises 8.2 and 8.3. Exercise 8.2 will help you identify and rank some long-term goals that have importance for you. Exercise 8.3 will help you assess how ready you are to begin working on your goals.)

A career that meshes with your values, interests, attitudes, and skills, but requires five or more years of training, can be considered your long-range career goal. The entry-level jobs that can prepare you for this career can be considered your short-term career goals. Thus, becoming a manager or executive would be the long-range career goal, whereas working toward a bachelor's degree in business management and/or becoming an assistant manager would be short-term goals.

Objectives are the specific and practical steps used to accomplish goals. Objectives are short-term "baby steps." They are visible and measurable signposts that indicate where we are relative to reaching our goal.

The more specific our objectives are, the higher the probability that we will accomplish them. A specific objective has some indication of the action, conditions, and amount of time it will take to achieve it. Most of us have said, "I'm going to lose weight." That's an example of a nonspecific objective. We know what the action is but we don't know how, when, and to what extent it will be accomplished. We rarely follow through with an unclear objective. Occasionally you will hear someone say, "I'm going to lose one pound this week by cutting out all bread, butter, and sweets from my diet." That's an example of a specific objective; the action, losing weight, is made specific with information on how much, when, and how it will be accomplished.

Four points should be remembered in setting goals. First, *consider what you are willing to give up* to get what you want. When most people make career changes, life in general changes for them. You may need to give up free time to take special courses. You may need to take a cut in pay (temporarily or permanently) to obtain better fringe benefits, security, and a potential chance for growth in another field, or you may need to give up being the old-timer and become the new kid on the block (and need to prove yourself again as a competent worker).

Long-range career goal vs. short–term career goal

=GOAL=
To explore career alternatives to teaching by July of this year.

=OBJECTIVES=

1. By February, I will start reading The Career Fitness Program.

2. Each week, I will read one chapter & do the exercises; I will finish the book by June 1.

3. By May, I will determine the strategies I will need to identify three jobs that use my talents.

4. By May, I will attend a job search workshop at the college.

5. By June, I will research three jobs by reading about them in the career center or library & by identifying three or more people working in those jobs locally.

6. By July, I will visit three of those people at their jobs.

Develop a timeline

Second, *give yourself a realistic timeline* to reach your goal. If you've incorporated baby steps (objectives) into your timeline, you are more likely to achieve your goals. A timeline is just a way of listing in chronological order all the objectives needed to accomplish your goal.

Once you've developed a timeline, it's a good idea to show it to a close friend or counselor and to sign and date it as if it were a contract. In actuality, this is a contract with yourself. At best, you will achieve your goals; at worst, you will need to revise them and alter the timeline. At this point, complete Exercise 8.17 to reinforce your ability to formulate specific objectives.

Third, *set your goals high*. Of course, the goal must be realistic enough to be achievable. Remind yourself that you are deserving and capable; if your initial steps are specific, clear, and small enough, you will achieve them. The example provided in the box on the previous page illustrates that each objective must have importance in itself and must help lead to the overall (larger) goal.

Finally, the fourth point about setting goals is quite simple indeed: *Reward yourself after completing each objective and after reaching each goal.* Some say that the mere accomplishment of the goal should be reward enough. However, most of us tend to be more motivated toward success when we have both internal and external reward systems. The internal reward is the feeling of success; the external reward is something outside of ourselves, e.g., crossing the objective off the checklist, a grade on a paper, recognition from a group of friends, dinner at a special place, or splurging on those athletic shoes you wanted. How do you reward yourself when you attain an objective or reach a goal?

Manage your time

One way that you can reward yourself is by learning to manage your time so that you can create the best possibilities for success. People who are successful in reaching their goals know how to manage their time. (Refer to the time management strategies box for hints on how to be more successful.) Many recent high school graduates and reentry students face new unstructured situations in college and need to schedule their time carefully to allow for study, work, leisure, and other responsibilities.

Time management strategies

1. Plan and set priorities each day.
2. Prioritize specific tasks.
3. Eliminate unnecessary work or tasks.
4. Have confidence in your judgment.
5. Work on your concentration.
6. Listen actively.
7. Focus on the present.
8. Accept the help of others.
9. Set firm deadlines.
10. Schedule relaxation time.
11. Build on successes.
12. Do something; get started!
13. Ask: What is the best use for my time now?

DECIDING ON A MAJOR

At this point you should be focusing your thoughts regarding your values, personality, interests, and skills toward either a college major or a few occupations that will express your career goals.

If you are thinking about a major, you will need to gather information about how jobs are related to college majors. The last chapter explained how to gather written information about careers; some resources may mention

majors related to specific careers. Whenever you meet people who have interesting jobs, do your own research by asking them if they have a degree and in what major. Since many people have majored in subjects seemingly unrelated to their jobs, your big choice will be to decide whether you should choose a major closely related to an interesting area of work, for example, a business major to become a manager, or if you should select a major that seems most interesting to you at this time in your life, for example, communications or psychology. The fact of the matter is that either major can lead you to a successful business career.

If all of your personal assessment does not suggest a specific major, you may need to sample some introductory courses to see if they appeal to you; for example, you might want to take a course providing an introduction to interior design, an introduction to management, or an introduction to engineering. It is better to sample several majors during one or two semesters than to prematurely choose one only to find out after several semesters that you don't really like that field.

Remember, many occupations do not have a strong relationship to a specific college major. Employers are looking primarily for candidates who are well-rounded individuals and who have done well in college no matter what their major. Therefore, identify a major that interests you and in which you can excel and enjoy the learning experience.

DECIDING ON TRAINING

If you are not interested in attending or completing four years of college but want to select a job that can best fulfill your career goals as soon as possible, then you have at least two issues to address: (1) job information and (2) training requirements. If the job information you have collected indicates that you are ready to enter the field, then you are also ready to read the chapters on job search strategy. If the job you want requires that you obtain further training, you will need to find out where to obtain it. Possible resources to use in obtaining this information were discussed in Chapter Seven. Using personal contacts or the yellow pages, you can call people working in the field of your interest, or the professional or trade association for that field, to obtain information on credible training centers. Usually people who work in a field know which schools have the best reputation. Public community colleges, technical junior colleges, and adult and proprietary schools also offer a variety of training programs. Be sure to

---

TOMORROW

She was going to be all she wanted to be . . . tomorrow.

None would be smarter or more successful than she . . . tomorrow.

There were friends who could help her—she knew,

Who'd be only too happy to see what they could do.

On them she would call and pay a visit or two . . . tomorrow.

Each morning she stacked up the letters she'd write . . . tomorrow,

And thought of the things that would give her delight . . . tomorrow.

But she hadn't one minute to stop on her way,

"More thought I must give to my future," she'd say . . . tomorrow.

The greatest of workers this gal would have been . . . tomorrow.

The world would have hailed her—had ever she seen . . . tomorrow.

But, in fact, she passed on, and she faded from view,

And all that was left here when living was through

Was a mountain of things she intended to do . . . tomorrow!

Anonymous

Define your goals and know how to reach them

compare the courses that you will be required to take with the preparation and skills necessary to perform the job. Making informed decisions is dependent upon acquiring accurate information.

DECIDING ON CHANGE

If you are exploring career opportunities as a result of company downsizing or family changes, the need for competent decision-making skills is perhaps even more imperative. All that you have learned about yourself thus far should give you the incentive and confidence to apply the decision-making skills discussed in this chapter. The exercises that follow will give you additional decision-making practice.

SUMMARY

Successful career planning involves two processes related to goals: (1) defining your goals and (2) knowing how to reach them. The more completely you plan out your objectives, the more likely you will be to achieve your goals. The key to the process is overcoming the hurdle of negative thinking. Block out the tendency to be self-critical. Dare to put aside your anticipation of failure, your fears and excuses, and your past habits. Allow yourself the right to create goals that energize you and take you beyond your past efforts.

The following exercises are designed to help you become aware of steps in the decision-making process and to encourage you to set some career and life goals. For example, you will be asked to decide what you want to do by the end of the current year and then one year from now. This can mean acquiring new skills or improving current skills, moving toward career advancement or career change, or staying where you are. Remember to try to picture in your mind what you want in your work life (e.g., type of work, responsibility, surroundings, salary, management relationship), and then focus on the exact steps necessary to reach your goals. If you can't picture the necessary steps, you need to gather more information (e.g., from people who have been in similar positions or from written materials about the field) so you can make attainable career decisions. Following the outline in the decision-making model (Exhibit 8.A), choose from alternatives, select the one that has the best possibility of success for you, create a plan of action, set specific objectives, and take action. As you attain objectives that move you toward your goal, reassess your decisions by taking in and processing information about how you feel in moving toward this goal. Be flexible, have alternatives, and understand that change may provide you with options (and challenges) that you never expected. Be honest with yourself. If you feel uncomfortable with your goal or your plan of action, enlist the help of a career guidance professional to assist you in formulating a goal that you can successfully attain.

The written exercises that follow help increase your awareness about how you make decisions. Exercise 8.1 asks that you rank yourself on two dimensions of decision-making style. There are no right or wrong answers. This is a chance to become aware of your personal style of decision making. Exercises 8.2 and 8.3 review goal setting. Exercises 8.4–8.7 assess whether you actually do what you say is important to you. Exercises 8.8–8.15 should clarify other factors that can affect your decisions. Exercise 8.16 asks you to think about some alternatives to your current life choices. Exercise 8.17 indicates your ability to recognize and state clear objectives (there are right and wrong answers). Exercise 8.18 encourages you to look for creative solutions. Exercise 8.19 asks you to list your time savers. Exercise 8.20 asks you to choose a long-term goal along with clear short-term activities that will start you toward the long-term goal now.

8.1 Ranking yourself

Place a check (✔) on each of the scales below to indicate your style of decision making.

cautious	_ _ _ _ _ _ _ _ _	risk taking
intuitive	_ _ _ _ _ _ _ _ _	logical
dependent	_ _ _ _ _ _ _ _ _	independent
influenced by others	_ _ _ _ _ _ _ _ _	self-motivated
feeling/emotional	_ _ _ _ _ _ _ _ _	rational
passive	_ _ _ _ _ _ _ _ _	active
quiet	_ _ _ _ _ _ _ _ _	assertive

8.2 Reviewing goal setting

In Chapter Two, we discussed long-term goals. Now let's try to become much more specific. List three specific long-term goals. Use additional paper if you have more than three.

1. ....

2. ....

3. ....

Let's assume you knew that you would not survive an earthquake six months from now. Would your short-term goals be any different? List at least three goals that relate to how you would live the next six months.

1. ....

2. ....

3. ....

Now you have a list of long-term and short-term goals. Deciding which ones are most important to you is the next step. This is called *setting priorities*. To do this, mark with the letter A those goals that are of most importance or value to you. Those of medium importance, mark with a B, and those of low importance, with a C. Let's look at the A goals first. With more than one A goal, you will want to rank them, for example, A_1, A_2, and A_3, with the A_1 goal being the most important to you at this time. Do the same for your B and C goals. Now rank your long- and short-term A, B, and C goals.

Activities are those actions we take to accomplish our objectives, which in turn get us closer to accomplishing our long-term goals. Take a separate sheet of paper for each of your three long-term goals, and list as many activities as you can think of to get you close to the goal. Don't question or judge the activities that come to mind; just list whatever they are. After you've listed these activities, ask yourself this question: Am I willing to commit five minutes in the next week to working on this activity? If your answer is no, then draw a line through the activity. It's okay if you don't want to spend the time on the activity; you don't have to make excuses. Your choice of the activities you're willing to commit five minutes to will enable you to choose the high-priority tasks. Now rank those activities you will do in the next week (A_1, A_2, A_3, etc.). Your activities are now organized. You're on your way toward meeting your goals. Make it an adventure and enjoy your accomplishments along the way.

8.3 Write a goal statement

a. Write a goal statement, describing either a short-term or a long-term goal. ....

....

....

b. Can you answer yes to the following questions about this goal?

1. Did I choose it personally?

2. Am I ready to make a written commitment to this goal?

3. Am I setting a deadline?

4. Is it within my control?

5. Have I thought through the consequences?

6. Is the goal based on my values?

7. Can I visualize it in considerable detail? (Is this goal specific?)

8. Will I work toward it?

9. Am I taking responsibility for this goal?

10. Is this goal measurable?

8.4 Task identification

Spending a maximum of five minutes, write down all the tasks you need to do in the next week.

8.5 One year to live

If you had only one year to live, which of the tasks listed would still be important to you?

8.6 Meeting your needs

How much of a week's work is spent reaching your own personal goals versus meeting others' needs?

8.7 Your energizers

What percentage of your daily activities gives you energy? List your energizing activities.

8.8 Recent decisions

What are some decisions you have made recently?

8.9 Priorities

Were some of these decisions more important than others? Why?

8.10 Irrevocable decisions

Give an example of a decision you made or might have to make that could be extremely difficult to change.

8.11 Harmful decisions

Give an example of a decision that might be harmful to you or someone you care about in some way.

8.12 Limiting decisions

Give an example of a decision you could make that might keep you from doing something you want to do.

8.13 Contingent decisions

Give an example of a decision that would have an effect on other decisions.

8.14 Values

What value or values were important to you in making the decisions listed in Exercises 8.10 to 8.13?

8.15 Factors adversely affecting decisions

The purposes of this exercise are to investigate factors that may unfavorably influence decision making and to determine whether any patterns are evident. First, on the lines provided below, write down three decisions you have made. Then, using the chart that follows, indicate which of the factors influenced you in making each decision, and to what extent they were present. To do this, use a ✔ to represent decision 1, an X for decision 2, and an O for decision 3. (Some sections of the chart may contain two or three symbols when you are done.)

Decision 1 (✔) ....

Decision 2 (X) ....

Decision 3 (O) ....

EXTERNAL FACTORS	SLIGHTLY PRESENT	MODERATELY PRESENT	STRONGLY PRESENT
1. Family expectations			
2. Family responsibilities			
3. Cultural stereotypes			
4. Male/female stereotypes			
5. Survival needs			
6. Other (specify)			

INTERNAL FACTORS	SLIGHTLY PRESENT	MODERATELY PRESENT	STRONGLY PRESENT
1. Lack of self-confidence			
2. Fear of change			
3. Fear of making a wrong decision			
4. Fear of failure			
5. Fear of ridicule			
6. Other (specify)			

After filling in the chart, look for patterns that may appear:

a. Do you experience more feelings related to internal or external factors as obstacles to making satisfying decisions?

....

....

b. If a particular factor is strongly present only once, but another factor is moderately present in two or possibly all three of your decisions, which of the two factors do you think is more significant in affecting your decision making?

....

....

8.16 What if . . .

a. Suppose you have lost all sources of support (e.g., you have been laid off or your family has withdrawn their support of your schooling). List three things you could do.

1. ....

2. ....

3. ....

b. How satisfying would these alternatives be to you?...

....

....

c. Suppose you have one year before losing the support. With one year to prepare, what would you do?

1. What alternatives might you choose?

2. What information would you need about your chosen alternatives?

3. What action would you take?

4. How satisfying would your one-year plan be?

8.17 Specific/nonspecific objectives

The following statements are objectives. Read each objective and decide whether the objective is specific or nonspecific. These are statements anyone might make; they don't necessarily apply to you. Imagine someone's standing in front of you in a line making each of these statements. With that in mind, mark each objective as "S" (specific) or "N" (nonspecific) to the left of the statement.

.... 1. I want to explore my interests.

.... 2. I want to get a good job.

.... 3. I'd like to get an idea of the job I'm best suited for.

.... 4. I'd like to take Spanish 1 next semester and for at least two years more, so I'll have another skill to use as a teacher.

.... 5. When I leave school, I want to get a job that pays at least $10 an hour.

.... 6. Tomorrow I'm going to make a 1-hour appointment to see Ms. Rogers in her office.

.... 7. I want to get at least a B on every history exam and earn a B as my final grade this semester.

.... 8. I'm going to ask Teresa to help me find some information about health careers in the Career Development and Placement Center right after class.

.... 9. I plan to move to an area where there are lots of jobs.

..............10. I want to be accepted by the state university when I graduate.

..............11. I want to find out more about myself.

..............12. I want to get along better with other people at work.

..............13. Next week I'm going to see my friends more.

..............14. I'm going to read one good book about social service careers tonight.

..............15. I want to get a good education.

(See page 154 for answers.)

8.18 Test your assumptions

a. Try to connect the following dots with only four straight lines and without lifting your pen.

b. Make a 6 out of IX by adding one line.

(See page 154 for answers.)

8.19 Time savers

List three things you do to save time.

8.20 Short- and long-term goals

Write down a long-term goal, and list two activities you can do in the next two weeks that will contribute to it.

8.21 Exercise summary

Write a brief paragraph answering these questions

What did you learn about yourself? How does this knowledge relate to your career/life planning? How do you feel? Go back to the decisions you listed on pages 149–150. Has your thinking changed regarding these decisions?

Answers to Exercise 8.17:

1. N	6. S	11. N
2. N	7. N	12. N
3. N	8. S	13. N
4. S	9. N	14. S
5. N	10. N	15. N

Answers to Exercise 8.18:

a.

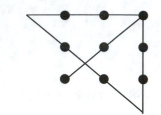

(The directions did not indicate that you must keep the lines *within* the pattern of dots.)

b. SIX

(The directions did not mandate a *straight* line.)

Go to page 161,
of the Part One Chapter Summaries,
and fill out the Chapter Eight exercise summary now.

PUTTING IT ALL TOGETHER TO REACH A TENTATIVE CAREER GOAL

The summary section on the following pages will be helpful to you as you progress through *The Career Fitness Program* and as you prepare to begin Part Two of the text.

First, as you complete each chapter, we encourage you to fill in the appropriate chapter summary here. Be as thorough as you can.

Second, when you reach this part of the text after completing Chapters One through Eight, review all your responses carefully. If your responses today are different from those you recorded when you initially read the chapter, record your current responses now.

Third, complete the exercises on pages 162–166, which will help you integrate all of this information and set a career goal.

Chapter One exercise summary

Refer back to original Chapter One answers.

1. I am ....

2. I need ....

   ....

3. I want ....

   ....

4. My current life stage in selecting a career could be summarized as ....

   ....

   ....

   ....

5. A check is placed next to the Holland Type most like me:

   .... Realistic   .... Social

   .... Investigative   .... Enterprising

   .... Artistic   .... Conventional

6. Five adjectives that best describe me are: ....

   ....

7. My favorite school subjects include ....

   ....

8. Five high-status occupations are ....

   ....

   ....

   ....

   ....

Chapter Two exercise summary

Refer back to original Chapter Two answers.

1. I am proud that ....

2. Five positive attitudes I bring to the job are ....

   ....

3. I admire the following characteristics in people: ....

   ....

4. I am working on developing the following qualities: ....

   ....

5. My affirmations are ....

   ....

   ....

Chapter Three exercise summary

Refer back to original Chapter Three answers.

1. I highly value ....

   ....

2. A problem in society that really concerns me is ....

   ....

3. My most important considerations in a job are ....

   ....

   ....

4. I am energized by the following types of activities (from my past jobs, volunteer experiences, or hobbies): ....

   ....

   ....

5. My ideal job would be (if you don't have a title, list the job tasks or activities) ....

   ....

   ....

Chapter Four exercise summary

Refer back to original Chapter Four answers.

1. Circle the term in each of the following pairs that best describes your personality type:

   extrovert/introvert   sensing/intuitive   thinking/feeling   judging/perceiving

2. Circle your top three Holland Interest Environments from Chapter Four:

   realistic   enterprising   investigative

   conventional   artistic   social

3. List the results of any assessment or inventories you have taken during the past year. For example:

   a. Strong Interest Inventory: Code letters ___ ___ ___ General Occupational Themes:

   ....

   Three highest Basic Interest Scales:

   ....

   ....

   ....

   Very similar/somewhat similar occupational scales (job titles). List five:

   ....

   ....

   ....

   b. Career Occupational Preference Survey (COPS), U.S. Interest Survey, or other interest inventory:

   List your three highest occupational groups from this survey or from any other interest inventory used:

   ....

   ....

   ....

   List five related job titles that sound interesting: ....

   ....

   ....

   ....

4. After reviewing your interests, list your three career choices:

   ....

   ....

   ....

Chapter Five exercise summary

Refer back to original Chapter Five answers.

1. Fill in the percentage of time during the day you would like to work with data, people, and things.

   .... data .... people .... things

2. Three of my accomplishments are

   ....

   ....

   ....

3. A summary of the skills I most enjoy using: ....

   ....

4. The skills I want to use in my future career are ....

   ....

5. The skills I hope to develop in the next few years are ....

   ....

Chapter Six exercise summary

Refer back to original Chapter Six answers.

1. The advantages of my age, sex, and background in looking for a job or working toward my career goal are ....

   ....

2. The disadvantages of my age, sex, race, or physical limitations in looking for a job or working toward my career goal are ....

   ....

3. Occupations that interest me (based on the trends described in Chapter Six): ....

   ....

   ....

   ....

   ....

Chapter Seven exercise summary

Refer back to original Chapter Seven answers.

1. List one job from Exercise 7.3. ....

2. Using the resources discussed in Chapter Seven, use a job you researched and list the titles or names of sources used in each category.

   a. Newspapers, bulletin boards, magazines

   b. Trade journals (name one)

   c. Directories (name one)

   d. Internet addresses used

   e. Which career and placement centers did you use?

Chapter Eight exercise summary

Refer back to original Chapter Eight answers.

1. I use the following decision-making strategies:

2. My limiting beliefs include

3. My belief about the future is

4. The best use of my time right now (according to time management strategies) is

5. A long-range goal related to my career is

6. A short-term goal related to my career is

7. External factors that can affect these career decisions include

8. Internal factors that can influence these career decisions include

Now complete the following exercises to integrate this information and set a tentative career goal.

Quick impressions

Read each category and respond quickly by recording the first three thoughts that come to mind in each one. Then list short- and long-term career goals on the next page.

Career values	Career interests	Career skills/abilities	Possible careers	Career-related, leisure-time pursuits

(continued)

Quick impressions *(continued)*

Short-term career goals and objectives	Long-term career goals and objectives	Supportive people to help me implement my career goals
1.	1.	
2.	2.	
3.	3.	
4.	4.	
5.	5.	

Review your Quick Impressions with three supportive people in your life. Ask for their input and help in working toward your goals. As a final step in confirming your career goal, complete the next exercise, "information integration and goal setting." Refer to Exhibit 8.A if you need a sample to help you.

Information integration and goal setting

Complete the form below using the following page as a guideline and sample.

Long-range career goal: ....

....

Present short-range career goal (one- to five-year goal):

I look forward to *majoring* or *getting training* in..

so that I can become ....

because I *value* ....

....

and my *interests* include ....

....

and this career would allow me to ....

....

Summary of strengths and weaknesses related to goal:

Personal strengths ("Your Type")	Personal weaknesses (need to improve)
Favorable external conditions related to career choice	Unfavorable external conditions related to career choice
Strategies to reach goal	Resources available to help reach goal

Alternative short-range career goals that would be equally satisfying:

....

....

Training needed to enter this career alternative:

....

....

Information integration and goal setting (sample)

Long-range career goal: *To enable people to use their resources.*

Present short-range career goal (one- to five-year goal):

I look forward to *majoring in or getting training in* *Psychology*

so that I can become *A social worker or counselor*

because I *value* *Helping others, serving people, being resourceful, variety, creativity, and continually learning*

and my *interests* include *Communication, holistic health, adult development, higher education, and career counseling*

and this career would allow me to *share, keep informed, serve people, be an expert*

Personal strengths that help me reach my career goal	**Personal weaknesses (need to improve)**
Have a B.A. *Willing to study* *Quick learner* *Self-confident* *Able to present before groups* *Eligible for credential programs* *Have already volunteered*	*Impatient* *Lack money for further education* *Fear taking Graduate Records Examination* *Need time management instruction*
Favorable external conditions	**Unfavorable external conditions**
Many education programs available *Many counselors retiring in next three years* *Already working* *Volunteer experiences are available* *Graduate programs exist*	*Not many openings now* *Not many paid positions available now* *Many people with this degree out of work*
Strategies to reach goal	**Resources to Reach My Goal**
Talk to graduate adviser *Obtain application to graduate school* *Discuss alternatives with adviser* *Identify volunteer opportunities* *Volunteer* *Seek part-time job related to counseling (e.g., teacher's aide)*	*Faculty* *Counselors* *College career and placement center*

If you are still confused about which career to focus on, start with the one that is most easily attainable. Work through your job search strategy in Part Two of this book using that career as your focal point. Once you understand the job search process, you can use it to explore additional career goals.

Now that you have selected a career goal and identified your strengths and weaknesses, answer the following questions:

1. What can you do now (or in the next six months) to address one or two of your weaknesses? List one weak area here, for instance, test anxiety, and list one method to help you improve, (e.g., see a counselor to learn how to reduce anxiety).

   Weakness: ....

   ....

   How to improve: ....

   ....

2. What can you do now (or in the next six months) to start working toward your career goal? List three activities you can do to move you closer to your goal, e.g., see a counselor to find out requirements for the major; sign up for major-related classes.

   To do:

   a. ....

   b. ....

   c. ....

PART TWO

JOB SEARCH STRATEGY

NINE

Targeting Your Job Search

Congratulations! You have finished the personal assessment portion of your career fitness program. You have reviewed and analyzed your skills, your interests, your personality, and your values, and you have tentatively selected some career options. They are tentative because you may find reason to alter your decisions as you continue to gather information. Just as adjustments occur in a physical fitness program based on your body's responses, so must adjustments occur in your career fitness program based on your "gut-level" responses.

The next step is to begin to design your job search strategy, which represents the second part of the career-planning process. Job search strategy involves the long-term process of acquiring the training, background, and experience needed to be competitive in the job market associated with your anticipated career goal. Simultaneously, you need to begin to identify potential employers for your skills and to develop a resume that reflects your background and your particular career goal. Finally, you need to learn how to present yourself in the best light in job interviews.

Your job search must be conducted consistently over a period of time. Studies indicate that it can take as long as seven months or more of searching to obtain the job you are seeking. Regardless of how certain or tentative you are currently feeling about your career alternatives, you must have a specific occupation in mind in

order to benefit from the remainder of this book. The goal of this chapter is for you to choose one of the occupations you have been considering. Then keep it in mind as you read and work through the following chapters.

The rest of this chapter will provide you with the information and skills to enable you to gain control over a competitive job market. In other words, you will learn many techniques to put yourself in the right place at the right time and to present yourself as the best candidate for your desired job. The underlying and most important concept, however, is focusing on what you want. Without this concentration you run the risk of being swayed by random opportunities and jobs that don't live up to your expectations. *Focusing* means that all new information should be evaluated and compared with your needs, values, interests, and skills. Remember, the first job you seek should not be considered an end in itself. It is one job on the way to several more that will compose your total career. As the dictionary defines *career*, it is a "pursuit of consecutive progressive achievement in public, professional, or business life." Additionally, career experts predict that the average worker can expect to make three to five career changes in a lifetime.

This approach assumes that you have identified a job objective for which you feel *100 percent enthusiasm*, that you will go after it with *100 percent determination*, and that you will interview for it with *100 percent of your heart*. This approach charges you with the responsibility to make things happen!

DESIGNING A COMPREHENSIVE JOB SEARCH STRATEGY

A comprehensive job search strategy involves much more than just researching to decide what your ideal job is, or simply identifying areas of employment in which you expect to find such jobs. It encourages you, once having made these basic decisions, to assertively locate and actually become employed in your ideal job. A comprehensive job search strategy stimulates you to consider a variety of aspects related to attaining your ideal job goal, such as whether you are likely to find your job in the geographical area where you live or want to live, and what sorts of activities and experiences will better qualify you for your career objectives. Equally important, job search strategy helps you to select and become involved in volunteer and entry-level activities that are the vital first steps toward your ultimate career goal. You can't always start right out in your ideal job, but guided by job search strategy, you can almost always start out in jobs and activities that

*A wise man will make more opportunities than he finds.
Sir Francis Bacon*

The assertive approach

will lead to your goals. Assuming that you have adequate skills and background and that you have identified a job for which you are 100 percent enthusiastic, the following approach will work for you.

First you must make a contract with yourself to complete all the tasks necessary to get the job. Next, you must become totally informed about the tasks and responsibilities of the job you are seeking. Much of this information can be gained from the written and electronic materials previously cited. Additionally, you will need to amplify the written information by making personal contacts with insiders.

Once you have identified your ideal job situation, an important part of your job search strategy is to investigate activities that may be indispensable first steps toward your goal. Such activities may be temporary, volunteer, or entry-level jobs in your chosen field. They can be very important in adding to your experience and making you a better candidate for your preferred job. For example, a student who wanted to move into the advertising business took a job as a receptionist in the executive suite of an advertising agency in New York. Of course, he had brushed up on his office skills to get this entry-level job, but he didn't plan to remain at that level for long. He kept his eyes and ears open for ways that he could contribute to the efficiency of the business. Within six months he had learned enough about the advertising business to interview at a competing firm and become assistant to an executive account manager.

One final suggestion before you conduct further research. You may find that your ideal job is years of education and experience away from you, or that you don't have the dedication or talent to make it in your ideal field. If so, you may be just as satisfied if you work in some job *related* to the career of your dreams. For example, behind every president of the United States there are advisers, speech writers, guards, secretaries, chefs, press representatives, and chauffeurs. Behind every rock musician there are disc jockeys, public relations representatives, recording technicians, piano tuners, album cover designers, sound editors, cutting designers, concert coordinators, costume and makeup artists, and background musicians.

There is some merit to the idea that if you stay around the field, constantly adding to your experience, you may be at the right place at the right time and get the job of your dreams. Every understudy in a play or musical has the chance to become a star some day!

Your comprehensive job search strategy

1. Commit 100 percent to your job objective.
2. Compare the tasks and responsibilities required in your chosen job at different companies and organizations.
3. Get involved in voluntary and entry-level jobs related to your ultimate goal.
4. Identify the hidden job market through personal contacts.
5. Use the Internet.
6. Utilize professional assistance, if necessary.
7. Conduct information interviews with people who are in a position to hire you. Approach all contacts with enthusiasm and sincerity and send thank-you letters to all contacts.
8. Network: let everyone know you are looking for a job (friends, neighbors, dentist, etc.).
9. Identify the needs of the organization. If the exact position you would like is not available, your task is to define a problem within the organization that you can help to solve with your unique skills.
10. Convince an employer that you have the skills he or she needs.

YOUR JOB SEARCH: GETTING STARTED

To improve the chances of getting your dream job, use a variety of strategies. Typical resources include newspaper want ads, trade journals, the Internet, sending resumes to potential employers through direct mail and e-mail, using permanent or temporary employment agencies, and volunteering or interning while in school. In addition, many hidden resources exist. The first section of this chapter focuses on common employment resources, while the latter part suggests ways to tap into those less apparent.

Understanding and Using Help Wanted Ads

Employment or "help wanted" ads are found in local newspapers, newspapers from your desired geographical area, trade journals, a supplement from *The Wall Street Journal*, association magazines and on the Internet. Most newspapers have classified advertising sections with separate employment sections. Other job listings are also found in the state employment department, county and city personnel offices, college placement centers, private employment offices, and the personnel offices of individual organizations.

Especially in larger cities, regularly reviewing the want ads over several months can lead to meaningful employment leads. Although it has been estimated that only 15 percent of jobs are found through ads, thousands of ads are published in large newspapers. You can increase your chances of obtaining a job by applying for a variety of job titles. People with accounting degrees may be eligible for junior accountant, management trainee, accounts payable, auditor, and securities broker, in addition to accountant.

Only 15–20% of all available jobs appear in employment ads

Another way to increase your chances of finding a good job involves combining a newsprint want ads search with your active accumulation of Internet information about companies. When you see a job opening at a firm that you've already visited, you should have a contact in that company to call and ask for more information about the opening. You may find that the ad is written with absolute qualifications but that the specific department will accept alternative experiences in lieu of some of the specific qualifications. Only people who have personal contacts would know such information.

Promoting Yourself Through Direct Mail and Computer

If you fail to find your ideal job in employment ads, you might try promoting yourself via mail. You may use the more traditional form of mail or you may choose to communicate electronically via the computer.

Postal mailings are quickly becoming outdated due to expense and low response. Some career fields lend themselves to this type of self-promotion better than others. For example, if you are a graphic artist or a freelance editor or writer, your potential employers may be more likely to peruse mailed-in resumes and sample work than employers in fields such as accounting and education. If creative promotion would be a plus in your field, then a direct-mail campaign may be an important part of your job search.

In the case of postal mailings, you will likely limit your campaign to those companies and organizations most likely to employ people in your career

field, due to the expense of blanket mailings. No matter what your field, devote time and energy to coming up with your list of target employers. (Use the sources of information we discussed in Chapter Seven, and also rely heavily on local business directories and even telephone directories.) To encourage response, include a stamped, self-addressed postcard for employers to use. Your postcard might include check-off statements such as "Sorry, no openings" and "Opening available; please contact _____," as well as blanks for the name, address, and telephone number of the organization.

In the case of electronic mailings (e-mail), you may be able to cover much more ground (for less money). Using the on-line programs available today, you can send your resume or other promotional material to specific groups and organizations, as in postal mailings. You can gain access to electronic mailing lists, lists of interest groups and discussion forums, and other means of targeting your promotion. Many resources are available explaining how to make good use of the electronic resume; refer to Chapter Ten for more information.

Understanding and Using Employment Agencies

Before you register with an agency, check carefully on its fees, the types of positions it handles, and its reputation. There is some controversy over the merits of a system that makes a profit by simply placing you on a job with limited concern for your satisfaction. However, there are good agencies that are very concerned about matching people with jobs that suit them.

Temporary employment agencies provide excellent ways to get back into the workforce or to test the climate in a variety of companies. The jobs available are no longer just clerical or entry-level. Many temporary employment agencies specialize in specific fields such as accounting or nursing. Some agencies place people part-time; some place people for short-term assignments. Agencies are placing even chief executive officers and college presidents in temporary, as well as full-time, employment.

For energetic, industrious workers, part-time and temporary assignments may lead to full-time employment and the opportunity to move up to better positions. Any job you hold may be the first step in a career. Exhibit a positive attitude, and do your best no matter what the position. However, for a specified period of time, you are probably under contract to the temporary agency and thus cannot be hired by the employer until the contract expires.

Volunteering

Xiao-ying found she was tired of going to college. She was beginning work in a master's degree program in anthropology when she realized that studying native tribes in the wilds of Africa would not enable her to make the personal contribution to other people's lives that she felt necessary for her own job satisfaction. With the help of a career counselor at the local YWCA and by talking with people working in her ideal setting, she became aware that working in a family-planning clinic would best suit her personal needs. So she volunteered for one year in a clinic and, in addition, conducted some studies on pregnancy and childbirth. Within the next year she had a full-time job in the education department of Planned Parenthood.

The importance of getting job-related experience cannot be overestimated. As can be seen in Xiao-ying's story, her volunteer experience supplemented her previous training. Many people have negative images of volunteering. They think volunteering means doing paperwork or "go-fer" work. However, you can create meaningful volunteer positions for yourself rather than taking whatever is available. To optimize your chances for obtaining such useful experience, go through a community voluntary action center, a college volunteer services office (sometimes part of the college placement office), a college cooperative education office, or a service learning office.

Volunteering, apprenticeships, and internships create opportunities

An even more intense volunteer experience for those who have the time and resources may be through the U.S. Peace Corps, VISTA, or the UN Volunteers. Such volunteer work requires a commitment of one to three years and provides room, board, benefits (including government service experience), and a living allowance.

The Peace Corps recruits individuals with varied academic backgrounds; for example, recruits may teach math and English in developing countries. Engineering graduates are especially valuable in the Peace Corps, with their math and science expertise, and civil engineers are needed to build water purification plants and roads.

Volunteering adds visibility and experience to your job search. However, volunteering does not relate only to jobs. Think about becoming a student member of a professional association. Student membership usually offers all the same benefits of regular membership but costs much less. Once in an organization, *volunteer* for committees and leadership positions, and gain visibility and recognition. The people in these organizations will soon be your peers. This is also an excellent method of making contacts for both jobs and letters of recommendation.

As a business student, Felipe wanted to focus on human resources development and training in industry. So he joined the American Society for Training and Development (ASTD). He volunteered to chair the student recruitment subcommittee and joined the Career Development Special Interest Group. Two years later, when interviewing for a job as assistant to a director of training, he found he knew people who had worked with the director, was able to learn about the firm from former employees who were ASTD members, and made an excellent impression in his interview.

Interning

Your college or university may help to arrange *internships* in some fields of study. Internships may be paid or unpaid and are usually restricted to students who have studied in the subject area of the internship. For example, a history major or a political science major may be given the highest priority among applicants for an internship in local or state government; a graphic arts, public communications, English, or communications major may be given priority for an internship in an advertising agency.

Some colleges have "internship offices," or "experiential education offices" that arrange internships of different types, including *fieldwork*, which involves work required as part of a major. (Prospective teachers usually must student teach, for example, to earn their degree or certificate.)

Internships 1996: On the Job Training Opportunities for Today's Job Market, Peterson's: Princeton, NJ, 1996. Arranged by career fields, this book includes detailed information on more than 1,500 organizations offering internships in the business, nonprofit, and government sectors. Included are short-term positions with businesses such as *The Wall Street Journal,* Proctor & Gamble, 3M, Aetna Life and Casualty, Sierra Club, and the U.S. Department of Energy.

Internships can be used to build extremely valuable experience and contacts. At Keuka College in New York, one political science major had *three* government internships before graduation. At that campus, each political science major takes a four-week field period either in January or during the summer. Students have worked for state assemblypersons, the lieutenant governor, and the Democratic Senatorial Campaign Committee in Washington, for example.

At Concordia College in Minnesota, students alternate semesters of work and study or work part-time while continuing classes in the school's cooperative education program. This gives them longer-term connections with an organization and allows them to learn more about the workplace and professional environments. Ramapo College in New Jersey, provided one of its students with overseas experience at a marketing firm in England. When she graduated she got a job as an assistant account executive at the New York office of Lloyds Bank PLC, the British bank chain.

Interns are generally closely supervised by college professors to help ensure they gain educational experience and benefit from the internship personally, while they provide services for the employer. Ideally, interns working as part of a college program enjoy a meaningful learning experience that provides them with skills that could not be learned from a book.

Another way for college students to get experience that may lead to a full-time position is through cooperative education programs. (At some schools, the terms *internship* and *cooperative education* are used synonymously, but others make distinctions between the two programs.) The Cooperative Education Association publishes a list of participating colleges and universities that have official co-op programs.

The URL (address) for the *Princeton Review Online* (www.review.com/careers/) is typical of many specific Web sites related to published materials. These sites are advertisements for related book(s) but contain a variety of career resources. Another way to get similar information is to go to Web sites of associations where information about paid and unpaid positions can be found. For example, the *National Multimedia Association of America* (NMAA) job bank can be found at http:// www.nmaa.org. You can also find this site by using a search engine such as Yahoo (http:// search.yahoo.com) or Magellan (http://searcher.mckinley.com) and type "career multimedia internship." When you use search engines you may get thousands of

The Princeton Review Online. America's Top Internships

Want to intern with the Academy of Television Arts & Sciences? How about the White House? The Princeton Review carries descriptions and application information for some of the best internship programs in the country. The site on eWorld describes the positions, requirements, compensation (they're not all unpaid), duration, deadlines, and other important info.

EWORLD

Go princeton review → Undergraduate Admissions → The Top Internships

WORLD WIDE WEB

URL http://www.review.com/career/ internships_worth.html

Source: *Netjobs* by Miller, K., and Goodwin, M. N.Y.: Michael Wolff & Co. 1996.

listings, many of which may be unrelated. Use more key words to narrow your search.

Internet has internship listings

STARTING YOUR OWN BUSINESS

One more way to get a job, of course, is to start your own business. In recent years, college students faced with limited job prospects have been starting businesses in record numbers. A reduction in corporate recruiters pitching jobs for graduates has led to new entrepreneurial pursuits and the rise of students *inventing* their own careers. Some examples include a myriad of Internet-related companies, organized walking tours in major cities with bilingual materials for foreign visitors, specialized photography to enhance pictorial magazines, and networks for improved services for persons with disabilities.

Become your own boss

Home Businesses

The U.S. Bureau of Labor Statistics (1996) counts over 8 million Americans out of over 14 million self-employed, who are working at home in a wide variety of careers. These numbers are growing each year as computer and Internet sites continue to expand. Approximately 25 percent of these home businesses are in the field of marketing and sales, with contracted services, professional, and technical jobs accounting for another 25 percent. A potential consumer population with huge and diverse needs encourages this trend in home businesses. Among home business owners, 45 percent are college graduates and 85 percent are married, with half having dependent children. The average household income is approximately $55,000 annually.

According to the Associated Press, freelancing, long associated with artists, writers, and performers, is a career option for people in all fields these days. Freelance opportunities are growing for specialists in accounting, marketing, management, and other traditional business functions. These growing opportunities are largely due to technological advances of the last decade or two; the proliferation and increased affordability of fax machines, cellular telephones, personal computers, and desktop/multimedia publishing capacities enable small businesses to compete for and service clients in a manner previously possible only for large businesses.

Freelance opportunities

Getting Help Starting Your Own Business

Career centers, libraries, and the Internet have useful information on starting a business. The Small Business Administration provides seminars and low-cost materials within local communities. A group called SCORE (Service Corps of Retired Executives) is composed of local retired businesspeople who lead low-cost workshops and offer free technical advice. Contact your local chamber of commerce for information about these resources. Also, a local community college or the extension/continuing education division of a local university may offer courses in small business administration or marketing. If colleges offer such courses, they may also have students available who get college credit by giving free technical assistance to newly formed small businesses.

If you would like to explore the possibility of beginning your own business, either home-based or traditional, do a thorough market research about the needs for your service. You will benefit greatly from consulting SCORE, statewide Small Business Development Centers, your local chamber of commerce, and Internet sites (which can be found by typing "small business" and "careers" or "entrepreneurs" and "careers" into a search engine) Finally, a healthy savings account will be needed to get you through many months until you can count on regular income from your enterprise. Better yet, try to begin building your new business while you are still employed (at least part-time) to ensure some income.

Related Web sites are http://www.inc.com and http://www.ideacafe.com. The first is a site for a magazine dealing with starting small businesses, and the second specializes in helping small business owners with marketing, market research, starting businesses, legal information, operations, accounting, and more. A useful government site can be found at "SBA Online": http://www.sbaonline.sbs.gov/gils/. Meanwhile a site that specializes in youth development and entrepreneurial leadership programs can be found at http://www.entreworld.org.

Franchise information

Here are three possible sources of preliminary information about franchises:

- Recorded information about franchises can be heard on a phone line operated by the Federal Trade Commission.

- *The Worldwide Franchise Directory,* published by Gale Research, is available at most libraries.

- A "Franchise Opportunities Guide" is available from the International Franchise Association.

- http://www.frannet.com

- http://www.sbaonline.sba.gov/workshops/franchises/

FRANCHISING

Franchising offers another means of owning and operating your own business. Franchising may appeal to individuals who have worked for large companies and those not quite ready to be full-fledged entrepreneurs. When you buy a franchise you become part of a larger structure; thus, you must do extensive research to ensure that your personality fits well with the goals and operations of this larger company.

USING COLLEGE PLACEMENT SERVICES

No matter what year you are in, there is much you can do to advance your career while still in college. First-year college students and sophomores should be taking courses in career exploration, exploring academic alternatives, setting goals, and making choices. Students further along in school should be pursuing internships, doing volunteer work, networking, and doing informational interviewing. Finally, students who are coming close to completing a degree should be working with their school's career planning and placement office.

Even though fewer companies are recruiting on college campuses these days, approximately 50 percent of new college graduates still find jobs via this method. If you have researched your career, done related volunteer work, completed an internship or held a part-time position or done well in your field academically, your appeal to these recruiters and other employers will be enhanced.

If the career planning office offers job search workshops covering resume writing and interviewing techniques, or the opportunity to videotape practice interviews, sign up for these services. Explore alumni contacts in the field you hope to pursue. While it is still easily accessible to you, use your college library to research career opportunities.

Be prepared to be flexible when considering job offers. During tight economic times, college graduates may find it difficult to find their ideal first job and may have to lower their expectations regarding starting salary. Read and inform yourself about today's opportunities and current salaries in your geographical area

Remember, a job that seems less than ideal may lead to one at which you can truly excel. For example, one university fine arts student became a recruiter at Prudential Life Insurance Company. Later, that art graduate's job involved purchasing art for Prudential Regional Headquarters!

During tight economic times, college graduates may decide that graduate school is the best bet and enter medical or law school or graduate degree programs in science, education, or business. If, when the time comes, you are genuinely interested in an advanced degree and the knowledge it will give you, this may be one option for you. However, if you find you are considering graduate school simply to avoid the "real world" and put off job hunting, consult a career counselor. The job market may or may not be better in two or three years. It would be wiser to devote your energies to finding out more about what you want to do and how you can accomplish your goals than to invest additional years in school.

> ### Job hotlines
>
> - Many companies and government agencies now have "job openings hotlines." A book titled *Job Hotlines USA* identifies over 1,000 telephone numbers. Numbers and organizations are listed both alphabetically and by geographic location.
> - WWW: http://www.ajb.dni.us/

INTERVIEWING FOR INFORMATION

Survey after survey on job hunting confirms a basic fact about job search strategy—namely, that the one best way to find out about a job and to get a job is through *people*. Now that you have reviewed the written sources of information on jobs, you are ready to begin conducting *information interviews*. These interviews help you develop contacts, sources of knowledge, and guides to meeting other people in a particular field. This network of people will keep you informed and connected to possible job openings. Once you gain some experience through information interviewing and networking, you will be ready to master the techniques involved in interviewing for a job.

Cultivating contacts

Information Interviewing—The Purpose

Information interviewing involves learning to identify people who are doing what you want to be doing and asking them questions related to their current jobs. Information interviewing serves several purposes. It helps you further refine your knowledge and understanding of the field you are exploring. It enables you to develop social skills related to feeling comfortable and knowledgeable while you are being interviewed. Information interviewing creates

the setting to develop contacts. These contacts are often helpful to your specific job search. The people you interview may themselves be in a position to hire someone like you for a job or they may simply hear about a job opening and pass the information on to you. Remember that your specific purpose in information interviewing is *not* to look for a job but to confirm your information about the field and to develop contacts that may be helpful in the future. When involved in an *information interview, you are asking* the questions. When on a *job interview, you are being asked* the questions.

Information interviewing is based on the premise that you have already read much of the written information related to a specific type of job and now need confirmation from people who are already doing that job. You want them to tell you basically what the field is really like before you commit your time, effort, and finances to the pursuit of a new field. Or, if you are already in the field, you want to know if one employer's environment would be more appealing to you than another's. Other information you can gain from such an interview involves much more than simply confirming the skills needed and the salary range. On one hand, you can find out if you like the people, if the atmosphere feels comfortable, or if the people are friendly and helpful. On the other hand, you may find that no one has time to talk to you, they keep you waiting, or they let the telephone constantly interrupt your interview, or they work in noisy cubicles. This information is available only through an on-site visit. Thus the overt goal of information interviewing is to collect information, but an additional goal is to make contacts and determine whether you have made an appropriate match between your personal needs and your career goal.

Information Interviewing—The Process

Identify people who are doing what you would like to do

The first step in the process of information interviewing is to identify people who are working in the fields that you've decided are interesting to you. It's especially helpful if you know a relative, friend, or neighbor involved in the field or at least someone who can refer you to a potential contact; it's always easier to talk to someone whose name is familiar. The hardest step is making the first phone call to a stranger or, even worse, a strange firm and asking for the name of a person doing that interesting job! Strangers will be more receptive to talking to you if you demonstrate the following characteristics.

1. Indicate that you are seeking personalized information about their field before you decide to enter it.
2. Confirm the person's job title by asking.
3. Sound enthusiastic and delighted to have reached this person.
4. Refer to the research you've already reviewed about this field or company.
5. Ask if you can have a specific amount of time to interview this person (e.g., 15 to 20 minutes).
6. Try to arrange the interview at the person's work site, so you can determine firsthand how it might feel to work there.
7. Keep to your agreed upon time frame.
8. Thank your interviewee, and follow up with a thank-you note.

As we noted, it's tough making that first phone call. Here are some specific examples of telephone "lead-ins" to help you get started. Remember to identify yourself, state your purpose, and ask for an appointment with the appropriate person. This straightforward approach is generally effective.

Example:

Hello, Mr. Jones, I am Diane Smith from Moorpark College. I'm doing some research in the field of houseplant maintenance service, and I'd like to stop by at your convenience to ask you a few questions. I'd appreciate about 15–20 minutes of your time. When may I stop by? Is Thursday at 2 P.M. all right?

or:

Hello . . . this is . . . This morning I talked to . . . about the opportunities in . . . and he spoke very highly of you. I'm calling to find out when you might have a few minutes to see me. Would it be convenient to meet with you in the morning or afternoon?

Information Interviewing Outline

Once you have located your contacts and made definite appointments to interview them, you need to consider in specific detail the best questions to ask to gain the maximum useful information as quickly and pleasantly as possible. Remember, you will be talking to busy people with many demands on their time; they will expect you to be, and it's to your advantage to be, as businesslike as possible. Finally, having made the telephone contact and set the date to meet, you should send a note confirming the information interview appointment.

Here is a framework to help you design your interview for an information field survey. You may think you already have answers to some of the questions, but personal interviews should help flesh out details and possibly fill in some gaps in your information that you don't realize are there. Try to choose your questions from the general categories of type of business, position classifications, position descriptions, work environment, benefits, and entrance requirements, as follows:

- **Type of Business**

  What are the services, products, or functions of the organization?

  Who utilizes the organization's services or products?

  Who are the competitors in this field?

  What sets the company apart or distinguishes it from others in the same industry?

  What are the projections for future development or new directions?

- **Position Classifications**

  In each major corporate division, what types of positions are available?

  What are the qualifications for entry-level and experienced positions? (Consider education, skills, abilities, etc.)

- **Position Descriptions**

  What duties and responsibilities are performed in the area in which you are interested?

What are some examples of projects currently under way and problems currently being solved?

What is a typical day like?

What contacts would there be (e.g., personal, telephone, e-mail) with other organizations?

- **Work Environment**

    What type of physical localities are involved: outdoors, indoors, travel? Is there pressure? Routine? Variety? How much supervision is there? Do flexible work schedules exist? Is overtime typical or atypical?

- **Benefits**

    How does compensation compare to education and ability level?

    What are the opportunities for advancement, promotions, or lateral mobility?

    What opportunities are available for advanced training, on-the-job training, or academic course work? Is there a tuition reimbursement plan?

    What other benefits are available? Possible benefits might include:

Medical/dental insurance	Profit sharing
Life, disability insurance	Retirement
Vacations, holidays	Preretirement planning
Expenses for moving, travel	Employee assistance programs
Outplacement	(counseling for work-related
Recreation, personal health	problems)
services	Job placement assistance (for
Child-care facilities	your spouse, when relocating)

- **Entrance Requirements**

    What suggestions do you have for an individual wishing to enter this field of employment?

    What other companies might employ individuals to perform this type of work? Could you refer me to someone else for more information about opportunities in this field?

Be prepared with questions

Moving from a general categorical framework to more specific detail, here is a sample list of typical questions you might ask in your information interviews.

1. What do you like most about your job and why?

2. What do you like least about your job and why?

3. How did you decide to get into this field, and what steps did you take to enter the field? What alternative ways can one enter this field?

4. What training would you recommend for someone who wanted to enter this field now? What skills and background are needed to get into this field now?

5. What is the salary range for a person in this field? Entry-level to top salary?

6. What personal qualities do you feel are most important in your work and why?

7. What are the tasks you do in a typical workday? Would you describe them?
8. What types of stress do you experience on the job?
9. What types of people survive and do well in this field?
10. Are resumes important in getting a job here?
11. What are the opportunities for promotion?
12. Is this field expanding? Taking any new directions?
13. What related occupations might I investigate?
14. Can you give me the names of three other people who share your enthusiasm for this kind of work? How can I contact them?
15. Is there anything else about this field that would be helpful for me to know?

When you approach professionals in your field of interest from a research point of view and *not* as if you want a job, they will often be happy to talk with you. Even the busiest executives will often find time for you. If one person doesn't have time, ask to be referred to another professional in the field. It is the secretary's job to protect the boss from distractions. When a secretary asks, "What is this call regarding?" you might respond, "I was referred to Jane by her associate Don Reid." Be certain to sound confident and friendly. It's best to call on a Tuesday, Wednesday, or Thursday between eight and eleven o'clock in the morning. If the person isn't in and you must leave a message, leave just your name and phone number.

Interviewing people who work in a field that interests you will provide you invaluable information, either confirming or revising your views. But even better, you will make contacts who may be able to help you actually find a job in the future. These contacts can suggest groups or associations to join, colleges to attend, and classes to take, as well as the current status of employment activity in their field. If you use this information wisely, you too can become visible in these inner circles. It's never too early to start.

Practicing Information Interviews

Some people prefer to practice information interviews until they become confident in approaching people about their career. If you need to practice, you might try one of the following approaches. Either you can interview someone you already know about a hobby that sounds interesting or you can ask people about their hobbies and careers at any informal gathering you attend. These informal activities tend to build your self-confidence in asking questions. Once you get started, you might find you enjoy interviewing for leads through other people.

Two interesting success stories may help you get started. Thomas Shanks, a college assistant professor of communications, tells how one of his students moved from California to New York. For three months, the student sent his resume everywhere and knocked on the door of every friend, relative, and remote acquaintance that he could find. He even found out which after-hours spots the television crowd preferred, and he frequented those places. He eventually got offers from all three networks. Another student, a freshman, was a business major with an interest in art. In November, the vice president of

Information interviewing leads to contacts and careers

ACTIVITY

INFORMATION INTERVIEWING OUTLINE

Below is an outline/review of the points we have discussed about information interviewing. Use this form as a guide in preparing for each interview you have.

1. Find someone with whom to start the interview process. Make sure you get the person's name. Call the person directly, by name.

   What is the name of the person you're going to call? ....

2. Make a specific appointment, for a specific length of time.

   When is your appointment, and for how long? ....

   ....

3. Make a list of specific questions, things you want to know about the job.

   Your questions for this interview. (See list on pages 180–181.) ....

   ....

   ....

   ....

4. Explain why you're calling for the interview. Some explanations:
   a. You want to know more about this kind of work before you decide that you're interested, or before you decide you should choose it as a career.
   b. You are getting ready for a job interview and would like to get some advice from someone in the field before the interview.
   c. You are interested in the field but haven't found much information on it and would appreciate someone filling you in on it.
   d. You are doing some research for a career class and would like some specific information in this field.

   Which explanation will you give when you call? ....

   ....

   ....

   (Create your own if you wish.)

5. Tell the employer who recommended that you call. (A reference helps.)

   Who is your reference for this interview? ....

6. After the interview, send a note thanking the person for the time and help.

   Date sent ....

industrial relations at an engineering firm gave a talk in her leadership class. After class she asked him about summer jobs with his firm (notice how early she did so). By January, he had arranged for her to interview in the graphic arts department of his firm. She got the summer job, one many graduates of art programs would have coveted.

Last, if you are a student or have access to a college campus, teachers often make fine resources. Many faculty members have interesting summer jobs or worked in other positions prior to becoming a teacher. They have valuable contacts. In turn, if you are a teacher interested in a career change, you might find a lead through a student. Many times a teacher can design a lesson plan to find out the occupations of parents and then invite parents to speak in their class about their career. These parents can become future contacts for both students and teachers!

NETWORKING

Networking refers to the process of developing and maintaining contacts. While conducting information interviews, you will meet many people. Besides gathering information, you are making contacts. Contacts, if cultivated and used wisely, can lead to or become potential employers. In a tight and competitive job market, contacts often make the difference between your being selected or being passed by. This is true for several reasons. Often jobs need to be filled before there is time to advertise. Additionally, as has been mentioned, the majority of new jobs that are available each year come from business leads that start off with relatives and neighbors. Most people hear about jobs by word of mouth. You need to let people know that you are looking.

Networking provides the edge

The term "network" is both a noun and verb. As a noun, a network is defined as a group of individuals who are connected to and cooperate with each other. As a verb, "to network" is to develop contacts and exchange information with other people for purposes of developing business or expanding one's career opportunities. The verb form often becomes action-oriented and is changed to "networking."

Your network can develop each day; anyone you know can be a good source. Each has friends and contacts and can make a difference in helping you secure an information interview. Think about it: the more people you get to know, the more information you gather. The more visible and proactive you are, the greater your chances will be in finding the right job. It may be a relative or neighbor who points you to a hidden job opening or provides you with valuable strategies.

You probably have many acquaintances willing to provide names and ideas to help you be successful in finding your preferred career. These friends and acquaintances may come from any of the following groups: clubs, organizations, health and sports team affiliations, teachers and professors (past and present), religious groups, coworkers, and previous employers. Exercise 9.1 will suggest people to contact.

One form of networking is to meet professionals where they gather. For example, if you are interested in human resources management (HRM), you will find HRM personnel at such association meetings as American Society for Training and Development (ASTD); if you are interested in personal

Join professional associations

communications services, read the trade journal, *Radio Communications Report*, to find out about local meetings or national conventions.

Attend conferences

Check the local business section of the newspaper to keep up on what's happening in your community. Review the list of groups using your city's convention center and plan on attending conventions related to your interests. For example, one trade show related to "theme parks" had 20,000 registrants and 800 exhibitors occupying 2,600 booths; it lasted four days. Students majoring in communications, radio-TV, theater arts, business, and computer science would all find experts related to their majors at such a conference. Such conventions usually offer reduced fees for attending only one day or entering the exhibit area only.

Sources for contacts

Many professional associations have related student groups or student sections. You should already know whether there are groups active on campus related to the field you want to pursue. If you don't, make this your first networking step. Use the resources listed in Chapter Seven to obtain association names and addresses, or ask your adviser. For example, a very complete source is *The Encyclopedia of Associations*, but the *Occupational Outlook Handbook* also lists names and addresses after each occupation. Consider writing an association to inquire about local meetings and the possibility of becoming a student member.

These are all ways of meeting professionals in your field of interest, a key factor in finding the job you want. A 1993 survey of 1,500 successful job applicants by *National Business Employment Weekly* found that 67 percent got their jobs through networking; 11 percent by answering an ad; and only 2 percent by sending out resumes and filling out applications.

While conducting information interviews or discussing people's careers at a conference, take advantage of these opportunities to find out what kinds of questions *they* were asked in interviews; ask what they considered to be the most difficult questions in their interviews. Another good question is to ask them what makes a candidate the best candidate. Their answers to questions like these will be helpful when you begin to practice for job interviews.

Moving Beyond the Fear of Networking

Many people are reluctant to develop contacts by networking. They may feel they are imposing on busy individuals whose time is precious. This hesitation can be overcome, however, by realizing that many people truly enjoy talking about themselves and their profession. Many remember their own difficulties in connecting to a new career and are, therefore, very receptive to others' request.

Remember that as you meet people, you are finding out about the real work these new contacts do and finding out if you feel comfortable with their environment. You should also be finding out if your skills would be helpful in solving problems or meeting needs in each workplace you visit while networking. Let the contact know what you can do for them—you may be just the person they need! One graphic design student visited the company of a graphic designer who had spoken in her art class. When asked if she had used Adobe Paint Program, she was very enthusiastic in her answer. She was hired for a summer job on the spot!

Some job seekers find it difficult to network because they are introverts by nature. To avoid a telephone conversation, consider writing an introductory note to ask for a brief meeting. Then, stick to the agreed-upon time. Knowing general conversational techniques helps. For instance, use mutual professional interest when making the contact.

Finally, be sure that every contact is made with courtesy and tact, and be prepared with specific questions. Thanking your contacts for assistance pays huge dividends in the future. The best networking is not simply a one-time association, but a continuing connection. Networking can positively affect your job search and every aspect of your life.

JOB SEARCH WHILE UNEMPLOYED

Although experts agree that it is best to look for a job while you are still employed, not everyone can be in that position. If you are unemployed and seeking employment, you will benefit by disciplining yourself to stick to a daily job search schedule. Otherwise, your best intentions may be thwarted by procrastination. Procrastination can then turn into the paralysis described in Chapter Eight related to poor decision-making strategies.

Create a disciplined job search to replace the work schedule missing from your life. You will be more productive if you begin the day as if you were going to work. Get dressed, have breakfast, and begin the day with a few hours of phone calls. Identify employers who can use your skills. Be aware that successful phone contacts rely on sheer numbers. The greater the number of calls made, the greater your chances of getting an interview.

Since many cold calls will result in responses such as "No one can speak to you today" or "Sorry, we have no openings," your daily routine must include predictably positive activities. For instance, plan a portion of your day to be spent at the library or on-line researching job information, a portion looking for leads, and a portion filling out job applications. Another important part of the day should include being with supportive people, for example, attending networking and association meetings (local newspapers have business sections that announce weekly association meetings), joining friends for lunch, and enjoying recreation. Keeping active will reenergize you and keep you visible to those who might be able to refer you to a job. Somewhere in your present circle of friends, coworkers, and acquaintances is someone who can link you with your next job. This process is further discussed under the topic of networking.

Part of your daily routine should be spent using the Internet

The final part of your day should be saved to return phone calls and e-mails, redraft letters, revise your resume and cover letter, and/or write specific thank-you letters to people you have met. Planning and preparation can make the critical difference in turning telephone calls into interviews and interviews into job offers. (See Chapter Eleven for interviewing techniques.)

Many unemployed people use the services of their state employment agency. (The unemployment office usually requires you to contact a minimum number of employers each week or month to remain eligible to collect unemployment insurance.) However, the state employment agency also offers workshops on job search strategy, assistance in writing a resume, and a computerized job bank. Some offices also conduct targeted group meetings for

workers in designated fields, for example, aerospace, automotive, banking, executive, manufacturing, and the like. Support groups may meet on a regular basis to offer both encouragement and leads.

PLANNING FOR ACTION

Lastly, effective job search strategy requires that you master the skills of goal setting and action planning. This means that you set objectives such as those indicated in the following suggestions and designate specific times to complete each one.

1. Schedule planning time.
2. Maintain a list of activities to get done, for example, write up a weekly calendar and enter each item per day or hour. A pocket calendar may be sufficient for one person whereas a notebook may work better for another.
3. Start a notebook with one section for contacts' names, addresses, and phone numbers and another section for notes about different companies.
4. Develop an Internet bookmark of often-used addresses. (A bookmark allows quick access to favorite sites.)
5. Review your progress by checking off completed activities.

Effective job search requires clerical and organizational skills. Every week you will need to update specific names, obtain more exact titles, and confirm addresses. This information can be kept in a file box or in your home computer. (Exhibit 9.A provides a sample contact record.) Being able to retrieve at a moment's notice the information you have been collecting can make the difference between faxing your resume or getting your resume in the mail today or tomorrow (which may be a day too late). The fastest way to update a resume is to have it stored in your own home computer or on a floppy disk for use in a personal computer at school, at a local copy center, or at a friend's home.

If you have access to a computer, software packages are available that will help you create a tracking system for all of your contacts and activities. One software program, for example, leads you through planning, analysis, targeted markets, and commitment to a schedule of tasks. After working through the program, you will have created a list of potential employers, a resume, and a cover letter, and will have prepared for the interview.

If you have a modem, consider investing in a service such as CompuServe, America Online, or Prodigy that provides access to computer bulletin boards. More and more companies are advertising job openings through these bulletin boards and even calling for electronic transmission of resumes (more about this later in Chapter Ten). Also, company insiders may provide information about job openings via these bulletin boards. A useful site for a general search of the web is http://www.search.com.

It is advisable to have a designated area in your home for all of your career information. Keeping careful records of all contacts made, applications submitted, resumes sent, interviews held, and correspondence sent and received will make your job search more effective and easier to manage logistically.

EXHIBIT 9.A

Sample contact file format.

1. Company: _____

Address: _____

Phone No.:	Contact Person & Title:	Type of Contact & Date:
Referred by:		Letter _____
		Phone _____
		Resume _____
Job Target:		Application _____
		Interview _____

Follow-up: _____

Conclusions: _____

---

2. Company: _____

Address: _____

Phone No.:	Contact Person & Title:	Type of Contact & Date:
Referred by:		Letter _____
		Phone _____
		Resume _____
Job Target:		Application _____
		Interview _____

Follow-up: _____

Conclusions: _____

---

3. Company: _____

Address: _____

Phone No.:	Contact Person & Title:	Type of Contact & Date:
Referred by:		Letter _____
		Phone _____
		Resume _____
Job Target:		Application _____
		Interview _____

Follow-up: _____

Conclusions: _____

---

4. Company: _____

Address: _____

Phone No.:	Contact Person & Title:	Type of Contact & Date:
Referred by:		Letter _____
		Phone _____
		Resume _____
Job Target:		Application _____
		Interview _____

Follow-up: _____

Conclusions: _____

---

5. Company: _____

Address: _____

Phone No.:	Contact Person & Title:	Type of Contact & Date:
Referred by:		Letter _____
		Phone _____
		Resume _____
Job Target:		Application _____
		Interview _____

Follow-up: _____

Conclusions: _____

IMPLEMENTING YOUR JOB SEARCH:
A LIFELONG VENTURE

The comprehensive approach to job hunting involves putting yourself in the right place at the right time again and again throughout your lifetime. It involves strategies that assist you in finding openings in your target area before the openings are publicly announced. In situations when you do not appear to be the ideal candidate, this approach will assist you in getting noticed and getting an interview.

Many times, this approach works best while you are still employed, because potential employers tend to defer unemployed inquirers to the personnel office. Ideally, before starting a job search you will have a specific field and job objective in mind. Let's say you have selected business administration and want to specialize in real estate finance. Your first decision is whether you want to work for a commercial bank, private developer, the government (such as an appraisal office or bureau of land development), or a related association that employs people to *interact* with the government. Following is an example:

Confirm your career objectives

Susan was an assistant to a county supervisor and found many of her assignments related to land development. While finishing work toward her bachelor's degree in business (attending college after work hours), she increasingly represented her supervisor when land developers appealed to the Board of Supervisors for zoning and code changes. When her supervisor did not run for reelection, Susan was hired as a director for the business-industry association to lobby the county for the industrialization of farmland. Within a few years, she became a consultant to land developers and interacted with her present boss, who hired her into his prospering real estate development firm as vice president of government relations.

High visibility helps

Even while working in an entry-level job, Susan met people working in the field of her interest, real estate. As an assistant to the county supervisor, she met people in government, nonprofit associations, and private industry. She maintained high visibility by speaking at community events, representing the supervisor when necessary, and joining related organizations and community clubs. When she wanted to make a job change, she had already identified and made contact with the types of places and people with whom she wanted to work.

Networking opens up the hidden job market

Susan had contacts who were insiders and could recommend her for jobs even before they were announced. But even more important, she had discovered the "hidden job market." She knew the needs of the business-industry association and could tell its people how her skills and contacts could benefit them. She was able to sell herself. She knew she had skills and contacts with government that could enhance her present employer's expansive plans. She was hired because she was able to describe the job she wanted to do in the firm and because her ideal job meshed with the vision of the president of the company. She actually created her current position.

Selected on-line employment databases

Searching "on-line" can be overwhelming. Thousands of Web sites are available for job searching, but you may feel comfortable with only a few. Find a service suited to you and remember, the more you target your search, the more efficient it will be. Rather than typing "job search," use terms like "entry-level job" or "job in advertising." Here are a few sites to get you started.

Sample Sites

The Monster Board (http://www.monster.com/home.html)

The *Monster Board* has a database with more than 48,000 job listings and includes a resume bank. There, you can develop your on-line resume and use it to apply for jobs. It will be matched to employers' needs at no charge.

America's Job Bank (http://www.ajb.dni.us/index.html)

JobBank USA is one of the largest and most diverse databases, with more than 250,000 jobs. This site provides resume writing, networking, and information services to job candidates, employers and recruitment firms. This is a free service to job hunters.

E-Span (http.//www.espan.com/)

E-Span offers job listings, resume tips, salary guides, and interactive practice interviews. *E-Span* distributes your resume for no charge. Be aware though that this distribution is *not* confidential.

JobSource (http://www.jobsource.com)

JobSource lets you search for jobs categorically and geographically; it offers career advice and direction. It also has a resume generator to help you format your profile with key words. Again, there is no security with this service, but it *is* free.

CareerMosaic (http://www.careermosaic.com)

CareerMosaic has its own database of job opportunities; it indexes postings from more than 20 job-related newsgroups and directs the user to on-line job fairs, employer profiles, and special resources for students. Instructions and tips about electronic resumes are provided. Again, this is free, but lacks security.

IntelliMatch (http://www.intellimatch.com)

IntelliMatch tries to match job seekers and employers and has a "power resume builder." The site uses the standard ASCII resume format. Unique to this service are its two levels of security: the "standard plan" blocks

your current employer from accessing your resume, and the "gold plan" requires your permission to release information to each potential employer.

Online Career Center (http://www.occ.com)

Online Career Center is the oldest and best known, and it's free. Job opportunities are searchable by title, key word, company name, and geographical region. The Career Manager lets you modify your resume at any time.

Nation Job Network (http://www.nationjob.com)

In addition to the standard search by job title or company name, this site features Personal Job Scout, which keeps an eye on listing updates and notifies you via e-mail about related jobs. Again, this service is free.

Virtual Job Fair (http://www.vif.com)

The *Virtual Job Fair* is especially useful for those looking for high-tech jobs. There are more than 15,000 jobs and links to career resources, magazines, and expos, as well as a resume-posting service.

Resumail Network (http://www.resumail.com)

Resumail Network has created a standard for electronic delivery of properly formatted resumes because its software is directly linked to employers' software. There is a fee for the software, but privacy is guaranteed. This site also has links to over 150 sites related to associations, career fairs, and other career information. Jobs may be searched by company or category.

On-line Services with Good Career Sections

America Online: (800) 827-6364
CompuServe: (800) 848-8990
Microsoft Network   (800) 386-5550
Prodigy: (800) 776-3449
Check with your local university for more on-line services.

Sample Browsers

Alta Vista: (http://www.altavista.digital.com)
Lycos: (http://www.lycos.cs.cmu.edu)
WebCrawler: (http://www.webcrawler.com)
Yahoo: (http://www.yahoo.com/business/employment/jobs)

SUMMARY

This chapter has discussed the comprehensive job search. It is important that you confirm your impressions about your ideal job. You won't know the accuracy of your researched information until you volunteer in the field, do part-time work in the field, or find a job that will put you around the people doing the type of job you really desire. Only then will you know how you feel about the real job environment. It also takes practice to remember to ask everyone you meet about his or her job. The more jobs you learn about, the more alternative choices you will have.

A large but hidden job market exists out there, and the people you meet through the process of information interviewing can help you uncover it by informing you about potential jobs before they are advertised.

The written exercises that follow serve to increase your ability to network effectively. Exercise 9.1 asks you to identify specific people who are part of your network. Exercise 9.2 suggests that you conduct information interviews. Exercise 9.3 helps you expand information about your job target by using practice information gathering, expert information gathering, and interviewing for employment strategies.

EXERCISES

9.1 Support network checklist

a. Fill in the names of people who might help you (use checklist below).

b. Specifically ask yourself: How can this person help? (Provide information, introduce me to someone, offer advice, write a reference, etc.)

Former employers: ....

Former coworkers: ....

Present employer: ....

Friends: ....

Relatives: ....

Civic group members: ....

Professional association members: ....

Alumni group members: ....

Religious group members: ....

Clients: ....

Counselors: ....

Teachers: ....

Clergy: ....

Neighbors: ....

Classmates: ....

Bankers: ....

Accountants: ....

Financial planners: ....

Insurance agents: ....

Real estate agent: ....

Stockbrokers: ....

Salespeople: ....

Retail store owners: ....

Medical professionals: ....

Other: ....

9.2 Information interviews

Select three individuals who work in fields that are interesting to you, and conduct brief information interviews using the list of sample information interview questions given in this chapter as your guide. Write a brief report of each.

9.3 Personal contact log

Prepare a log of personal contacts (at least five) that you make using the approaches described in this chapter under Information Interviewing and Practicing Information Interviews. Focusing on your own job target, see how much information and how many new contacts you acquire. Use the appropriate format below for each type of contact made.

Name .... Job Target ....

Practice information gathering

Hobby or interest ....

Contact ....

Information gathered as a result of the interview ....

....

....

Other possible contacts ....

Expert information gathering

Occupational interest ....

Contact (who, where employed, how you found this person) ....

....

Information gathered ....

....

New contacts ....

....

Any contradictions ....

....

Conclusions ....

....

Interviewing for employment, apprenticeship, or volunteer experience

Choice of possible work site ....

....

What do you want (job, apprenticeship, volunteer experience)? ....

....

Who is in a position to hire you? ....

Your approach (telephone, letter, in person) ....

Outcomes and follow-up ....

....

9.4 Exercise summary

Write a brief paragraph answering these questions

What did you learn about yourself? How does this knowledge relate to your career/life planning? Did you use the Internet? Was it helpful in locating job information? What was most useful?

TEN

Preparing a Winning Resume

LEARNING OBJECTIVES

At the end of the chapter you will be able to . . .

Understand the advantages of developing a resume

Identify guidelines for resume preparation

Write a resume and cover letter

Every good fitness program includes a chart that indicates visually where you started, where you are currently, and where you are going. In a career fitness program, this chart is called a resume. Eventually, in the course of job hunting, you will be asked to present a resume to a prospective employer. Some career counselors warn that the resume isn't going to get you an interview unless you already have a good contact inside the company; others suggest that a good resume can help you get your foot in the door. These days, a resume can be transmitted electronically via computer to reach thousands of potential employers at once. In any case, your resume will be an essential job search tool. A resume is:

1. A systematic assessment of your skills in terms of a specific job objective.
2. A memory jogger useful in an interview in responding to the following common requests/questions by interviewers:
   a. Tell me about yourself.
   b. Why should I hire you?
   c. What skills do you bring to this job?
3. An aid in filling out application forms.
4. A marketing device used to gain an interview.

This chapter offers guidelines for writing a resume and distributing it electronically. The chapter presents three sample formats: functional, chronological, and a creative combination. Additionally, the importance of cover letters and application forms is addressed. Once you have completed this chapter you will be prepared to compile your own winning resume.

THE RESUME

The purpose of the resume is to get an interview. Like an advertisement, the resume should attract attention, create interest, describe accomplishments, and provoke action. Brevity is essential; one page is best, two are the limit. The resume tells the prospective employer what you can do and have done, who you are, and what you know. It also indicates the kind of job you seek. The resume must provide enough information for the employer to evaluate your qualifications, and it must interest the employer enough so that you will be invited for an interview.

Writing a well-constructed resume requires that your research be completed before compiling the resume. You need to keep in mind the type of employer and position as well as the general job requirements in order to tailor your resume to the specific requirements and personality of the employer. To be most effective, your resume should be designed to emphasize your background as it relates to the job being sought. It should also look neat, clean, and organized. This means word-processed with no errors, and then laser-printed or photocopied on high-quality paper.

By now you should have completed all the necessary research. Utilize the information gathered in Chapter Seven, "Information Integration," and Chapter Nine, "Targeting Your Job Search." Integrate your answers with the categories listed in the resume review on the next page.

Portfolios

The portfolio is an expanded resume. It is usually a folder containing the basic resume and samples of your work related to the job objective. It is a good idea to be storing work samples now. For instance, a marketing specialist will send a potential employer a resume along with fliers, brochures, and ads created in past jobs. For a marketing student with limited experience, the folder could include copies of term papers, proposals completed for classes, and homework assignments related to the job objective. Portfolios are useful to have during information interviews, when you are at association meetings and "networking," or upon request in an interview.

Life is a mirror and gives back to us the reflection of our own self.
Joseph Batten

Resume/portfolio review

Review this information mentally. It will help you to write a complete resume.

A. PERSONAL DATA
1. Name
2. Address
3. Phone

B. CURRENT JOB OBJECTIVE

C. EDUCATION (This category may follow category D, "Work Experience," on your actual resume, depending upon which is more relevant to the position sought.)
1. High school and college
   a. Favorite subjects
   b. Samples of best work in classes related to job objective
   c. Extracurricular interest
   d. Offices held
   e. Athletic achievements
   f. Other significant facts (e.g., honors, awards)
2. Other (military, volunteer, correspondence, summer, languages, technical skills, licenses, and/or credentials)

D. WORK EXPERIENCE (May precede category C, "Education," on actual resume.)

Refer to your experiography or your skills analysis.

Employer

Length of employment

Position

Skills and accomplishments (May be called out in a bulleted list following "Job Objective.")

Samples of best work if relevant

E. PUBLICATIONS
F. ASSOCIATIONS, VOLUNTEER WORK, AND COMMUNITY INVOLVEMENT
G. SPECIAL SKILLS (e.g., language proficiency, computer skills)

Preparation for Composing Your Resume

Although stating an objective is considered optional by some experts (because it can be stated in your cover letter), it is to your advantage to include it on the resume. In actuality, one resume should be designed for each job objective. Remember, there are no jobs titled "anything."

The job objective is a concise and precise statement about the position you are seeking. This may include the type of firm in which you hope to work (e.g., a small, growing company). A clear objective gives focus to your job search and indicates to an employer that you've given serious thought to your career goals. When time does not allow you to develop a resume for each of several different jobs that interest you, the job objective may be emphasized in the cover letter (which will be discussed at the end of this chapter) and omitted from the resume.

A job objective is sometimes referred to as "goal," "professional objective," "position desired," or simply "objective." It can be as specific as "community worker," "personnel assistant," or "junior programmer"; it can be as general as "management position using administrative, communications, and research skills" or "to work as an administrative assistant in a creative atmosphere and have the opportunity to use my abilities." The more specific the objective statement, the better, because a clear objective enables you to focus your resume more directly on that objective. The effect is pointed, dramatic, and convincing.

A resume summarizes your particular background as it relates to a specific job. It summarizes your career objectives, education, work experience, special skills, and interests. Visualize a pyramid or triangle with the job objective at the top and everything beneath it supporting that objective.

In writing the rough draft of your resume, prepare 5" x 8" index cards for each job you've held (see Exhibit 10.A). The index card should contain the following information:

Front of card

1. Name, address, phone number of employer, and immediate supervisor at work site.

2. Dates employed (month/year to month/year).

3. Job title.

4. Skills utilized. (Review the skills discussion, Chapter Five)

Back of card

Duties divided into functional areas.

In choosing information to include in your resume, avoid anything that may not be considered in a positive light or that has no relationship to your ability to do the job (e.g., marital status, number of children, political or religious affiliation, age, photos). When in doubt, leave it out. One clue: In the next chapter you will be given information about illegal questions in an interview. If it's illegal in an interview, then it's unnecessary in a resume.

Put the most relevant information first

Using Action Words

Remember that your writing style communicates the work activity in which you have been involved. Use phrases and document experiences that both involve the reader and make your resume outstanding and active. Following are basic guidelines for selecting your "power" words.

Select "power" words

EXHIBIT 10.A Front and back of resume index card. The format can easily be adapted for use in creating a computer file.

Elaine's Espresso House
555 Stevens Circle   April 1996–December 1997
Roanoke, VA 23640
(540) 555-1211

Supervisor: Position:
Joe Smith   Bookkeeper & Shift Supervisor

Skills Utilized:
Related well with continuous flow of people. Attentive to detail; organized; energetic.
Bilingual—Spanish/English

Functions:

Management	—Coordinated service with customer needs, payroll, scheduled employees.
Communications	—Welcomed guests. Directed staff in performing courteous and rapid service. Responded to and resolved complaints.
Bookkeeping	—Maintained records of financial transactions. Balanced books. Compiled statistical reports.

- Choose short, clear phrases.
- If you use sentences throughout, keep them concise and direct.
- Use the acceptable jargon of the work for which you are applying. Remember: You want your prospective employer to READ your resume.
- Avoid general comments such as "My duties were . . ." or "I worked for . . . ." Begin with action words that concisely describe what your tasks were; for example:
  Implemented new filing system.
  Developed more effective interviewing procedure.
  Evaluated training program for new employees.
- List the results of your activities; for example:
  Reduced office filing by 25 percent.
  Developed interview evaluation summary form.
  Increased efficiency in delivering services.

Action words

Here are some examples of action words that could be used in your resume.

accomplished	evaluated	negotiated
achieved	expanded	organized
analyzed	facilitated	oriented
arranged	guided	planned
built	implemented	processed
controlled	improved	produced
created	increased	proved
demonstrated	initiated	raised profits
designed	inspired	reduced costs
developed	interpreted	researched
directed	invented	sold
effected	led	supervised
encouraged	managed	supported
established	motivated	wrote

For additional action verbs, see the *Identifying Your Skills* section, Chapter Five, including the *Assessing Your Skills* activity.

- Don't dilute your action words with too many extraneous activities. Be SELECTIVE and sell your BEST experiences.
- Target your words on the employer's needs.

Using the Right "Key Phrases"

In many large companies, human resource personnel now scan resumes into computer files and databases for storage and later retrieval. According to a 1995 poll by a management consulting firm, 31 percent of 435 human resource professionals indicated their firms used "resume banks" for recruiting. Many experts say the percentage of large and mid-size companies using such programs is far higher, with employers such as Walt Disney World Company and MCI Communications Corp. leading the way in their use of resume banks. A growing biotechnology firm, Amgen, Inc., receives more than 225 resumes a day, about 60 percent in conventional paper format and 40 percent by e-mail or fax. All end up in an automated tracking system. The manager of employment systems at Amgen, Inc. says automated tracking allows the company to consider all applicants for all available jobs—which is especially important in a growing company. When an opening occurs, employers search their banks and databases for resumes using certain key phrases relevant to the position. For example, a company looking for "B.S., Information Systems, dBase, Lotus 1-2-3," would first retrieve resumes containing these key words.

Depending upon the field in which you hope to work and the type of companies you will apply to, this information may be vital to your writing a resume that gets retrieved during a "key word" search. In such cases, the appearance and style of your resume will be less significant than the manner in which you describe your specific skills: be certain to use concrete nouns to summarize past experience.

References

The expression "References available upon request" is usually sufficient on a resume and is typically placed at the end. Although you don't have to list specific names on the resume, you should have at least three people in mind who can talk about your work habits, your skills, and your accomplishments. When you are job hunting, ask these people in advance if you may use them as references, informing them of your job objective so that they will be prepared if a prospective employer calls. Many college placement centers act as a clearinghouse for the collection of resumes and references. You establish a file and the center sends out your resume and references when you make a request. The placement center often makes this service available for alumni, and it may have reciprocal agreements with other colleges across the country.

THE APPEARANCE OF YOUR RESUME

Resume appearance counts

The appearance of this document is important. Your resume must be typed clearly, spaced well, and visually attractive. Remember that many employers skim only the first page of a resume. Thus it is crucial that your material be strategically placed so that what is most likely to be read is most relevant to the job desired. Employers have been known to receive hundreds of resumes each day, giving them only minutes to review each one. Therefore, even if you must use two pages, the first is more crucial. Experts advise against using a resume preparation service. An employer can usually spot a "canned" resume and might assume that the applicant lacks initiative or self-confidence. The time you spend writing your resume will be time well-spent. It will give you the opportunity to summarize what you have to offer to an employer.

Personal computers and resume writing or word processing software can help turn an average-looking resume into a class act. If possible, store your resume and cover letter on a floppy disk or in hard-drive memory for easy retrieval and updating. Many duplicating shops have personal computers available for an hourly fee.

Although offset printing was once the preferred method of producing resumes, quick copies made at professional copy centers are now acceptable if they are reproduced on high-quality equipment and are clean and free of smudges. Use an attractive bond paper for these copies of your resume; usually a neutral color such as ivory or white is best. Copy centers typically have a wide selection of stationery available. It is often useful to have a career counselor, potential employer, family member, or friend review a draft of your resume before duplicating your final copy. Ask for a careful check for content, format, grammar, spelling, and appearance. Even if you plan to send your resume electronically via computer, make sure it is completely error-free.

ELECTRONIC RESUMES

Whether you prepare your resume yourself or have it prepared professionally, once you have a document to be proud to send to potential employers, you will need to make slight modifications to create the scannable version. Electronic resumes are entered into a resume bank, which means they are subject to electronic, as well as human, scanning. You may need to create two or more versions of your resume, emphasizing various skills and key words.

You will find this process easier if your resume is on computer disc. You are then free to copy it and make changes to the copy. This allows you to keep your hard work safe and protected in the original file. If your resume is prepared professionally, you may also want to have the service prepare an electronic version. They will provide you with a disc containing the file, so you may create the electronic version yourself if you feel competent to do so. The key is to work from a copy—not the original!

Another reason to have your resume on disc is that employers and on-line resume distribution services often have different requirements for file formats and design specifications. The Web site for an on-line resume distribution service or potential employer will provide you with company-specific details; it may also offer assistance in preparing this very important promotional piece about you. The human resource department of a potential employer may also be able to provide you with electronic resume information.

Although it is highly recommended that your "traditional" resume be no more than one page, your electronic resume may be longer. The computer will easily scan more than one page. It uses all the information on your resume to determine if your skills match available positions. The computer searches for key words. Those key words can often be found in a general job description matching the position title for which you are applying. They also appear in classified ads and job postings. Or you may be able to glean some during information interviews. Be sure to write your resume to reflect the skill needs of the position—another reason why you may want to prepare multiple versions of your resume.

Please refer to the accompanying box, "Guidelines for Preparing and Submitting Electronic Resumes," for detailed "how-to" information. You may wish to learn more about electronic resumes. Your career center, many books on the subject, and resume Internet sites (see Chapter Nine) are excellent sources for additional information.

Guidelines for preparing and submitting electronic resumes

- Your resume will be viewed with 80-character lines and 24 lines to a "screen page."
- Use an 8 ½" x 11" page format. (If you plan to fax it, print it on white paper.)
- Use an easy-to-read typeface ("font") such as Times, Helvetica, or Palatino at a point size of 10 or 12.
- Avoid tabs (use the space key), underlines, boxes, columns, italics, and shading.
- Use boldface type and bullets to emphasize words.
- Use key skill words from a job description or advertisement.
- Some resume banks offer "fill-in-the-blank" templates, complete with instructions.
- E-mail a copy of your resume to yourself to see what it looks like. (You can do this from an Internet site that allows you to create your own resume using their format.)

Resume guidelines

NAME
Address
Phone Number

Job Objective

State and describe as specifically as possible. Refer to the *Dictionary of Occupational Titles* for appropriate descriptive vocabulary.

Education

Depending on your job objective and the amount of education you have had, you may want to place this category directly after Job Objective. (However, if your job experience is more relevant to the position being applied for or if your education is not recent, you will want to list job experience *prior* to education.) Most recent education should be listed first. Include relevant credentials and licenses.

Example: As employers, educational institutions are usually more concerned with appropriate degrees than other employers. Include special workshops, noncredit courses, and self-taught skills when they are appropriate to your job objective.

Experience

Describe *functionally* (by activities performed) your experience relevant to the particular job for which you are applying; start with the most relevant and go to the less relevant. Include without distinction actual job experience, volunteer experience, your work on class projects, and school and class offices held. Alternatively, show your experience *chronologically*, listing your most recent professional experience first.

There is no need to stress dates unless they indicate that you have been continuously advancing toward this job objective.

Use action verbs; do not use full sentences, unless you decide to write your resume as a narrative.

Use the *Dictionary of Occupational Titles* to help you describe accurately what you have done, always keeping in mind how your experience relates to your job objective. Remember to use words and skills related to your job objective to describe yourself in the cover letter and during the interview. (See Chapter Five.)

Special Skills

Put this optional category directly after Job Objective if you feel that your professional experience does not adequately reflect the talents you have that best support this job objective.

Examples: Facility with numbers, manual dexterity, patience, workshops you have led, writing ability, self-taught skills, language fluency.

References

Available on request.

(Use references only if you have space and if the names are well known to potential employers.)

TYPES OF RESUMES

To reiterate, there are three general types of resume: functional, chronological, and combination. Comparing the following two sample work experience entries (taken from Exhibits 10.E and 10.K) will give you some idea of the basic difference between functional and chronological resumes, which we referred to in the box on resume guidelines. The next part of this chapter will discuss all three types in detail. The combination resume, as the name implies, is a combination of functional and chronological.

Sample functional entry under professional experience:

- *Budgeting/Financial*
  Analyzed and coordinated payroll recordkeeping, budgeted expenditures, requisitioned supplies, prepared attendance accounting reports, and initiated budget system for $10,000 of instructional monies allocated to the school.

Sample chronological entry under professional experience:

- *Cashier*
  Builders Emporium, Wadsworth, Texas 76199, 1995–1997
  Operated cash register and made change, worked well with public, motivated fellow employees, encouraged customers to buy products.

The Functional Resume

A functional resume presents your experience, skills, and job history in terms of the functions you have actually performed rather than as a simple chronological listing of the titles of jobs you have held. Like any resume, it should be tailored to fit the main tasks and competencies required by the job you are seeking. Essentially, you redefine your past experiences according to the functions in the job for which you are applying. You should select and emphasize those activities from previous employment that relate to the specific job sought and de-emphasize or omit irrelevant background.

For example, an administrative assistant might perform some administration, communication, and clerical functions. A secretary for an elementary school rewrote his resume to highlight these categories. In order to better define the skills used in his secretarial job, he researched the job description of executive secretary and office manager in his school personnel manual and located the description of administrative assistant in the *Dictionary of Occupational Titles*. (See "Suggestions for Job Descriptions" on the next page.) He then compiled his resume to show how his executive secretarial responsibilities related to the administrative assistant position desired. (See the functional resume in Exhibit 10.E, at the end of this chapter.) Review the organizational divisions described in Chapter Seven to assess how your past work or life experience can be described in such categories as marketing, human resources, finance, community services, or research and development.

Suggestions for job descriptions

Descriptions in the *Dictionary of Occupational Titles* and in some personnel manuals provide a source of helpful phrases and statements to use in describing your own job history and experience. The following two descriptions, for example, would be useful to you in composing a functional resume for a job in business. However, you would use only relevant sentences, adapting them to your personal background.

Examples:

OFFICE MANAGER

Coordinates activities of clerical personnel in the organization. Analyzes and organizes office operations and procedures such as word processing, bookkeeping, preparation of payrolls, flow of correspondence, filing, requisitioning of supplies, and other clerical services. Evaluates office production, revises procedures, or devises new forms to improve efficiency of work flow. Establishes uniform correspondence procedures and style practices. Formulates procedures for systematic retention, protection, retrieval, transfer, and disposal of records. Plans office layouts and initiates cost reduction programs. Reviews clerical and personnel records to ensure completeness, accuracy, and timeliness. Prepares activity reports for guidance of management. Prepares employee ratings and conducts employee benefit and insurance programs. Coordinates activities of various clerical departments or workers within department.

ADMINISTRATIVE ASSISTANT

Aids executive in staff capacity by coordinating office services such as personnel, budget preparation and control, housekeeping, records control, and special management studies. Studies management methods in order to improve work flow, simplify reporting procedures, and implement cost reductions. Analyzes unit operating practices, such as recordkeeping systems, forms control, office layout, suggestion systems, personnel and budgetary requirements, and performance standards to create new systems or revise established procedures. Analyzes jobs to delineate position responsibilities for use in wage and salary adjustments, promotions, and evaluation of work flow. Studies methods of improving work measurements or performance standards.

If you are applying for a specific job, ask the human resources department for a copy of the job description; then tailor your resume to the skills listed in that description.

Creative functional resume

Beginning or returning workers who have had no paid experience often find it particularly hard to make their activities sound transferable to the world of work. They dismiss their experience as "academic work" or "homemaking," which they mistakenly think differs markedly from work in business. However, they usually have been performing business functions without realizing

it. People without paid work experience and people returning to the job market after taking time out to be homemakers can persuade employers to recognize their ability and practical experience if they describe their life in categories such as these.

Management

- Coordinated the multiple activities of five people of different ages and varying interests, keeping within tight schedules and continuous deadlines.
- Established priorities for the allocation of available time, resources, and funds.

Office Procedures

- Maintained lists of daily appointments, reminders, items to be purchased, people to be called, tasks to be accomplished.
- Handled all business and personal correspondence—answered and issued invitations, wrote stores about defective merchandise, made hotel reservations.

Personnel

- Recruited, hired, trained, and supervised household staff; negotiated wages.
- Motivated children to assume responsibilities and helped them develop self-confidence.
- Resolved problems caused by low morale and lack of cooperation.

Finances

- Established annual household budget, and monitored costs to stay within expenses.
- Balanced the checkbook and reconciled monthly bank statements.
- Calculated take-home pay of household staff, made quarterly reports to the government on social security taxes withheld.

Purchasing

- Undertook comparison shopping for food, clothing, furniture, and equipment, and purchased at various stores at different times, depending upon best value.
- Planned meals according to savings available at different food stores.
- Shopped for insurance and found lower premiums than current coverage, resulting in substantial savings.

Pros and cons of the functional resume

The functional resume is especially useful if you have limited work experience or breaks in your employment record, or if you are changing fields. You need not include dates or distinguish paid activities from nonpaid volunteer activities. By omitting or de-emphasizing previous employers' names, you downplay any stereotyped assumptions that a prospective employer may make about previous employers (McDonald's, the PTA, a school district). Similarly, highlighting skills and de-emphasizing job titles helps direct the future

employer to the fact that you are someone with specific abilities that may be useful in the present job opening. This format also can emphasize your growth and development.

To use this format effectively, you must be able to identify and write about your achievements. This sometimes requires the assistance of an expert resume writer. Additionally, some employers may prefer resumes that include exact dates and job titles.

Exhibits 10.E, 10.F, 10.G, and 10.H (at the end of this chapter) are examples of functional resumes for various positions.

The Chronological Resume

The chronological resume is the traditional, most often used resume style. It lists your work history in reverse chronological order, meaning the most recent position or occupation is listed first. The work history should include dates employed, job title, job duties, and employer's name, address, and telephone number.

Pros and cons of the chronological resume

The chronological resume is most useful for people with no breaks in their employment record and for whom each new position indicates continuous advancement or growth. Recent high school and college graduates also find this approach simpler than creating a functional resume.

As dates tend to dominate the presentation, any breaks or undocumented years of work may stand out. If your present position is not related to the job you desire, you may be eliminated from the competition by employers who feel that current experience is the most important consideration in reviewing resumes. However, if you emphasize skills in your present job that will be important to the new position, this will be less of a problem.

Exhibits 10.I, 10.J, 10.K, and 10.L (at the end of this chapter) are examples of chronological resumes tailored for various positions.

The Combination Resume

If you have major skills important for success in your desired job in addition to an impressive record of continuous job experience with reputable employers, you can best highlight this double advantage with a *combination* of the functional and chronological styles of resume. This combination style usually lists functions followed by years employed with a list of employers. The combination style also satisfies the employer who wants to see the dates that you were actually employed. See Exhibits 10.M and 10.N.

COVER LETTER GUIDELINES

Want to turn off a prospective employer? Send a resume with no cover letter. Or send a form letter addressed to "Personnel Manager." Or address your letter "Dear Sir," only to have it received by a female manager.

A cover letter is used to announce your availability and introduce the resume. It is probably one of the most important self-advertisements you will write.

The cover letter should indicate you have researched the organization and are clearly interested in a position there. Let the person to whom you are writing know what sources you used and what you know about the firm in the first paragraph—to get his or her attention and show your interest.

You may have heard people say, "It's not *what* you know, but *who* you know that counts." This is only partly true, but nonetheless important. You can often get to know someone with only a little effort. Call, or better yet, visit the organization and talk to people who already hold the job you want. Be tactful and discreet, of course. You're not trying to eject them from the position. Ask about training, environment, salary, and other relevant issues. Then in your cover letter, mention you talked with some of the firm's employees and these discussions increased your interest. You thereby show the reader you took the initiative to personally visit the company and that you "know someone," if only casually. This is all part of "networking," as discussed in Chapter Nine.

Basic principles of letter and resume writing include being self-confident when listing your positive qualities and attributes, writing as one professional to another, and having your materials properly prepared.

First, address your letter to a specific person, name spelled correctly and with the proper title. These details count. Your opening paragraph should contain the "hook." Arouse some work-related interest. Explain (very briefly) why you are writing. How did you become interested in that company? Summarize what you have to offer. Details of your background can show why you should be considered as a job candidate. The self-appraisal that went into preparation of your resume tells what you *can* and *like* to do and where your strengths and interests lie. Your research on the prospective employer should have uncovered the qualifications needed. If your letter promises a good match—meaning your abilities matched with the company's needs—you've attracted attention.

Keep your letter short and to the point. Refer to your resume, highlighting relevant experiences and accomplishments that match the firm's stated needs. Ask for an interview. Indicate when you will be calling to confirm a convenient time for the interview. Let your letter express your individuality but within the context of the employment situation.

The cover letter should be individually typed for each job desired. Always review both cover letter and resume for good margins, clarity, correct spelling, and accurate typing. Appearance does count! Review the sample cover letters in Exhibits 10.P through 10.U.

APPLICATION FORMS

A final type of form, accepted sometimes as a substitute for a resume, is an *application form*. The employment application is a form used by most companies to gain necessary information and to register applicants for work (see Exhibit 10.B). This information becomes a guide to determine a person's

Filling out application forms

1. Fill out the application form in ink—or use a typewriter.

2. Answer every question that applies to you. If a question does not apply or is illegal (see Chapter Eleven) you may write *N/A,* meaning *not applicable,* or draw a line through the space to show that you did not overlook the question.

3. Give your complete address, including zip code.

4. Spell correctly. If you aren't sure how to spell a word, use the dictionary or try to use another word with the same meaning.

5. A question on job preference or "job for which you are applying" should be answered with a specific job title or type of work. Do not write "anything." Employers expect you to state clearly what kind of work you can do.

6. Have a prepared list of schools attended and previous employers. Include addresses and dates of employment.

7. Be prepared to list several good references. It is advisable to ask permission of those you plan to list. Good references include:
   a. A recognized community leader
   b. A former employer or teacher who knows you well
   c. Friends who are established in business

8. When you write or sign your name on the application, use your formal name—not a nickname. Your first name, middle initial, and last name are usually preferred.

9. Be as neat as possible. Employers expect that your application will be an example of your best work.

suitability for both the company and the job that needs filling. You should observe carefully the following guidelines.

You will probably be asked to fill out an employment application form, usually before the interview takes place. Therefore, it is good practice to arrive at the employment office a little ahead of the time of your interview. Bring along a pen and your resume or personal data sheet. You will be asked to provide your name, address, training or education, experience, special abilities, and possibly even your hobbies and interests. Practically all application forms request that you state the job you are seeking and the salary you have received in the past. Most firms require an applicant to complete an application form.

Many times the employer wants to make certain rapid comparisons and needs only to review the completed company employment application forms on file. For example, Ms. Ford needed a stenographer who could type fast. She examined many application forms of people who had word processing skills. *By referring to the same section each time,* she quickly thumbed through dozens of applications, eliminating all candidates who had only average speed. Thus, there was no need for her to examine resumes or read dozens of letters to find out exactly how fast each candidate could type.

Neatness Counts

The way in which an application form has been filled out indicates the applicant's level of neatness, thoroughness, and accuracy. If two applicants seem to have equal qualifications but one's form is carelessly filled out, the application itself might tilt the balance in favor of the other applicant. Unless your handwriting is especially clear, print or type all answers. Look for "please print" instructions on the form.

Sometimes you may apply for a job by mail, and a form will be sent to you. The application form should be carefully, completely, and accurately filled out. You should then return it to the company, and may also attach a copy of your resume. When you have completed the application, go over it again. Have you given the information asked? When an item asked for is not applicable, have you written in *N/A?*

Sample employment application.   **EXHIBIT 10.B**

Date _____

PERSONAL INFORMATION:

Name _____
          Last   First   Middle

Address_____
            Street   City   State   Zip

Telephone Number (_____) _____   Are you over 17 years of age? ☐ Yes ☐ No

POSITION WANTED:

Job Title _____ Date Available _____ Salary Desired _____

Check any that apply: ☐ Full Time   ☐ Part Time   ☐ Day Shift   ☐ Night Shift

EDUCATION:

Begin with high school; include any military school you may have attended:

NAME OF SCHOOL	LOCATION OF SCHOOL	DEGREE OR COURSE OF STUDY

List any Academic Honors or Professional Associations:
_____

WORK EXPERIENCE:

List last three employers. Start with the current or most recent.

Name and Address of Employer _____

Dates Worked _____ Pay _____ Reason for leaving _____

Job Title _____ Job Description _____

Name and Address of Employer _____

Dates Worked _____ Pay _____ Reason for leaving _____

Job Title _____ Job Description _____

Name and Address of Employer _____

Dates Worked _____ Pay _____ Reason for leaving _____

Job Title _____ Job Description _____

Computer Skills (describe)   Typing Speed _____ *wpm*
      (if applicable)   (if applicable)

Do you have any physical condition or handicap that may limit your ability to perform the job applied for? ☐ Yes ☐ No
If yes, what can be done to accommodate your limitation?

Have you ever been convicted of a felony? ☐ Yes ☐ No If yes, give kind and date.
A conviction will not necessarily disqualify you from employment.

Are you legally entitled to work in the U.S.? ☐ Yes ☐ No Can you provide proof of citizenship after employment? ☐ Yes ☐ No

Are you a veteran? ☐ Yes ☐ No If yes, give dates:

List the names of three references whom we may contact who have knowledge of your skills, talents, or technical knowledge:

	(1)	(2)	(3)
Name and Relationship (*Supervisor, Teacher, etc.*)			
Address			
Telephone & Area No.			

I certify, by my signature below, that any false or omitted important facts in my answers on this application may be cause for dismissal.

_____
Applicant's Signature   *Date*

SUMMARY

This chapter has provided diverse examples of resumes, cover letters, letters of introduction, and application form reminders. Putting the resume together is now your job. Use the exhibits and ideas in the following written exercises as well as the tips throughout the chapter to assist you in getting your resume into shape.

The written exercises that follow will enable you to prepare a resume as well as critique it. Exercises 10.1 and 10.2 help you to organize pertinent information about yourself. Exercise 10.3 asks you to draft a resume. Exercise 10.4 reminds you to save copies of work for a portfolio. Exercises 10.5 and 10.6 provide guidelines for critiquing your own resume and obtaining valuable feedback from others. Exercise 10.7 reminds you to write a cover letter and get feedback before sending it.

EXERCISES

10.1 Resume review sheet

Fill in the boxed review sheet on the following page. The answers will help you prepare a complete resume.

10.2 Create a card file

Create a card file (or a computer file) describing your work experiences, using Exhibit 10.A as a guide. This gives you a chance to write your job tasks in functional terms.

10.3 Write your resume

Choose the format desired and write your own resume, referring to Exercise 10.1 for data. Refer to the suggestions in the chapter and the samples that follow this chapter.

10.4 Save sample work for a portfolio

Start now to keep a folder of the best work you have done in work-related classes and past jobs, internships, and volunteer positions.

Resume/portfolio review sheet

A. PERSONAL DATA

   1. Name ....

   2. Address ....

   3. Phone ....

B. CURRENT JOB OBJECTIVE ....

C. EDUCATION

   1. High school and college ....

      a. Favorite subjects ....

      b. Work samples ....

      c. Extracurricular interests ....

      d. Offices held ....

      e. Athletic achievements ....

      f. Other significant facts (e.g., honors, awards) ....

   2. Other (military, volunteer, correspondence, summer, languages, technical skills, licenses and/or credentials) ....

D. WORK EXPERIENCE

Refer to your experiography or your skills analysis.

   1. Employer ....

      Length of employment ....

      Position ....

      Skills/accomplishments/work samples ....

   2. Employer ....

      Length of employment ....

      Position ....

      Skills/accomplishments/work samples ....

   3. Employer ....

      Length of employment ....

      Position ....

      Skills/accomplishments/work samples ....

E. PUBLICATIONS ....

F. ASSOCIATIONS, SPECIAL SKILLS, AND COMMUNITY INVOLVEMENT ....

G. REFERENCES (Do not include specific names on resume, but do homework regarding possible references *now*.)

10.5 Critique your resume

Use the resume checklist and critique form (Exhibit 10.C) to evaluate your resume.

EXHIBIT 10.C

Resume checklist and critique form.

	STRONG	AVERAGE	WEAK	PLANS FOR IMPROVEMENT
1. *Resume format.* Does it say "READ ME"?				
2. *Appearance.* Is it brief? Did you use an interesting layout? Type clearly? Use a correct format?				
3. *Length.* Are the key points concise?				
4. *Significance.* Did you select your most relevant experiences?				
5. *Communication.* Do your words give the "visual" impression you want? Is the job objective clearly stated?				
6. *Conciseness.* Does your information focus on the experiences that qualify you for the position?				
7. *Completeness.* Did you include all important information? Have you made a connection between the job desired and your experience?				
8. *Reality.* Does the resume represent you well enough to get you an interview?				
9. *Skills.* Does your resume reflect the skills necessary for the job?				

10.6 Ask others to critique your resume

- Ask other people to give you feedback about your resume (e.g., career counselors, people who have been receptive to you during informational interviews, teachers, friends, etc.)
- Use the following checklist of "Dos and Don'ts" to help others give you feedback.

EXHIBIT 10.D

Resume "DOs and DON'Ts"

DO

- focus your job objective to illustrate specific skills and responsibilities.
- interest your reader with significant employment, education, accomplishments, and skills.
- present yourself positively, honestly, and assertively.
- keep the resume to no more than two pages.
- use an attractive and readable layout, including top quality paper, for a professional appearance.
- have your resume carefully proofread prior to its final printing.

DON'T

- be too wordy or use buzzwords and unnecessary verbiage.
- provide personal data on your age, race, marital status, religion, or other privacy issues.
- suggest abilities or objectives beyond your reach or qualifications.
- make reference to a desired salary or income.
- state a reason for leaving a previous job.
- provide names of references in the resume.

10.7 Write a cover letter

Referring to Exhibits 10.P–10.U, write a cover letter to accompany your resume. Ask others to critique it, as you did in Exercise 10.5 with your resume.

10.8 Exercise summary

Write a brief paragraph answering these questions

What did you learn about yourself? How does this knowledge relate to your career/life planning? How do you feel?

EXHIBIT 10.E

Functional resume for administrative assistant position.

SAMUEL GILDAR
P.O. Box 1111
Cincinnati, Ohio 14528

Day Phone: (513) 555-1212
E-mail: sgildar@aol.com

GOALS

To work as an administrative assistant in a creative
atmosphere and have the opportunity to use my abilities.

SUMMARY OF EXPERIENCE

Ten years of increasing responsibility in the area of office management involving organization, problem solving, finances, and public relations.

MANAGEMENT

Initiated and organized procedures used in the office, coordinated activities of clerical personnel, and formulated procedures for systematic retention, protection, transfer, and disposal of records. Coordinated preparation of operating reports, such as time and attendance records, of performance data. Reviewed, composed, and answered correspondence. Directed services, such as maintenance, repair, supplies, mail, and files. Aided executive by coordinating office services, such as personnel, budget preparation and control, housekeeping, records control, and special management studies.

PUBLIC RELATIONS

Coordinated communication with state, county, and district officials as well as district and local employees, student body, staff members, and parents in our community. Planned and coordinated social functions for school, staff, and two social clubs. Promoted sales of jewelry, gourmet foods, and liquors in sales-related jobs.

PROBLEM SOLVING

Made decisions according to district policy in the absence of the principal. Worked under constant pressure and interruption while attending to student problems regarding their health and welfare. Liaison between school and community, resolving as many problems as possible before referring them to superior.

BUDGETING/FINANCIAL

Analyzed and coordinated payroll recordkeeping, budgeted expenditures, requisitioned supplies, prepared attendance accounting reports, and initiated budget system for $10,000 of instructional monies allocated to the school.

CREATIVE

Created newscopy and layouts using PageMaker and QuarkXPress. Designed fliers, posters, calendars, and bulletins sent home from school to parents. Personal hobbies include ceramics, oil painting, sculpting, and interior design.

EMPLOYERS

Cincinnati Unified School District
1115 Old School Road
Cincinnati, Ohio 14528
(513) 555-2345

Cincinnati Blue Cross
5900 Erwin Road
Cincinnati, Ohio 14526
(513) 555-3698

EXHIBIT 10.F

Functional resume for management position.

OLIVIA MARTINEZ
2406 Adams Avenue
Los Angeles, CA 90025
213-555-0862
e-mail: om@msn.com

PROFESSIONAL OBJECTIVE:

Management position utilizing administrative, communications, and research skills.

SUMMARY OF SKILLS:

Administrative

Designed and implemented evaluation program for compensatory education project.

Coauthored grant proposal

Served as liaison between volunteers and university administration

Directed registration program and coordinated staff at registration desk, Western Psychological Association Annual Convention, 1996

As student senator, initiated Earth Day activities and helped establish faculty evaluation program

Communication

Planned discussion sections, provided guidance to students, cowrote and graded examinations for undergraduate courses in developmental psychology and statistics

Prepared tutorials in science and study methods and offered educational guidance to economically disadvantaged high school students

Participated in human growth seminar led by clinical psychologist, trained in therapy methods, and helped devise therapy program for young people

Research

Designed and conducted study investigating memory in 4-year-olds.

Studied mathematical structure underlying Piagetian developmental theory.

Implemented computer simulation model of certain cognitive behaviors of children. Analyzed and categorized data for cognitive anthropologist and psychologist.

EDUCATION:

M.A., August 1997 Developmental Psychology, University of California, Los Angeles, California. California State Graduate Fellow, National Science Foundation Honorable Mention.

B.A., 1995 Psychology, University of California, Irvine. *Summa Cum Laude*, Outstanding Scholar, Honor Scholar.

EXPERIENCE:

Teaching Assistant and Reader. Psychology Department, University of California, Los Angeles, August 1994–June 1997.

Administrative Assistant. Psychology Department, California State University, Fullerton, February–June 1993.

Business Manager, Education Motivation. Community Projects Office, University of California, Irvine, August 1991–January 1992.

Research Assistant. Departments of German and Russian, University of California, Irvine, October 1990–June 1991.

REFERENCES WILL BE FURNISHED UPON REQUEST

EXHIBIT 10.G

Functional resume for a teacher changing careers.

STACY L. MOLLARD

1001 Gainsborough Street
Chicago, IL 60664

312-555-3581 (home)
312-555-4343 (work)

POSITION OBJECTIVE:

Employee Training Specialist

QUALIFICATIONS IN BRIEF:

B.A. in English, Mundelein College, Chicago.

Six years' elementary teaching with experience in communications, human relations, instruction, and supervision.

Bilingual.

EXPERIENCE SUMMARY:

COMMUNICATIONS:

Conducted staff development workshops. Presented new curriculum plans to parent groups, sent periodic progress reports to parents, and developed class newsletter. Presented workshops in parent effectiveness training at state and local conferences.

HUMAN RELATIONS:

Directed effective problem solving/conflict resolution between individual students and student groups; initiated program of student self-governance; acted as liaison between families of diverse cultural, ethnic, and economic backgrounds and school personnel/services; and conducted individual and group conferences to establish rapport with parents and discuss student progress.

INSTRUCTION:

Developed instructional modules to solve specific learning problems; developed instructional audiovisual materials; used audiovisual equipment such as overhead, opaque, and movie projectors and audio and videocassettes; did extensive research in various curricula; served as a member of curriculum development committee; introduced new motivational techniques for students.

CURRENTLY EMPLOYED:

Austin Elementary School, Chicago, Illinois

COMMUNITY INVOLVEMENT:

Board member, Chicago Community Services Center

Allocations Committee, Chicago United Way

REFERENCES:

Available upon request

EXHIBIT 10.H

Functional resume for high school graduate.

RICHARD ROTH
66 Cheyenne Dr.
Billings, Montana 46060
(712) 555-1212

Professional Objective

Administrative assistant position utilizing administrative, bookkeeping, and communication skills.

Summary of Skills

Administrative
Answered phones, scheduled appointments, sorted mail, filed
Implemented new filing system
Software programs used include ClarisWorks 3.0, Lotus 1-2-3, Word, WordPerfect 6.0, dBase, Quicken, and Windows 97
Maintained appearance of office

Bookkeeping
Handled cash register
Closed cash register at the end of the evening
Recorded cash transactions

Communications
Customer service, peer counselor for 2 years
Assisted in dental office
Demonstrated proper dental hygiene to children
Fed, clothed, and entertained children

Education
Billings Community College, Transfer Program, 1995 to present, Dean's List
Billings High School, graduated 1995

Experience
Lombard Medical Group, Billings, MT, October 1995–present
Sandy Murphree, Billings, MT, 1990–present
Oakbrook Dental, Billings, MT, June 1995–October 1995
Fantastic Sam's, Billings, MT, June 1994–August 1994
Blue Wave, Billings, MT, December 1993–June 1994

References will be furnished upon request.

EXHIBIT 10.1

Chronological resume for high school graduate with limited experience.

JOHN JONES   1050 Baez Street
(602) 555-1221   Mesa, AZ 85201

OBJECTIVE: An entry-level position as a *(list one or two related job titles)*
                   that affords opportunities to learn and progress.

SUMMARY: Three years of part-time and summer employment related to
                   sales, public contact, and accounting while attending high
                   school.

EDUCATION: *(List your most recent education first.)*
                   1996 Red Mountain High School, Mesa, Arizona
                   Graduated with emphasis in mathematics and business.
                   Courses included:

Word processing	Trigonometry
Excel	Geometry
English	Business math
Journalism	Accounting principles
Algebra	

EXPERIENCE: *(List most recent experience first.)*
                   1996–1997 Mesa General Store, Mesa, Arizona

                   <u>Salesperson</u>. Sold apparel in men's and children's depart-
                   ments.

                   1995–1996 Tower Records & Video, Mesa, Arizona

                   <u>Counterperson</u>. Assisted customer selections. Handled mone-
                   tary transactions.

                   1993–1995 Miscellaneous employment: babysat for four
                   families with one to four children. Stayed with children week-
                   ends and while parents were on vacation, and assumed full
                   responsibility for normal household routines.

HONORS: *(If you had a high grade point average, include it. List offices
                   held in a student or community organization. List publications.
                   If none of these apply, omit this section from your resume.)*

ACTIVITIES: Future Business Managers Association, Journalism Club,
                   Student Tutoring Association, Young Republicans Club

EXHIBIT 10.J

Chronological resume for office management position.

THUY NGUYEN

532 Castilian Court   (206) 799-1212 (Home)
Seattle, Washington 98102   (206) 555-1212 (Work)

OCCUPATIONAL OBJECTIVE:

A position as office manager leading to increased responsibilities for business operations.

SUMMARY OF QUALIFICATIONS:

Three years of increasingly responsible experience in different positions.

BOOKKEEPER   Hungry Hunter and El Torito Restaurants
                                                Seattle, WA 1996 to present

Kept records of financial transactions, entering them in computer. Balanced books and compiled reports to show statistics, such as cash receipts and expenditures, accounts payable and receivable, and other items pertinent to operation of business. Calculated employee wages from time cards and updated computerized records.

RESTAURANT GREETER   Hungry Hunter Restaurant
                                            Thousand Oaks, CA 1994–1995

Welcomed guests, seated them in dining area, maintained quality of facilities. Directed others in performing courteous and rapid service; also assisted in settling complaints. Related well with the continuous flow of people, coordinating the service with customers' needs.

SPECIAL ACCOMPLISHMENTS:

National Forensic League, vice president (third place, statewide oratory competition); Athletic Association (gymnastic team); Honor Roll and Dean's List; Alpha Gamma Sigma; *Who's Who Among American High School Students,* 1993–1994.

EDUCATION:

Seattle Pacific University, Seattle, WA

Majoring in Business Administration

GPA: 3.5 on a 4.0 scale

REFERENCES:

Available upon request

EXHIBIT 10.K

Chronological resume for bank teller position.

ELEANOR RUTLEDGE
3388 North Dallas
Wadsworth, Texas 77065
909-555-0026

JOB OBJECTIVE: A position as a bank teller that offers opportunities to learn and progress.

EDUCATION: 1997—Glencoe College, Dallas, Texas
Courses included:

Accounting	Sociology 1
Business Computers	English 1A

1994–1997—Wadsworth High School, Wadsworth, Texas.
Courses included:

Windows 95	Algebra
English	Geometry
Public Speaking	

SPECIAL SKILLS: Facility with numbers, manual dexterity, patience, excellence in telephone communications, organization of fundraisers for church group.

EXPERIENCE: 1995–1996—Cashier, Builders Emporium, Wadsworth, Texas. Operated cash register and made change, worked well with public, motivated fellow employees, encouraged customers to buy products.

1992–1995—Miscellaneous employment: babysat for local families; assumed full responsibility while parents were away, helped children with their homework.

REFERENCES: Available upon request

EXHIBIT 10.L

Chronological resume for community worker position.

SARITA SANDHA
980 Victory Blvd.
Brooklyn, NY 11321
(405) 555-4150

JOB OBJECTIVE:	**Public Representative or Community Service Worker**
SUMMARY OF QUALIFICATIONS:	Six years' experience in public relations, media work, and writing press releases and newsletters. Organized concerts, rallies, walk-a-thons, and volunteer-a-thons. Basic qualifications in office procedures: phone networking, word processing, mailing, leafletting, outreach, and public speaking.
EDUCATION:	**Brooklyn College, currently attending, 1996–present** Sociology major. Additional specialized institute training at Loyola Marymount University in social organizing. **Alemany High School, graduated 1993** Two years as teacher's aide in New York City School System. Interrelated with a variety of cultural groups.
EXPERIENCE:	**1993–1996 Community service organizations in New York** Organized, educated, persuaded, created social change, and performed security work. **1991–1993 Self-employed** Managed and maintained family residence. **1990–1991 Receptionist and secretary** Interviewed applicants for positions in sales and maintained records.
SPECIAL SKILLS:	Interact easily with diverse people while under pressure. Knowledge of fund-raising practices. Self-motivated. Experienced in analyzing and working with issues and strategies underlying a particular campaign. Computer literate.
REFERENCES:	Available upon request

EXHIBIT 10.M

Combination resume for sales executive position.

JOHN BENNETT
304 Amen Street
Columbia, South Carolina 29260

(803) 555-3692 (w)
(803) 555-1126 (h)
E-mail: jben@msn.com

OBJECTIVE

MARKETING DIRECTOR

SALES PROMOTION

Designed and supervised sales promotion projects for large business firms and manufacturers, mostly in the electronics field. Originated newspaper, radio, and television advertising. Coordinated sales promotion with public relations and sales management. Analyzed market potentials and developed new techniques to increase sales effectiveness and reduce sales costs. Created sales training manuals.

As sales executive and promotion consultant, handled a great variety of accounts. Sales potentials in these firms varied from $100,000 to $5 million per annum. Raised the volume of sales in many of these firms 25 percent within the first year.

SALES MANAGEMENT

Hired and supervised sales staff on local, area, and national bases. Established branch offices throughout the United States. Developed uniform systems of processing orders and maintaining sales records. Promoted new products, as well as improved sales of old ones. Developed sales training program. Devised a catalog system involving inventory control to facilitate movement of scarce stock between branches.

MARKET RESEARCH

Originated and supervised market research projects to determine sales potential, as well as need for advertising. Wrote detailed reports and recommendations describing each step in distribution, areas for development, and plans for sales improvement.

SALES

Retail and wholesale. Direct sales to consumer, jobber, and manufacturer. Hard goods, small metals, and electrical appliances.

EMPLOYERS

1995–Present	B. B. Bowen Sales Development Co., Columbia, South Carolina	Sales Executive
1993–1995	James Bresher Commercial and Industrial Sales Research Corp., Oakland, California	Senior Sales Promotion Manager
1990–1993	Dunnock Brothers Electronics Co., San Francisco, California	Order Clerk, Salesworker, Sales Manager

EDUCATION

University of California, Berkeley, B.S.; Major: Business Administration

REFERENCES AVAILABLE UPON REQUEST

EXHIBIT 10.N

Combination resume for programmer trainee position.

ALBERT CHAN
111 East Maple
Minneapolis, Minnesota
(508) 866-1592

JOB OBJECTIVE: Applications programmer trainee

QUALIFICATIONS   Flowcharted, coded, tested, and debugged interactive
BY EXPERIENCE: programs for the HP3000. Created a system of five COBOL pro-
                        grams from a system problem statement and flowchart. Built a
                        KSAM file for use by the system. Designed system flowcharts
                        and wrote other documentation for improved payroll system
                        for previous employer, as Systems Analysis course project.

                        Tutored students in visual BASIC and COBOL, working with
                        Hispanics, Vietnamese, and reentering adults, as well as other
                        students.

                        Currently searching a bibliographic database as a volunteer
                        at Minneapolis Public Library and designed library's web
                        page.

EDUCATION: 1997 Associate in Science in Computer Science,
                        Minneapolis Central College.

                        3.6 GPA in computer science classes.

                        1996 B.A. in English, Florida Southern College.

                        Graduate work in research methods.

                        Supported self through college by security work at various
                        firms. Gained secret clearance while at IBM Federal System
                        Division.

SPECIAL SKILLS: Attentive to detail, organized, work well with little supervision,
                        enterprising, enjoy problem solving and interacting with others
                        to plan projects, work well under pressure, able to see relation-
                        ships between abstract ideas, good at communication, con-
                        cise.

COMMUNITY SERVICE   Organized CROP Walks (fund-raisers for Church World Service),
EXPERIENCE: which resulted in raising $6,000 in 1994 and $10,000 in 1995.

                        Chaired the planning committee, recruited members, mapped
                        walk route.

                        Obtained parade permits and business tax exemptions.

                        Wrote press releases and walkers' instruction sheets.

REFERENCES: Available upon request

EXHIBIT 10.0

A poorly constructed resume. See corrected version following.

Omit entirely ➜ **❶** PROFESSIONAL EXPERIENCE AND TRAINING OF SARA CRANE: SOCIAL CASE WORKER

Place name, address, phone on top of page in correct format ➜ **❷** 4234 S. Platt Avenue, Salt Lake City, Utah 84100 (801) 765-4321

List as job objective, with specific summary ➜ **❸** Social Case Worker with RN degree wants a responsible position with a large medical firm that could benefit from my experience in both nursing and social work.

EXPERIENCE

Edit and highlight key responsibilities ➜ **❹** 1990–present . . . Family caseworker. Working through Parker General Hospital Services in Salt Lake. Worked directly with families at their homesites. Met with family and formulated a plan after consultation and comprehensive investigation of needs. Developed assistance and support as appropriate with follow-up services.

Same as #4 ➜ **❺** 1985–90 . . . RN and convalescent services. Grandjunction, Utah. treating patients with disablties. Reviewed financial aspects and fee payments, all inpatient and outpatient services, and full family participation in health program to ensure cooperation and support.

EDUCATION

Omit years (if over 10) and reduce excess words ➜ 1986–89 . . . Bachelor of Science. Social Work. BRIGHAM YOUNG School of Social Work. Training in all areas of social work including internships in pediatrics, psychiatric, rehabilitation, and gerontology sections.

❻

1982–85 . . . Registered Nurse. Baker College, Salt Lake City, Utah. General nursing curriculum including family health concerns. Took additional courses in specialized nursing for retired patients and also advanced psychiatric techniques. I realized that my experience and interests were becoming directed into social work.

PROFESSIONAL AFFILIATIONS
The National Association of Case and Social Workers

Too wordy and unrelated to job objective. Edit to highlight language ability. ➜

INTERESTS
❼ Travel and reading. Conversational abilities in Spanish and French including reading knowledge. Good cook and enjoy theater productions. Any references regarding my education or work experience may be requested at any time. **❽**

Separate and edit ➜

A corrected resume (from Exhibit 10.O)

SARA CRANE
4234 S. Platt Avenue
Salt Lake City, Utah 84100
(801) 765-4321

JOB OBJECTIVE

Social Caseworker utilizing skills developed as a Registered Nurse and Financial Planner

EXPERIENCE

Family Caseworker. Family General Hospital, Salt Lake City, Utah, 1990–Present.

Report to Social Services Director of largest family assistance program in Salt Lake City, attached to hospital intake services. Duties include:
- interviewing family members at the hospital and in their homes to determine needs.
- investigating claims and proposing plans for assistance.
- counseling and guiding families in special circumstances, including personal and health issues.
- providing follow-up treatment and reports.

Convalescent Service as an RN. Grandjunction Hospital, Grandjunction, Utah, 1985–90.

Reported to Health Services Center with following responsibilities:
- interviewed patients' families to determine financial capabilities.
- arranged fee structures.
- planned outpatient plan and referral services.
- counseled families for inpatient and/or convalescent needs.

EDUCATION

Bachelor of Science, Social Work, Brigham Young University, School of Social Work, Provo, Utah.
Internships in pediatric, psychiatric, rehabilitation, and gerontology sections.

Registered Nurse, Baker College, Salt Lake City, Utah.
Full training in general nursing with specialization in psychiatric nursing. Workshops in family health led to social work career path.

SPECIAL SKILLS/AFFILIATIONS

Fluency in Spanish and French. Membership in the National Association of Case and Social Workers.

References available upon request.

EXHIBIT 10.P

Resume cover letter guidelines.

Address
City, State Zip
Date

Name of Person
Company Name
Street Address or P.O. Box
City, State Zip

Salutation: (Dear M... ....: or Greetings:)

THE FIRST PARAGRAPH SHOULD INDICATE WHAT JOB YOU ARE INTER-ESTED IN AND HOW YOU HEARD ABOUT IT. USE THE NAMES OF CON-TACT PERSONS HERE, IF YOU HAVE ANY.

SAMPLE ENTRY Your employment advertisement in Tuesday's News Chronicle indicating an opening for an administrative assistant is of special interest to me. Mary Smith, who is employed with your firm, suggested I write to you. I have heard that Rohn Electronics is a growing company and needs dynamic employees who want to learn and contribute to the firm.

THE SECOND PARAGRAPH SHOULD RELATE YOUR EXPERIENCE, SKILLS, AND BACKGROUND TO THE PARTICULAR POSITION. REFER TO YOUR ENCLOSED RESUME FOR DETAILS AND HIGHLIGHT THE SPE-CIFIC SKILLS AND COMPETENCIES THAT COULD BE USEFUL TO THE COMPANY.

SAMPLE ENTRY During the last five years, I worked as office manager. In this position, I improved office efficiency by investigating and selecting word processing equipment. I understand that your opening includes responsibilities for supervising and coordinating word processing procedures with your home office. I was able to reduce my firm's operating costs over 30 percent by selecting the best equipment for our purposes.

THE THIRD PARAGRAPH SHOULD INDICATE YOUR PLANS FOR FOL-LOW-UP CONTACT AND THAT YOUR RESUME IS ENCLOSED.

SAMPLE ENTRY I would appreciate the opportunity to apply my skills on behalf of your company. For your examination, I have enclosed a resume indicating my education and work experience. I will call your office early next week to determine a convenient time for an appointment to further discuss possible employment opportunities.

Sincerely,

NOTE: Don't forget to sign the letter.

Your first and last name
Enclosure (or Attachment)

EXHIBIT 10.Q

Cover letter for community health worker position.

March 4, 1998

Mr. Harvey J. Finder
Executive Director
Lung Association of Alma County
1717 Opportunity Way
Santa Ana, California 92706

Dear Mr. Finder:

I am interested in the position of community health education program coordinator
with the Lung Association of Alma County. I feel that my education, skills, and desire
to work in this area make me a strong candidate for this position.

My education has helped me develop sound analytical abilities and has exposed me
to the health care field. My involvement with health care and community organizations has provided me with a working knowledge of various public and private health
institutions, which has increased my ability to communicate effectively with health
care professionals, patients, and the community at large. This combination of education and exposure has stimulated my interest in seeking a career in the health field.

Please review the enclosed resume and contact me at your convenience regarding a
personal interview. If I do not hear from you in the next week, I will contact you. I
look forward to talking with you.

Sincerely yours,

Denise M. Hunter
18411 Anticipation Drive
Northridge, California 91330
(213) 555-0217

Encl.

EXHIBIT 10.R

Cover letter for a teacher with business background.

532 Glendora Avenue
Anytown, Indiana 45420
April 1, 1998

Ms. Joan Addeman
Director of Personnel
ABC Corporation
Anytown, MO 90000

Dear Ms. Addeman:

I am applying for the administrative assistant position currently available at your firm. I have been impressed for some time with the outstanding reputation that ABC Corporation holds in our community.

As you read my resume, please note that my twelve years of business experience directly relate to the needs of your company. One of my greatest assets is seven years in motivational psychology related to personnel management and public school teaching. I am aware that strength in business and management is considered important in your firm, and I would like the opportunity to discuss with you, at your earliest convenience, how we might work together for our mutual benefit.

Enclosed is my resume for your review. I will telephone your secretary next week to see when we might set up an appointment to further discuss the administrative assistant position and any other ways that I could serve your corporation.

Sincerely,

Gerald Burnes

Encl: Resume

EXHIBIT 10.S

Cover letter for electronic technician position.

412 Melbrook Avenue
Omaha, Nebraska 77050
June 17, 1998

Mr. Lloyd Johnson
Sonat Technical Supervisor
Lear Electronic Company
1229 Van Owen
Knoxville, TN 37917

Dear Mr. Johnson:

I am interested in working for your company as an electronics technician in the field of systems installation and calibration.

During my tour of duty in the service, I became acquainted with many of your electronic systems aboard ship and was extremely impressed with their design and documentation. I have since pursued a course of studies at Hastings College to increase my competence in the field of electronics. For these reasons, I feel I would be an asset to your company.

I have enclosed a copy of my resume for your consideration. I will contact you by telephone next week to set up a meeting to discuss employment opportunities with your company.

Sincerely yours,

Emilio Reyna

Encl.

EXHIBIT 10.T

Cover letter for public relations position.

1234 Evanston Avenue
Cambridge, IL 61238
May 16, 1997

Mr. Harrison MacBuren
Director of Personnel
North Hills Mall
Cambridge, IL 61238

Dear Mr. MacBuren:

I am very interested in the position currently available in your public relations department for an assistant to the director of public relations.

As you can see by my resume, my previous administrative experience would be a definite asset to your company. I feel that a vital part of any public relations job is the ability to deal with people. This is a skill I have acquired through many years of volunteer work.

I would like to meet with you to discuss how we might work together for our mutual benefit. I will be contacting you within the week to arrange a convenient meeting time.

Sincerely,

George Herounian

Encl.

EXHIBIT 10.U

Cover letter for marketing manager position.

1736 D Street NW
Washington, D.C. 20006
(202) 555-8192
May 1, 1997

Ms. Emma Major, President
Vendo Corporation
1742 Surf Drive
Fort Lauderdale, Florida 33301

Dear Ms. Major:

I was intrigued by the write-up about your new portable vending centers in *Sales Management* magazine. I think it is an extremely good idea.

As you will note from the enclosed resume, my marketing, planning, and sales management experience could be of great assistance to you at this early stage in your project. Enclosed are some specific marketing ideas you might like to review. I would like to make arrangements to meet with you in Florida during the week of May 15 to discuss some of these ideas.

Because of my familiarity with the types of locations and clients you are seeking, I am sure that if we were able to work together in this new venture, the results would reflect my contribution.

I am looking forward to meeting with you and will call next week to arrange for an appointment.

Very truly yours,

Janet Perrill

Encl.

EXHIBIT 10.V

Letter of introduction.

TO WHOM IT MAY CONCERN:

This will introduce Mary Smith, a trusted and valued member of my staff for the past two and a half years.

During this time she has held a key position, performing a variety of secretarial tasks, as well as having full charge of the ordering procedures, maintenance work, and updating in our career resources library. She is keen at spotting deficiencies and was instrumental in developing a more efficient system of updating our materials.

She has been recognized by other members of the staff, including the counselors and our program director, the dean of student personnel, as being outstanding in poise, appearance, and reliability. Additionally, and probably most important, she has been exceptionally effective in working with the students, faculty, and professionals who use the resources of our center.

Mary is a good organizer, capable of dealing with concepts and goals and devising systems approaches to problem solving. She is loyal and discreet in dealing with unusual situations and those calling for confidentiality.

If there is anything more you feel you would like to discuss regarding Mary's qualifications, please feel free to contact me.

Very truly yours,

Her Past Employer

ELEVEN

Interviewing Successfully

nce you begin to feel comfortable with the notion of networking and practice interviewing, you are ready to begin preparing for the "Olympic Finals"—the interview.

BEFORE THE INTERVIEW

Here are the three most important tips to take into consideration as you approach your first interview or refine your current interviewing style: *prepare, prepare, prepare.*

Some of the best preparation for the interview occurs when you research the prospective employer. Your goal is to show the employer why you will be the best person for the job, relating your personal strengths and past accomplishments to this particular enterprise. Specifically, you want to tell the employer how you can help with current problems or function as a valuable member of the organization. To find out more about a prospective employer and the job you're interviewing for, call or write the organization to request a current publication, such as an annual report, that describes the organization, along with the job description. You may find recent newspaper or magazine articles about the company in your library's computerized retrieval system or

through such computer networks as Prodigy, America Online, or CompuServe. Also refer to Internet sources in Chapter Nine for company information locations on the World Wide Web. If the firm does business with the government, you may also find relevant information in the library's government section.

Before the interview, or at least early into it, try to find out what the essential responsibilities of the job are. Make a mental note of them, and throughout the interview, feed back the kind of information from your background that shows you can handle these responsibilities.

Don't let a formal job description disqualify you for a job. Remember that job descriptions are only guidelines, and, once in a job, you are allowed to imprint your own style. Additionally, it is expected that over 50 percent of the work in any job is learned on the job. Thus, your ability to express what your skills are, how you can contribute to the company, and your willingness to learn new skills is as important as being able to do each task listed in the job description. In fact, if you can already do each task described, you might be labeled as overqualified and not get the job!

Your resume and cover letter become the written and mental outline upon which you elaborate to translate your skills into potential benefits to the employer. Use your resume as a point of reference; write on index cards the key points you want to remember and convey during the interview. It's fine to bring these cards with you to your interview.

In applying for jobs, a male increases his chances by trying to enter a field that has previously been primarily a female domain (e.g., nursing). Similarly, a female increases her chances if she applies for a position that has previously been primarily a male domain.

Don't be afraid to reapply and reinterview at the same company. Your interview skills will probably have improved in the meantime, and different areas may be interested in you for different positions.

Be creative if you are applying for a creative job (advertising, design, sales, art), but be conservative if you are applying for a conservative job (banking, insurance, accounting).

Before the interview, verify the particulars. Write down the interviewer's name, the location, and the time and date of your appointment. Last-minute nervousness can block such details from your memory. Plan on arriving 15 minutes early.

Apprehension, tension, and anxiety are a normal part of the preinterview jitters. Relaxation techniques, deep breathing, and chatting with the receptionist may help.

If you are turned down for the position, consider calling to get information to improve subsequent interviews: "I realize that this

The person who gets the job isn't always the person who is best qualified but rather the person who is best prepared to find potential jobs and interview for them.

Ask for feedback is a bit unusual and I am aware that you've chosen someone else for the job, but could you spend a few moments giving me some ideas as I continue my job search?" You could end up with some valuable leads; it's worth a try!

Interviewing becomes easier as you gain practice. Don't be overly discouraged if you don't get the first job for which you interview. Interviews and even rejections are actually invaluable opportunities to reassess and reaffirm your qualifications, strengths, weaknesses, and needs.

In the competitive job market of today, you can maximize your chance of successful interviewing by doing practice interviews and being prepared to answer an employer's typical questions. Always be prepared to support your general answers with specific examples from your experience. Your interviewers will remember your examples! *Consider using a video camera to sharpen your interviewing skills.* Ask a friend or classmate to be the interviewer. Using the questions below and those found on page 243, practice your responses. Then play the tape and use the interview critique form on page 248 to evaluate your performance and improve your answers for the next interview.

The sample questions below are representative of the types of questions commonly asked in an employment interview. Review these, and be prepared beforehand to answer such questions.

1. *Tell me about yourself.*

   Refer mentally to your resume; do not assume that the interviewer has even read it! Briefly recap your skills and experiences as they relate to this particular job.

2. *Why do you want this job? Why did you apply here?*

   Refer to information about *this job* and *this company* or institution that makes it particularly appealing to you. Do not give the impression that you're here just because the firm has a job opening. Refer to the company's history, products, and services. Let your interviewer know that you have researched the organization.

3. *Why should I hire you?*

   "Because, with my skills, experience, positive attitude, and enthusiasm, I am obviously the best person for the job. I agree with your philosophy and feel that I will fit in. I will be an asset to your enterprise." (Reemphasize your strengths.)

4. *What are your career plans? Where do you see yourself five years from now?*

   Employers generally like to think you will be with them forever; you can't make any promises, but you can indicate you would like to be with a company that allows you to grow, asks you to assume more responsibility, and challenges you continuously. That challenges them to be that kind of place!

5. *Are there any questions?*

   You might ask just what kind of person the interviewer is really looking for, then show how you fit the bill. Or you might clarify expected follow-up, or add some information. "When can I expect to hear about the position?" "Oh, yes, I forgot to mention earlier that. . . ." "I would like to reiterate that. . . ." (See the box on page 249 for sample questions to ask at the interview.)

Leave the interviewer convinced that you are ready and able to do the job. Never answer a question "no" without qualifying it positively. "Are you familiar with Excel?" "No, but I have mastered other software, and I'm certain I won't have any problems learning." "Can you 10-key?" "No, I didn't realize it was part of the job description. If it's necessary, I can learn. Just how much numerical data entry will be involved?"

6. *What salary do you expect?*

If you have done your homework, you should have an idea of the general range for the position. Find out whether this company has a fixed salary schedule. You may want to defer the matter until you know more about what the job entails. If the interviewer does not mention salary, it is best not to bring up the subject at a first interview.

7. *Don't you think you are too young/old for this position?*

In either case, phrase your answer so it is an advantage. Example:

Too young: Show how the job best lends itself to a young person—one who can face the challenges with youthful vigor and a fresh point of view.

Too old: Point out how your years of experience and previous success give you the confidence and wisdom to handle extensive responsibility with the mature judgment required by this position. Talk about maturity, *not* age.

8. *Why did you leave your last job?*

If asked why you left your last position, avoid mentioning a personality conflict. Rather say, "I felt I had gone as far in that company as possible and I was ready for more responsibility, challenge, hours (etc.)." If your work history reflects many job changes, explain how you have transferred existing skills and learned new skills that can now benefit these employers.

INTERVIEW GUIDELINES

The interview—and ultimately, a job—is the goal of your job search strategy. Generally, people who are interviewed are assumed qualified to do the job; the question becomes one of an appropriate meshing of personalities. Both the interviewer and interviewee are relying on their communication skills, judgment, intuition, and insight. It is a two-way process. While you are being evaluated, you should be evaluating the position and the people offering it. Remember that a good interview is a dialogue, an exchange of information.

An interview is a two-way process

Take a good look at yourself. Employers are becoming increasingly broad-minded about clothes and hair, but few are totally "liberated." If you are serious about getting a job, then you had better look and dress the part. No interviewer will tell you what you are supposed to wear, but the person will measure your maturity and judgment partially by your appearance. Remember that the first impression is often a lasting one. It's often not the best qualified person who gets the job, but the one who makes the best impression. *You never get a second chance to make a good first impression!*

If possible, drive by the interview site a day or two before so you'll know where it is, where to park, and how long it takes to get there. Plan to arrive for your interview at least fifteen minutes early. Establish a friendly relationship with the secretary or receptionist. Develop a firm handshake (practice),

and use it when being introduced. Practice good eye contact. Above all, try to relax. Remember, you will be talking about someone you know very well—you!

You may have to handle some trick or stress questions; be prepared beforehand with responses that feel comfortable to you (see the sample questions on page 243). If a question seems inappropriate, you may ask: "How does this information relate to or affect my employment here?" This may prompt an employer to express the real concerns, such as your record of stability on the job, age, child-care needs, or commitment to the job and company. You may even consider bringing up these relevant issues. Often seemingly unimportant conversation is an attempt to put you and the interviewer at ease or to assess your ability to socialize.

Body language can speak louder than words

Remember that many interviewers are just as nervous about the process as you. Feel free to make the first attempts to break the ice; when you try to relieve another's anxiety, yours becomes secondary. Note the office decor, the cordial welcome, whatever makes sense. If you are nervous, you will find that focusing on the question "What would it be like to work here?" rather than "How am I being perceived by them?" will relax you. Relax in the chair; a rigid posture reinforces your tenseness. Actually, a slightly forward position with head erect indicates interest and intimacy. Maintain eye contact. In answering questions, use your knowledge of yourself to transmit the idea that you are the best person for the job; allow strengths such as goodwill, flexibility, enthusiasm, and a professional approach to surface. Bring samples of your work if they are related. On an index card, note your strengths or key selling points in addition to the questions you may have and some cue words like "smile, speak up, relax"; review them from time to time, especially just before you go into the interview. Forthright statements about what you do well, with examples of accomplishments, are of key importance. Talk with pride, honesty, and confidence about your accomplishments and your potential, your interest and commitment, and your readiness to learn on the job.

Express yourself *positively*. You are selling yourself; allow your personal *energy* and *enthusiasm* to surface.

SEGMENTS OF AN INTERVIEW

Although every interview is different, most follow a general pattern. A typical half-hour session can be roughly divided into four segments.

1. The first five or ten minutes are usually devoted to establishing some rapport and opening the lines of communication. Instead of wondering why the interviewer is taking valuable time chatting about the weather, your parking problems, etc., relax and enjoy the conversation. He or she will get to deeper subjects soon enough. The interview begins the moment you introduce yourselves and shake hands. Don't discount the initial period. Your ability to converse, expressing yourself intelligently, is being measured.

Establish initial rapport

2. The adept interviewer will move subtly from a casual exchange to a more specific level of conversation. The second part of the interview gives you a chance to answer some "where, when, and why" questions about your background—to supply information that does not appear on your resume.

Now is the time to describe some extracurricular activities or work experience that may explain your less-than-perfect GPA. Or to talk of changes you effected as president of a campus organization or community group. This is your chance to elaborate on your strong points and maximize whatever you have to offer. Don't monopolize the conversation; let the interviewer lead. But don't confine your statements to yes or no answers. Ask some questions to let the interviewer know you have researched the firm thoroughly and have a keen interest in the position.

The interviewer will be interested not only in what you say, but how you say it. Equally as important as the information you communicate will be the demonstrated evidence of logical organization and presentation of thoughts. The interviewer will be mentally grading your intelligence, leadership potential, and motivation.

3. Part three begins when the interviewer feels your skills and interests have been identified and can see how they might fit the organization. If a good match seems possible, the interviewer will discuss the company and the openings available.

4. At the end of an interview, try to find out where you stand. "How do you feel I relate to this job?" "Do you need any additional information?" "When can I expect to hear from you?"

Ask questions

After you leave, take 10 or 15 minutes to analyze how you did. What questions did you find difficult? What did you forget to say? How can you improve on the next interview? You might even keep a diary or log with written notes on each of these concerns as well as a list of the specific interview questions asked and a note about how you responded. Also list any specific things that you can do in following up with an employer to increase your chances of getting the offer you want. If you feel you forgot to mention something or there was a misunderstanding, correct or elaborate on these points in a letter or telephone call. Type a thank-you letter to the interviewer, recalling a significant fact or idea of the interview that will set you apart from the other applicants. Write the letter while the interview is still fresh in your mind. One paragraph is usually sufficient.

PRACTICE QUESTIONS

The following are questions that have been asked during interviews, intended to create a *stress* response. Often they are asked out of pattern, intended to throw you. The interviewer sometimes is more interested in *how* you respond than in what you say, to observe how you react and how you think on your feet. Decide which of the following questions are likely to be asked of you in your situation. PRACTICE!

1. What kind of job do you expect to hold five years from now? Ten years? Twenty years?

2. Why do you want to work for this company?

3. Why did you choose this company over our competitors?

4. Why did you choose your particular field of work?

5. What do you know about this company?
6. Describe your perfect job.
7. What qualifications do you have that make you feel you will be successful in your field?
8. What are your salary expectations?
9. What determines a person's progress in a good company?
10. Do you prefer working with others or by yourself?
11. Describe how you handle stress.
12. How do you react to criticism?
13. What interests you about our product/service?
14. What is your major weakness? (What are three of your strong points? Three of your weak points?)
15. Are you willing to go where the company sends you? Travel? Relocate?
16. What kind of supervision gets the best results from you?
17. What are your own special abilities?
18. Do you object to working overtime?
19. What is your philosophy of life?
20. Do you have any objections to a psychological test or interview?
21. What are the main elements needed to develop a team spirit?
22. What are your career goals?
23. What are the things that motivate you?
24. In what ways will this company benefit from your services?
25. If you were me, why would you hire you?
26. How would you describe yourself as an employee?

HOW TO HANDLE ILLEGAL QUESTIONS

Certain hiring practices, employment application form questions, and specific interviewing procedures are illegal under the Fair Employment Practices Act, the Americans with Disabilities Act, and other governmental regulations. Review Table 11.A on the following pages to familiarize yourself with the subject matter and specifics of the illegal issues.

If the question is on an application, you always have the option to put *N/A* in the blank. If you are asked illegal questions in an interview, try to anticipate the concerns a potential employer might have about hiring you and bring them up in a manner that is comfortable for you.

Example:

Interviewer: "Do you have any children?"

Interviewee: "I guess you are wondering about the care of my school-aged children. I'd like you to know I have an excellent attendance record. You are welcome to check with my past employer, and, besides, I have a live-in sitter. Additionally, I have researched the needs of this position and can assure you that I have no family responsibilities that will interfere with my ability to do this job."

TABLE 11.A

Preemployment inquiries: lawful and unlawful.

SUBJECT	ACCEPTABLE PREEMPLOYMENT INQUIRIES	UNACCEPTABLE PREEMPLOYMENT INQUIRIES
Photograph	Statement that a photograph may be required after employment.	Requirement that applicant affix a photograph to application form. Request that applicant submit photograph at applicant's option. Requirement of photograph after interview but before hiring.
Race or Color		Complexion, color of skin, or other questions directly or indirectly indicating race or color, such as color of applicant's eyes and hair.
Citizenship	Request that applicant state whether residency status is: (a) U.S. citizen (b) Legal right to remain permanently in the United States. Statement that, if hired, applicant may be required to submit proof of citizenship.	What is your country of citizenship? Inquiry whether an applicant or applicant's parents or spouse are naturalized or native-born U.S. citizens; date when applicant or parents or spouse acquired citizenship. Requirement that applicant produce naturalization papers or first papers.
National Origin	Inquiry into applicant's proficiency in foreign language must be job-related.	Applicant's nationality, lineage, national origin, descent, or parentage. Date of arrival in United States or port of entry; how long a resident of the United States. Nationality of applicant's parents or spouse; maiden name of applicant's wife or mother. Language commonly used by applicant: "What is your mother tongue?" How applicant acquired ability to read, write, or speak a foreign language.
Education	Inquiry into academic, vocational, or professional education of an applicant and schools attended.	Any inquiry asking specifically the nationality, race, or religious affiliation of a school.
Name	Inquiry about having worked for the company under a different name. Maiden name of married female applicant, assumed name, or change of name, if necessary to check education or employment records.	Former name of applicant whose name has been changed by court order or otherwise.

(continued)

TABLE 11.A Continued.

SUBJECT	ACCEPTABLE PREEMPLOYMENT INQUIRIES	UNACCEPTABLE PREEMPLOYMENT INQUIRIES
Address or Duration of Residence	Inquiry into place and length of residence at current and previous addresses.	Specific inquiry into foreign addresses that would indicate national origin.
Gender		If not based on a bona fide occupational qualification, it is extremely difficult for gender to be considered a lawful subject for preemployment inquiry.
Birthplace	Requirement that applicant submit, after employment, a birth certificate or other proof of legal residence.	Birthplace of applicant, applicant's parents, spouse, or other relatives.
Age	Requirement that applicant submit, after employment, a birth certificate or other document as proof of age.	Requirement that applicant produce proof of age in the form of a birth certificate, baptismal record, employment certificate, or certificate of age issued by school authorities.
Religion		Inquiry into applicant's religious denomination, affiliation, church, parish, or pastor, or which religious holidays observed. Applicant may not be told, "This is a Catholic/Protestant/Jewish/atheist, etc., organization."
Work Day and Shifts	Request that applicant state days, hours, or shift(s) available to work.	It is unlawful to request applicants to state days, hours, or shift(s) that they can work if it is used to discriminate on basis of religion.

Anticipate concerns and address them

Not only will employers appreciate your sensitivity to their concerns, but your statement provides you with an additional opportunity to sell yourself and to evaluate whether this position is one that you want to consider. It is often advisable for you, the interviewee, to bring up any issue that may be on the employer's mind but that, because of legal concerns, will not be addressed unless you mention it. Such issues as age, children, spouse's feelings about this position, gender, disabilities, and qualifications can all be addressed by you in such a way as to enhance your chances of getting the job. Basically, you want to show how your age, qualifications, gender, or disability will be an advantage to your employer. This requires some thinking on your part before the interview, and the payoff—getting the job you want—is well worth the effort.

BODY LANGUAGE

Your body language speaks just as loudly as your words. Eye contact is crucial. Remember that at a distance of five or six feet from another person, you can be looking at the person's nose or forehead or mouth and still maintain the sense of eye contact. Try it with friends.

Present yourself assertively

Voice tone, volume, and inflection are important. A soft, wispy voice will seldom convince another that you mean business; a loud or harsh voice tends to be blocked out. Listen to yourself on a tape recorder or, preferably, watch yourself on videotape. How do you sound to yourself? Remember, however, that our own recorded voice always sounds odd to us, so ask others for their comments. Lessons in voice and diction are available in most schools. Try varying your voice pitch and volume while reading something into a tape recorder. You may find a range that sounds better.

Don't chew gum!

Try accenting your words with appropriate hand gestures to gain emphasis. Before the interview, analyze your practice interviews. Consider the option of being videotaped during a practice interview. The instant feedback is very helpful, particularly if you use the format set out in Table 11.B to critique your performance. If you are in a class, practice with one or more classmates, evaluating your own and your classmates' interview techniques according to the critique form.

VIDEO INTERVIEWING

Some companies are beginning to use video as a prescreening and screening tool. Video interviewing occurs most often in the fields of education, government, and private manufacturing. According to *EEO BiMonthly (Equal Employment Opportunity* magazine, Nov.–Dec. 1996), six factors are important to consider:

1. Are you articulate? How do you come across on videotape?
2. Be prepared; practice what you will say before you are taped.
3. If you are a person who usually plays off another's body language in an interview, you will need to practice to make your answers and conversation flow as if you were actually talking to someone.
4. Dress professionally and conservatively; pay attention to the colors and patterns you wear. Solid colors work best on video.
5. Communicate with enthusiasm and confidence through facial expressions and voice tone.
6. Do not exaggerate your movements. Overdone gestures can be distracting and may even cause "waves" in the air.

LEARNING FROM THE INTERVIEW

As much as they are interviewing you, you are in turn interviewing the representatives of a company. Ideally, you will do only about 40 percent of the talking. In the remaining time, you can listen and assess whether or not you want to work for that company. Although an interview tends to be rather formal,

TABLE 11.B

Interview critique form.

Name _____
(individual being interviewed)

	Very good	Satisfactory	Fair—could be better	Needs Improvement	Comments
1. Initial, or opening, presentation (impression).					
2. Eye contact.					
3. Sitting position.					
4. General appearance: grooming (hair, makeup, shave, beard, mustache, etc.), clothing.					
5. Ability to describe past work experiences, education, and training.					
6. Ability to explain equipment, tools, and other mechanical aids used.					
7. Ability to explain skills, techniques, processes, and procedures. Ability to emphasize how skills are related to job.					
8. Ability to explain personal goals, interests, and desires.					
9. Ability to explain questionable factors in personal life (functional limitations, frequent job changes, many years since last job).					
10. Ability to answer questions or make statements about company or job applying for.					
11. Ability to listen attentively to interviewer's questions and to notice and respond to interviewer's body language.					
12. Manner of speech or conversation understandable (voice, tone, pitch, volume, speed)?					
13. Physical mannerisms (facial expressions, gestures).					
14. Enthusiasm, interest in this job.					
15. Attitude (positive?), confidence.					
16. Overall impression? Would you hire this applicant?					

you can still gain a feeling about the climate of the organization. Entering its offices, you can observe the receptionist, support staff, people talking or not talking in the hallways. The colors and decor of the furnishings should generate a positive or negative impression.

Take note of the punctuality of the interview (assuming you are on time or early), the arrangement of the seating in the interview room, and the dress of the interviewers. The entrance and handshake are important first impressions. Some companies deliberately set up awkward or uncomfortable situations to observe your response. They may ask tough questions just to see how well you think on your feet. If you can maintain your composure and enthusiasm in the interview, they will probably conclude that you are able to work equally as well under stress.

In selecting your own questions, you might ask who the last person in the position was and what happened to him or her; if the person resigned, you may ask why. Another related question would be "Given the current economy, how have careers at my level been affected?" You may also ask about the background of your potential supervisor and professional mobility within the company. Although you want to emphasize your interest and commitment to the position for which you are interviewing, these questions can illustrate your interest in a future with the company.

A final bit of information that you should gather or confirm about the company relates to its *corporate culture*. Corporate culture refers to the personality of the potential employer. Primarily you want to seek employment with a firm that is likely to meet your personality needs. Do you need a competitive environment in order to thrive? Most likely a job in a high school or a government position won't satisfy those needs. Do you need security? The aerospace field may be a bit too unsteady for you. The prime question that is related to corporate culture and that you may ask during an interview is "Can you explain the management style or philosophy of your company?" If you want to have the opportunity for input into management, you might also ask about the use of quality circles or the potential for the use of total quality management in the organization. If you are hoping to enter the field of business but have little relevant background, it might help to take a college

Sample questions to ask at the interview

Going one step further than just *answering* the interviewer's questions involves being prepared to take the initiative in *asking* several questions.

- Could you describe the duties of this job?
- Where does this position fit into the organization?
- What type of people do you prefer for this job?
- Is this position new?
- What experience is ideally suited for this job?
- Was the last person promoted?
- To whom would I be reporting? Can you tell me a little about these people?
- What have been some of the best results you have received from these people?
- Who are the primary people I would be working with?
- What seem to be their strengths and weaknesses?
- What are your expectations for me?
- May I talk with present and previous employees about this job?
- What are some of the problems I might expect to encounter on this job, e.g., efficiency, quality control, declining profits, evaluation?
- What has been done recently regarding . . .?
- How is this program going?
- What is the normal pay range for this job?
- If you don't mind, can I let you know by (date)?
- What kind of on-the-job training is allocated for this position?

class or read a book on the world of business so that you can ask intelligent questions about business practices.

FACTORS INFLUENCING HIRING

We have seen that many things must be considered in preparing for an interview. Some of these factors we can control; other considerations are beyond our control. Look over the box on page 251 to distinguish between the two.

The College Placement Council (1994) identified sixteen traits recruiters seek in job prospects. To make an outstanding and lasting impression, emphasize the traits listed below during any contact with a company (e.g., informational or formal interview). As you review the list, check each item you feel comfortable discussing in an interview.

1. Ability to communicate.   _____
2. Intelligence.   _____
3. Self-confidence.   _____
4. Willingness to accept responsibility.   _____
5. Initiative.   _____
6. Leadership abilities.   _____
7. Energy level.   _____
8. Imagination.   _____
9. Flexibility.   _____
10. Interpersonal skills.   _____
11. Ability to handle conflict/stress.   _____
12. Self-knowledge.   _____
13. Competitive spirit.   _____
14. Goal and achievement level.   _____
15. Education and skill level.   _____
16. Personal direction.   _____

Each of the traits you checked can strengthen your chances for a successful interview. Those you did not check are areas for additional homework prior to preparing the final version of your resume and going to the interview.

A greater range of jobs now require a college degree. Often a degree will be required primarily because so many applicants have degrees. Even your liberal arts degree can compete with a specialist degree in business if the following factors are taken into consideration:

1. You have an excellent grade point average.
2. You have a record of extracurricular activities (club or community involvement). It's especially good to have had leadership positions.
3. You worked your way through college (it helps even more if the work was at the company with which you seek full-time employment or at least in the same field).
4. You've made some contacts within the firm who can serve as positive references.
5. You either minored in business or, at least, selected business courses as electives (e.g., accounting, economics, marketing, information systems).

OUT OF YOUR CONTROL

Too many applicants.

Cannot pay you what you are making.

Indecisiveness on part of business owner.

Only trying to fill a temporary position.

A current employee changed plans and decided not to leave.

Introduction of new personnel policies.

Death of a company management employee.

Looking for a certain type of person.

Lack of experience on part of interviewer.

Accepting applications only for future need.

Looking for more experience.

Looking for less experience.

Your skills are more than are needed for the position.

Company management decided that morning on a temporary freeze on hiring—for many business reasons.

Illness of interviewer.

Change in management.

Further consideration of all applicants.

A more important post must be filled first.

Factors you can control or guard against

- A poor personal appearance.
- An overbearing, overaggressive, conceited attitude; a "superiority complex"; being a know-it-all.
- An inability to express oneself clearly; poor voice, diction, or grammar.
- A lack of career planning; no purpose or goals.
- A lack of interest and enthusiasm; appearing passive, indifferent.
- A lack of confidence and poise; nervousness, being ill at ease.
- An overemphasis on money; interest only in best dollar offer.
- A poor scholastic record; just squeaking by.
- An unwillingness to start at the bottom; expecting too much too soon.
- Making excuses; evasiveness, hedging on unfavorable factors in record.
- Lack of courtesy; being ill-mannered.
- Talking negatively about past employers or coworkers.
- Failure to look interviewer in the eye.
- A limp, fishlike handshake.
- A sloppy application form.
- Insincerity; merely "shopping around."
- Wanting job only for short time.
- Lack of interest in company or in industry.
- Emphasizing whom you know over what you can do.
- An unwillingness to be transferred.
- Intolerance; strong prejudices.
- Having narrow interests.
- Arriving late for interview without good reason.
- Never having heard of company.
- Failure to express appreciation for interviewer's time.
- Failure to ask questions about the job.
- Directing a high-pressure style at interviewer.
- Providing vague responses to questions.

6. You have defined goals, exude enthusiasm and confidence, and can verbalize these characteristics in an interview.

For example, Walt Disney World Company employs thousands of new college graduates each year; more than one-third hired are liberal arts graduates.

Generally attributed to all college graduates, but especially to liberal arts graduates, are intellectual ability (verbal and quantitative) and skills in planning, organizing, decision making, interpersonal relations, leadership, and oral communication. The less your major is related to the job desired, the more you must be able to discuss your transferable skills.

Summary—reviewing the interview process

Preparation
- Resume—contacts—letters of reference.
- Interview log—contacts—initial contact letters written.
- Letters out—make appointments—contacts.
- 3" x 5" cards on each interview.
- Attitudes—"You can do it"—visualize that you have the job.
- Dress the part.
- Know your resume—bring extra copies to the interview.
- Know something about the company (Dunn and Bradstreet—Moody's—Standard & Poor's—Fortune 500—annual report—magazine articles).
- Have five or six good questions—know when to ask them.
- Keep a computer "log" or journal.
- Keep control.
- Be on time! ! !

The introduction
- Maintain good posture, shake hands, breathe.
- Use good eye contact and posture.
- The first four minutes are key—establish rapport—generate the proper chemistry.
- What can I do for you?—major strengths question—tell me about your background.
- Be positive—convert negatives to pluses.

The interview
- Smile.
- Supply information, refer to your resume.
- Seek the next interview (or the job).
- Overcome any objections—try to anticipate objections.
- Keep answers brief.
- Ask questions about the field.
- Know the rules—when a decision will be made.
- Ask for the job if it exists.
- Be positive.
- When would you like my answer?

After the interview
- Debrief yourself—make notes (name, address, phone, impressions; if a panel of interviewers, write down names and positions of all panel members). Add to computer journal.
- Formally thank the employer or panel chairperson by letter.
- Plan a follow-up strategy—if you don't hear from them, call and ask if a decision has been made.
- Don't be defeated—keep interviewing!

Alternatives
- Continue learning and searching.
- Consider volunteer work to gain more experience.
- Join or create a job support group.
- Keep current and updated.

Sample thank-you letters

Use these sample thank-you letters as a guide and write your own to an imaginary or real interviewer.

19574 Delaware
Detroit, MI 48223
February 8, 1998

Ms. Dorothy Smith
Michels' Manufacturing Corporation
1928 North Berry Street
Livonia, MI 48150

Dear Ms. Smith:

Thank you for your time this morning. I was certainly impressed with the efficiency, friendliness, and overall climate of Michels' Manufacturing Corporation.

Now that you've told me more about Michels' recent contract with the U.S. Tank Command, I feel my degree in industrial engineering and two years of part-time work in task force analysis should be of value to you.

I hope you will consider me favorably for the position of junior project engineer.

Sincerely,

Steven B. Boyd

1010 Yourstreet Avenue
Elizabeth, New Jersey 07208
July 12, 1997

Mr. John Jones
Widget Manufacturing Company
345 Widget Avenue
Newark, New Jersey 07210

Dear Mr. Jones,

Thank you for an interesting and informative interview on July 12, 1997. The position of manufacturing representative is of considerable interest to me, as I am most impressed with Widget's excellent growth record.

One point was not brought out in our interview that may be of interest to you. In my previous position with Ferrals Manufacturing, I took ten weeks of intensive training in billing and credit, skills that would directly relate to the position as you described it.*

Again, thank you for the time you spent interviewing me.

Yours truly,

Rosario Ortega

---

*NOTE: This is your chance to mention anything helpful to your campaign that you forgot to tell the employer in the interview. However, the point should be brief and precise.

IF YOU DO NOT GET THE JOB

Should you find that, despite your solid efforts, you do not get the desired job, remember that all your dedicated preparation will pay off in time. The next interview will be easier; you will benefit from your experience. The key is to keep a positive attitude and not to give up. Keep your goals in mind and remember that persistent people achieve their objectives by focusing on the target and believing in the future.

Unfortunately, continuing unemployment can undermine a person's confidence. You will be better prepared to handle temporary setbacks and rejection if you remember that your situation is far from unique; everyone with a job was once a job searcher. As you persist in your job search, remind yourself that you *will* find a job and build a career.

How well you cope with stress and rejection will depend on your attitude and actions. Put any anger or frustration you feel to positive use. Concentrate on your strengths; review them each day. A healthy diet, physical exercise, and adequate rest are obvious prescriptions for overcoming worry and anxiety.

One of the best antidotes for feeling depressed is doing something to help someone else. You have time, talents, and skills that will mean a great deal to others. And remember, each time you volunteer, you gain valuable experience and contacts.

Finally, try to accomplish something every day. Accomplishments are activities that make you feel good about yourself. Even minor tasks such as cleaning out a closet or refining your resume can invigorate you and give you new direction.

When you take care of yourself and strive to maintain a positive attitude, your self-image is enhanced and you improve your chances of success.

The written exercises that follow serve to prepare you for a job interview. Exercise 11.1 asks you to review and be ready to answer sample questions. Exercise 11.2 asks you to practice and critique an interview.

EXERCISES

11.1 Question review

Review the interview questions listed under Practice Questions, and be prepared to answer all of them.

11.2 Practice interview

Arrange a practice interview with a friend, colleague, career counselor, or potential employer (someone you've met during your information interviewing). If possible, have the practice videotaped so you can review your performance. Use the Interview Critique Form (Table 11.B) to evaluate your practice session.

11.3 Exercise summary

Write a brief paragraph answering these questions

What did you learn about yourself? How does this knowledge relate to your career/life planning? How do you feel?

TWELVE

Future Focus

*At the end of the chapter you will be
able to . . .*

Recognize the role of the future in
your current career-planning
efforts

Understand the philosophy of personal empowerment and career
flexibility

*Create your own
career future*

At the threshold of a new century, one thing is certain. The only predictable future is the one you create for yourself. The new employee contract guarantees you nothing but the opportunity to remain employed—provided your skills are current and in demand. This stark reality translates into the need for constant self-renewal, continuous learning, and deliberate, lifelong networking.

This book has provided tools to help you identify who you are; define what you want to do; research, identify, and develop your skills; and create a context in which you are able to find meaningful work. Following the book's guidelines puts you in full control, for you are creating your own possibilities instead of spending time preparing for the "predicted future" only to find that it does not exist.

You are responsible for your own development. Learning to learn will be the most essential survival skill of the new millennium. If you are constantly on the lookout for new ways to use your current skills and new skills, you will remain in demand in the job market. Even if you feel content and secure in your current position, you must constantly be aware of emerging trends, opportunities, and danger signals that may impact your situation. In essence, make the world your classroom; learn something new from everything you do!

Your future is determined by the choices you make in the present. For that reason, this book has emphasized the development of your decision-making skills. This takes the focus away from *predicting* your future and puts the emphasis on *creating* your future. As we enter the 21st century, the world is in flux, and you are continually changing so why shouldn't your career evolve as well? No longer are people staying in one job until retirement. Unfortunately, however, it is human nature to resist change. Thus, many people do not turn to career counselors or books about career change until they are terminated from what had supposedly been a secure job. If you are wise enough to prepare for change before it is forced upon you, you have a head start. The time to seek the career of your choice is while you are already employed or still in school!

Life transitions and unemployment can lead to feelings of desperation and a closed or confused mind. The anxiety and confusion generated by a life crisis make career planning difficult, if not impossible. If you are unemployed or underemployed, you are likely to feel depressed, lethargic, and hopeless about the future. It is precisely during this time that you need to totally immerse yourself in the career-planning process. During times of personal transition and uncertainty, this process will give you a structure to cope with anxiety and depression and to reconnect with your dreams and passions. Each time you begin a job search, review the accomplishments and skills you recorded in this book. This may help relieve your apprehension about another job search. You will be reminded of the skills you have and the many alternatives that can be equally satisfying career goals. Your emotional intelligence will enable you to recognize that the uncertainty of transition provides you with fertile ground on which to learn and grow. In fact, a change of direction *now* may become the *best* opportunity of your lifetime.

In the course of re-evaluating your personal strengths and skills, your self-confidence will blossom. You will regain a sense of purpose and direction by setting meaningful and achievable goals. Through networking, information interviewing, and volunteering, your interaction with people will enable you to choose, confirm, or change current goals and be energized and inspired by people who are doing the kind of work you find challenging and rewarding.

Exercising your options may take more effort than crystal ball gazing, but the results are worth it. Finding a career is a full-time effort. We hope you have pulled, stretched, and grown in the process.

It is a very funny thing about life; if you refuse to accept anything but the best, you very often get it.
W. Somerset Maugham

Risking

To laugh is to risk appearing the fool.

To weep is to risk appearing sentimental.

To reach out for another is to risk involvement.

To expose feelings is to risk exposing your true self.

To place your ideas, your dreams before the crowd is to risk their loss.

To love is to risk not being loved in return.

To live is to risk dying.

To hope is to risk despair.

To try is to risk failure.

But risks must be taken because the greatest hazard in life is to risk nothing. The person who risks nothing does nothing, has nothing, is nothing. One may avoid suffering and sorrow, but one simply cannot learn, feel, change, grow, live, or love. Chained by certitude and safety, one becomes enslaved. Only the person who risks is free.

Anonymous

References

CHAPTER ONE

Bridges, William. 1995. *Jobshift: How to Prosper in a Workplace Without Jobs.* Menlo Park, CA: Addison Wesley.

Holland, John. 1985. *Making Vocational Choices: A Theory of Vocational Personalities and Work Environments.* 2nd edition. Englewood Cliffs, NJ: Prentice Hall.

Sheehy, Gail. Joelle Delbourgo (Ed.) 1996. *New Passages: Your Life Across Time.* New York: Ballantine.

Super, Donald E. 1957. *The Psychology of Careers.* New York: Harper.

CHAPTER TWO

Cousins, Norman. 1995. *Anatomy of an Illness as Perceived by the Patient: Reflections on Healing and Regeneration.* New York: W. W. Norton.

Dyer, Wayne. 1992. *Real Magic.* New York: Harper Collins. pp. 97–102.

Gawain, Shakti. 1995. *Creative Visualization.* Mill Valley, CA: Whatever.

Goleman, David. 1995. *Emotional Intelligence.* New York: Bantam Press.

Kauffman, Draper L., Jr. 1976. *Teaching the Future: A Guide to Future Education.* Palm Springs, CA: ETC.

CHAPTER FOUR

American College Testing Program. *Career Planning Program Handbook,* 1077, p. 12, 1981.

Planning Your Career, ACT Adult Booklet, p. 14, 1981.

Appalachia Educational Lab, Inc. 1980. *Worker Trait Group Keysort Deck.* Bloomington, IL: McKnight.

Golden, Bonnie, and Kay Lesh. 1997. *Building Self-Esteem: Strategies for Success in School and Beyond.* 2nd edition. Upper Saddle River, NJ: Prentice Hall.

Holland, John. 1985. *Making Vocational Choices: A Theory of Vocational Personalities and Work Environments.* 2nd edition. Englewood Cliffs, NJ: Prentice Hall.

Jung, Carl. 1923. *Psychological Types.* New York: Harcourt Brace.

Keirsey, David, and Marilyn Bates. 1984. *Please Understand Me: Character and Temperament Types.* Del Mar, CA: Prometheus Nemesis.

Lawrence, Gordon. 1993. *People Types and Tiger Stripes: A Practical Guide to Learning Styles.* 3rd edition. Gainesville, FL: Center for Applications of Psychological Type, Inc.

Myers, Isabel. 1962. *Manual: The Myers-Briggs Type Indicator.* Palo Alto, CA: Consulting Psychologists.

Government Printing Office. 1988. *Guide for Occupational Exploration*. (Supplement to the Dictionary of Occupational Titles, Vol. 2). Washington DC: Gov. Printing Office (1990 Edition Published by Circle Pines, MN: American Guidance Service).

U.S. Department of Labor Employment and Training Administration. 1979. *Interest Checklist*. Washington, DC: U.S. Employment Service.

CHAPTER FIVE

Dictionary of Occupational Titles. 1992. Washington DC: Employment & Training, U.S. Department of Labor.

Elliott, Myrna. 1982. *Transferable Skills for Teachers*. Moorpark, CA: Statewide Career Counselor Training Project. (a paper)

Handy, Charles. 1994. *The Age of Paradox*. Boston, MA: Harvard Business School.

SCANS (Secretary's Commission on Achieving Necessary Skills): What Work Requires of Schools: A SCANS Report for America 2000. June, 1991. Washington, DC: U.S. Department of Labor.

School to Career Handbook. 1995. Sacramento, CA: California Community Colleges.

CHAPTER SIX

Byrne, John A. et al. 1993. "Virtual Corporation: The Company of the Future will be the Ultimate in Adaptability." *Business Week*, February 8, pp. 98–103.

Employment and Earnings. January, 1994. Washington, DC: U.S. Department of Labor, Bureau of Labor Statistics.

Hammonds, Keith et al. 1994. "Rethinking Work." *Business Week*. October 17, pp. 75–117.

Kaplan, Karen. 1996. Tech's Top 10. *L.A. Times*: "Cutting Edge Careers." February 26, pp. 28–29.

Kiechel, Walter. 1993. "How We Will Work in the Year 2000: Six Trends That Will Reshape the Workplace." *Fortune*. May 17, pp. 38–66.

Occupational Outlook Handbook, 1996–7. Washington DC: U.S. Department of Labor, Bureau of Labor Statistics.

Occupational Outlook Quarterly. Fall, 1994. Washington, DC: U.S. Department of Labor, Bureau of Labor Statistics, pp. 29–31.

Money Magazine, March 1996. "Top Ten High-Income Home Businesses."

Scheetz, L. Patrick. 1995. *Recruiting Trends 1995–6*. East Lansing, MI: Collegiate Employment Research Institute, Michigan State University.

U.S. Department of Labor, Women's Bureau. 1996. "20 Facts on Women Workers." *Statistical Abstracts of the United States*. Washington, DC: U.S. Bureau of Labor Statistics.

CHAPTER SEVEN

Messmer, Max. 1995. *Job Hunting for Dummies*. Chicago, IL: IDG Books Worldwide.

CHAPTER EIGHT

Douglas, Merril and Donna. 1993. *Manage Your Time, Your Work, Yourself.* New York: AMACOM.

Gelatt, H. B. 1992. *Creative Decision Making Using Positive Uncertainty.* Menlo Park, NJ: Crisp.

Stamp, Dan. "Managing Priorities." Executive Excellence, No. 1. January 1996, pp. 6–7.

CHAPTER NINE

Associated Press. 1993. "Internships." *Daily News*, November 14, Classified Section.

Bolles, Richard N. 1997. *What Color Is Your Parachute? A Practical Manual for Job Hunters and Career Changers.* Revised edition. Berkeley, CA: Ten Speed.

Career America. Washington, DC: U.S. Office of Personnel Management.

Gilbert, Sara D. 1997. Internships 97: The Hotlist for Job Hunters. 2nd edition. New York: Arco.

Kennedy, Joyce, and Thomas J. Morrow. 1995. *Electronic Job Search Revolution.* 2nd edition. NY: Wiley & Sons.

Lauber, L. 1993. *The Government Job Finder.* Garrett Park, MD: Garrett Park.

National Business Employment Weekly. Published quarterly. P.O. Box 300. Princeton, NJ 08543.

Peterson's Internships 1997. 1997. New York: Peterson's Guide Pub.

Smith, L. 1993. *Great Careers: The Fourth of July Guide to Careers, Internships, and Volunteer Opportunities in the Non-Profit Sector.* Garrett Park, MD: Garrett Park.

Wolff, Michael. 1997. *Netjobs: Your Guide to Getting the Job You Want.* (2nd ed.) Wolff New Media.

CHAPTER ELEVEN

Beatty, Richard. 1995. *The Interview Kit.* New York: John Wiley & Sons.

Hirsch, Arlene. 1994. *Interviewing.* New York: John Wiley & Sons.

Martinez, Michelle. "Video Interviewing." *EEO Bimonthly*, volume 27 #6, pp. 8, November/December, 1996.

Pearson, H. 1981. *Your Hidden Skills: Clues to Careers.* Mowrey.

Washington, Tom. 1992. *The Hunt: Complete Guide to Effective Job Finding.* Mt. Vernon Press.

CHAPTER TWELVE

Barner, Robert. 1994. "The New Career Strategist: Career Management for the Year 2000 and Beyond," *The Futurist*, September–October, pp. 8–14.

Bibliography

American College Testing Program. *Career Planning Program Handbook*, 1077, p. 12, 1981.

America's Top 300 Jobs: A Complete Career Handbook. 5th edition. JIST Works. 1996.

Appalachia Educational Lab., Inc. *Worker Trait Group Keysort Deck.* Bloomington, IL: McKnight, 1990.

Basta, Nicholas. *Major Options.* New York: Harper Collins, 1991.

Boldt, Laurence G. *Zen and the Art of Making a Living: A Practical Guide to Creative Career Design.* NY: Penguin Group, 1993.

Bolles, Richard N. *What Color Is Your Parachute? A Practical Manual for Job Hunters and Career Changers.* Revised edition. Berkeley, CA: Ten Speed, 1997

Bolles, Richard Nelson. *Quick Job Hunting Map.* Berkeley, CA: Ten Speed, 1996.

_____ . *Quick Job Hunting Map.* Berkeley, Calif.: Ten Speed, 1996.

Bridges, William. *Job Shift.* NY: Addison-Wesley. 1995.

California Community Colleges, Chancellor's Office. *School to Career Handbook.* 1995.

Career Opportunities News. Garrett Park, MD: Garrett Park.

Careers: Doubling Up on Degrees. *U.S. News & World Report*, Oct. 22, 1990.

Carter, Carol. *Majoring in the Rest of Your Life.* New York: Noonday, 1990.

Cetron, Marvin, and Davies, O. *American Renaissance: Our Life at the 21st Century.* New York: St. Martins, 1990.

Coxford, Lola. 1998. *Resume Writing Made Easy.* 6th edition. Upper Saddle River, NJ: Prentice Hall.

Dorsey, Ivory. *Redefining Success.* Santa Monica, CA: The Training Network, 1994.

Edwards, Paul and Sara Edwards. *The Best Home Businesses for the 90s: The Inside Information You Need to Know to Select a Home-Based Business that is Right for You.* : 2nd edition. Los Angeles: J.P. Tarcher, 1995.

Eikleberry, Carol. *The Career Guide for Creative and Unconventional People.* Berkeley, CA: Ten Speed Press, 1995.

Elliott, Myrna. *Transferable Skills for Teachers.* Statewide Career Counselor Training Project. Moorpark, CA: 1982.

Eyler, David R. Resumes That Mean Business. NY: Random House, 1996.

Fein, Richard. *Cover Letters! Cover Letters! Cover Letters!* Franklin Lakes, NJ: Career Press, 1997.

Gelatt, H. B. *Decisions and Outcomes.* College Entrance Examination Board, 1973.

Godfrey, Joline. *Our Wildest Dreams: Women Entrepreneurs Making Money, Having Fun, Doing Good.* New York: HarperCollins, 1992.

Golden, Bonnie, and Lesh, Kay. *Building Self-Esteem: Strategies for Success in School and Beyond.* 2nd edition. Upper Saddle River, NJ: Prentice Hall, 1997.

Gray, James. *The Winning Image: Present Yourself with Confidence and Style for Career Success.* NY: AMACOM, 1996.

Handy, Charles. *The Age of Paradox.* Boston: Harvard Business School, 1994.

Herzberg, Frederick. *Work and the Nature of Man.* New York: World, 1966.

Hill, Napoleon. *Think and Grow Rich.* New York: Fawcett, 1987.

Hirsch, Arlene S. *Love Your Work and Success Will Follow: A Practical Guide to Achieving Total Career Satisfaction.* NY: John Wiley & Sons, 1996.

Holland, John. *Making Vocational Choices: A Theory of Vocational Personalities and Work Environments.* 2nd edition. Englewood Cliffs, NJ: Prentice Hall, 1985.

Interest Checklist. Developed by U.S. Department of Labor, Employment and Training Administration, U.S. Employment Service, 1979.

Irish, Richard K. *Go Hire Yourself an Employer.* New York: Doubleday.

Jones, Laurie Beth. *The Path: Creating Your Mission Statement for Work and for Life.* NY: Hyperion, 1996.

Jung, Carl. *Psychological Types.* New York: Harcourt Brace, 1923.

Kauffman, Draper L. Jr. *Teaching the Future: A Guide to Future Oriented Education.* Palm Springs, CA: ETC, 1976.

Kaye, Beverly L. *Up is Not the Only Way: A guide to developing workforce talent.* Palo Alto, CA: Davies-Black Publishing, 1997.

Kreigel, Robert, and Kriegel, Marilyn. *The C Zone.* Garden City, NY: Fawcett, 1985.

Levinson, D. J. *The Seasons of a Man's Life.* New York: Alfred A. Knopf, 1978.

Martin, Charles. *Looking at Type and Careers.* Gainesville, FL: Center for Applications of Psychological Type, Inc., 1995.

Maslow, Abraham. *Motivation and Personality.* 2nd edition. New York: Harper & Row, 1970.

Moreau, Daniel. *Take Charge of Your Career: How to Survive and Profit from a Mid-Career Change.* New York: Kiplinger, 1991.

Naisbitt, John. *Megatrends 2000: Ten New Directions for the 1990s.* New York: Avon, 1993.

National Business Employment Weekly: Managing Your Career, College Edition. *The Wall Street Journal,* Winter/Spring 1990.

1994 Career Guide. *U.S. News & World Report,* September 17, 1993.

Occupational Outlook Quarterly. 1995–96. U.S. Department of Labor, Bureau of Labor Statistics.

Parker, Jana. *Resume Catalog, 200 Damn Good Examples.* Berkeley, CA: Ten Speed, 1995.

Phelps, Stanlee, and Austin, Nancy. *The Assertive Woman, A New Look.* San Luis Obispo, CA: Impact, 1997.

Rifkin, Jeremy. *End of Work.* NY: Putnam Publishing Group, 1995.

Simon, Sidney B., Howe, Leland W., and Kirschenbaum, Howard. *Values Clarification*. New York: Warner Books, 1995.

Super, Donald E. *The Psychology of Careers*. New York: Harper, 1957.

Yate, Martin. *Career Smarts: Jobs with a Future*. NY: Random House, 1997.

OTHER BOOKS AND NEWSLETTERS TO CONSIDER FOR GENERAL INTEREST:

Basta, Nicholas. *Major Options*. New York: Harper-Collins, 1991.

Career Opportunities News. Garrett Park, MD: Garrett Park Press. Six issues annually.

Career Planning and Adult Development Newsletter. Twelve newsletters and four journals annually. San Jose, CA: CPAD Network.

DiMarco, Cara. *Life Transitions: Finding Your Way Over, Around, and Through Life's Challenges*. Upper Saddle River, NJ: Prentice Hall, 1995.

The Executive Moonlighter. New York: John Wiley & Sons, 1990.

Jaffe, Dennis T., and Scott, Cynthia D. *Self-Renewal*. National Book Network, 1995.

_____ . *Rekindling Commitment: How to Revitalize Yourself, Your Work, and Your Organization*. San Francisco: Jossey Bass, 1994.

Jeffers, Susan. *Feel the Fear and Do It Anyway*. New York: Fawcett Columbine, 1987.

Journal of Career Development, ed. Gysbers, Norman. New York: Human Sciences Press.

Moreau, Daniel. *Take Charge of Your Career: How to Survive and Profit from a Mid-Career Change*. New York: Kiplinger Books, 1991.

Pedras, K., and Pedras, R. *Jobs '97*. Englewood Cliffs, NJ: Prentice Hall, 1997.

Sheehy, Gail. *New Passages*. New York: Ballantine, 1996.

Siebert, Al. *Survivor Personality*. Berkley: Perigee Books, 1996.

Siebert, Al and Gilpin, Bernadine. *Adult Student Guide to Survival and Success*. Practical Psychology Press, 1997.

Task Force Report on Self Esteem. "Toward a State of Esteem." Sacramento, CA: California State Department of Education, 1991.

USEFUL

Job Bank USA
1420 Spring Road, Suite 480
McLean, VA 22102

Index